MONOGRAPHS

1

Massimo Gemin   Filippo Pedrocco

GIAMBATTISTA
TIEPOLO

Paintings and Frescoes

arsenale editrice

Massimo Gemin • *Filippo Pedrocco*
GIAMBATTISTA TIEPOLO
Paintings and Frescoes

Designed by
Michela Scibilia

Translated by
Gregory Dowling (chapters 1-2)
Holly Snapp (chapters 3-6)

Coordinator and editor of the English translation
Rosella Mamoli Zorzi, Director of Post-graduate Course
in Literary Translation, University of Venice

Types
Weiss and **Meta**

Printed in Italy by
EBS Verona

First edition
October 1995

Copyright © 1995
Arsenale Editrice srl, San Polo 1789, I – 30125 Venice (Italy)

ISBN 88-7743-155-5

Photographic Acknowledgments

Bergamo, Curia vescovile
Bergamo, Studio fotografico Da Re
Boston, Museum of Fine Arts
Casarsa della Delizia (PN), Foto Elio Ciol
Chicago, The Art Institute of Chicago
Dachau, Wolf-Christian von der Mülbe
Gerscheim, Foto Zwicker Berberich
London, Courtauld Institute Galleries
London, Walpole Gallery
Madrid, Prado Museum
Madrid, Royal Palace
Milan, Studio fotografico Giancarlo Costa
Mortegliano (Udine), Foto Riccardo Viola
New York, Piero Corsini Inc.
New York, The Metropolitan Museum of Art
Pasadena, Norton Simon Foundation
Peissenberg, Artothek Kunstdia-Archiv
Rovigo, Dino Marzola
San Francisco, M.H. de Young Memorial Museum
Stuttgart, Staatsgalerie
Udine, Foto Seguini
Venice, Archivio fotografico Arsenale Editrice
Venice, Archivio fotografico Osvaldo Böhm
Venice, Cameraphoto
Venice, Istituto Santa Maria della Pietà
Venice, Studio fotografico Francesco Turio Böhm
Venice, Studio fotografico Mark Edward Smith
Washington, National Gallery of Art

The publisher would like to thank the following
for their valuable assistance
Adam Butler, Walpole Gallery, London
Barbara Morandini and Giuseppe Bergamini, Civici Musei
e Gallerie di Storia e Arte, Udine
Troy Moss, Isabella Stewart Gardner Museum, Boston
Julien Stock, Sotheby's, London
Sergio Tazzer, Rai, Venice
Antonio Tommaseo, Istituto Provinciale Infanzia
Abbandonata, Venice
and
Anna Maria and Francesco Caporossi
Cecilia Collalto Falk
Alessandra and Alessandro Zoppi

The Authors would like to thank
all those who have made this book possible
through their valuable assistance
in archives and public and private collections.

Special thanks are due to Terisio Pignatti,
who has read the text with great care and attention.

The Authors would also like to thank
Cinzia Boscolo and Maddalena Redolfi
for their painstaking editorial assistance.

For Ottavia

Contents

Würzburg 1750–1753

The last decade in Italy 1753–1762

Tiepolo in Spain 1762–1770

Illustrations

GIAMBATTISTA
TIEPOLO

Paintings and Frescoes

Tiepolo's formation and early works
1710-1729

[1] The baptism certificate was published for the first time by G.M. Urbani de Gheltof (1879, pp. 2-3) and later verified by F. Pedrocco on behalf of M. Levey (1986, pp. 3, 291, n. 2); it is in the *Liber baptizatorum* in the parish Archive of San Pietro di Castello (n. 18, p. 6). It reads: "16 aprile 1696 / Gio. Batta figlio del sig. Domenico q. Zuanne Tiepolo, mercante, e della Signora Orsetta, giogali; nacque li 5 del pass.o: sta in C.S. Dom.co C. il N.H. Gio. Donà fu di C. Nicolò B.P. Gasparo Solta canonico nostro".

[2] A. Zorzi (1984, pp. 208-212, 221-223, 253, 319-320).

[3] See, for example, the details of this area in the two different editions of the aerial-view map of Venice by M.S. Giampiccoli: cf. G. Romanelli, *Venezia Ottocento*, Rome 1977, ill. 38.

1.
opposite
Memento Mori
(Age and Death).
Venice, Gallerie
dell'Accademia.

Tiepolo's family and social environment

Giambattista Tiepolo was born in Venice in the *sestiere* of Castello on 5 March 1696 and was baptized forty days later, on 16 April, in the church of San Pietro di Castello[1]. San Pietro was not his parish church. As he was born in Corte San Domenico, near the church and monastery of the same name, which were pulled down in 1807 to make way for the Napoleonic gardens, he could have been a parishioner of San Francesco di Paola, which became a subsidiary church after the viceroy's decrees at the beginning of the nineteenth century, or of Sant'Anna, San Giuseppe di Castello, Sant'Antonio di Castello or San Nicolò di Bari: all of which were suppressed as parish-churches and some of them demolished before 1810[2]. A plaque above the archway that leads into the courtyard reads: "In this courtyard stood the house where the painter Giovanni Battista Tiepolo was born in March 1696". The plaque is modern and the word "stood" ("*sorgeva*") suggests that the building has been pulled down. However, if one studies the maps immediately before and after the demolition-work under Napoleon[3], it is clear that the plans for the public Gardens hardly touched the area and the buildings are the same today as they were then. Therefore, even though we do not know the exact number of the house Giambattista was born in, we can state that it must have been one of the simple buildings that still look onto the little courtyard today.

The baptism took place in San Pietro, the church that remained the cathedral of Venice until 1807, and there was probably an element of self-promotion in this choice: for godfather, the family managed to avail themselves of the services of Giovanni Donà, a Venetian nobleman; his presence threw a little luster on the Tiepolo family, who were not noble, even though there are still those who insist on a possible relationship with the Tiepolos enrolled in the *Libro d'oro*. Apart from the fact that none of the patrician genealogies includes the Tiepolo family of Corte San

Domenico, two family-groups with that surname in seventeenth-century Venice were as likely to be related to one another as two Smiths in London today. The presence of the nobleman Donà is a little over-emphasised by Levey, especially in view of his claim that the area in Castello "has its own sense of being a little Venice within a greater one"[4]. In fact, all the parishes and *contrade* were "little Venices"; small worlds identical to the larger world they belonged to. There is thus nothing surprising in the fact that members of the ruling class should have mingled with their inferiors on such occasions as baptisms or weddings, or indeed in everyday life. Even today one only needs to walk around the city to notice that no area of cheap or lower-class housing is without its nobleman's palazzo. The patrician, by living in direct contact with his fellow citizens, played the role of a social filter, a symbol of inter-class harmony, as well as serving the central power by exerting a controling force.

The mother, who had given birth to five children before Giambattista, was called Orsetta (Orsola); we do not know her surname. His father, Domenico Tiepolo, son of Giovanni, in the baptism certificates published by Urbani de Gheltof[5] is described first as a "ship's Captain", then *"Parcenevole di vascello"*, which is to say the owner of a share in a commercial vessel, and finally, in the record concerning Giambattista, "Merchant". A steady rise up the social ladder: passing from the bridge of a ship to the position of an entrepreneur investing capital in maritime traffic and living off dividends, and finally a regular merchant. This improvement in social status is confirmed by the fact that at the baptism of his third child, Eugenia Giulia, the godfather was the nobleman Francesco Mocenigo, son of Giovanni, of the branch of the Carità, while the godfather of Giovanni Francesco, the fourth child, was Giovanni Dolfin di Andrea of the San Pantalon branch. When Giambattista was born, the family was thus extending its connections with the nobility, and in particular with the Dolfin family of San Pantalon, who were to assist Giambattista greatly in the role of patrons. The family's financial condition was one of modest prosperity, typical of the middle classes, the lower ranks of whom were forever dependent on incomes subject to sudden reverses of fortune: *"vita d'entrada, vita stentada"* (a life of income is a tough life), says Goldoni[6].

And the family suffered just such a reverse when Giambattista was only a year old. Domenico died on 10 March 1697, leaving his wife Orsetta with a patrimony that may have enabled the family to get by for a while, but which was not self-perpetuating, since it does not seem to have been invested in interest-earning securities, and the six children were too young to take over their father's business network. The eldest son, Antonio Maria, was not yet ten, and in a city where the financial security of families was mainly based on the steady circulation of money, the children's future was now a problem.

Giambattista was not born into an artistic family like other painters at the turn of the seventeenth and eighteenth centuries, who thus found their careers more or less guaranteed; nor did Giambattista's family seem to know any more about painting than any other family of the mercantile bourgeoisie. The aristocratic families often had great collections, covering every inch

[4] M. Levey (1986, p. 4).
[5] G.M. Urbani de Gheltof (1879, pp. 2-4).
[6] C. Goldoni, *La casa nova*, act II, scene III.

2.
The Apostles Thomas and John.
Venice, Ospedaletto.

of wall-space with pictures in a sort of *horror vacui* , which struck many non-Venetian visitors as being in the poorest taste[7], and there were a few wealthy intellectuals such as Anton Maria Zanetti il Vecchio[8] who possessed collections. The middle-classes, however, rarely owned more than one or two paintings and prints and a few books. Such meager possessions were hardly sufficient to foster, let alone determine an artistic vocation. But Venice played a major role in importing and exporting artistic objects of the most varied sort – and not only objects: from the end of the seventeenth century, the city's artistic talents were always ready to serve the international market and the new art-patrons in Europe[9]. As in the sixteenth century, it was increasingly easy to make ends meet as a painter, and, if one had talent, it could even be a lucrative job. For these reasons, in 1710 Tiepolo was taken on as an apprentice at the famous studio of Gregorio Lazzarini, at San Pietro di Castello, not far from his house.

Questions of method

The principal source of information on Tiepolo's youthful works – let us say from when he started work in Lazzarini's studio (1710) to shortly after 1717, when he parted from his first master – is the *Vita di Gregorio Lazzarini*, written by Vincenzo Da Canal in 1732 and published for the first time under the editorship of Giannantonio Moschini in 1809[10]. Da Canal writes:

"G. B. Tiepolo son of Domenico, merchant in ship's goods, born on the fifth of March of the year 1697, now a famous name, was his [Lazzarini's] pupil although he departed from his diligent manner, since all spirit and fire he embraced a more rapid and resolute one. This appears in the *Apostles*, which at the age of nineteen years he painted above the niches of the church of the Ospedaletto. He was the painter for the Doge Cornaro at San Polo, in whose rich home (...) he presided over the distribution of paintings, as well as making several 'sovra-porte' with *portraits* and *pictures* of good taste. At the age of twenty in competition with other painters he painted on canvas *Pharaoh Submerged*, a work that was applauded on the day of San Rocco, when it was exhibited. He frescoed a *Sala* in Palazzo Baglioni at San Cassiano (...). At Vascon, a villa in the Trevigiano, he painted *The Story of St. Lucy* in the ceiling of the church (...). At Biadene, in the Trevigiano again, in the church of M. Assunta, built by the N.H. Proccuratore Pisani, he did *his first frescoed work...*"[11].

Ever since then the critics have sifted Da Canal's words carefully in the hope of unearthing more information on the early phases of Tiepolo's career, but sometimes confusing the original statements of the source with the "notes" added by the nineteenth-century editor. Very few definite facts have emerged from these attempts, which are rendered even more difficult by the fact that until his fresco-work for the Patriarchate in Udine, in the mid-1720s, only two works are dated directly on the surface of the paintings: the so-called *Repudiation of Hagar* in the Rasini collection in Milan[12] and the *St. Lucy in Glory* at Vascon.

Thus the actual order of Tiepolo's early works is by no means certain; the sequence varies according to the opinions of different scholars and also according to more general changes of taste. It is like attempting to put together the fragments of a precious vase that has been shattered: one starts by assembling the largest, most obvious pieces, one passes onto the smaller shards and finally, by trial and error, one attempts to add the tiny fragments, inserting them wherever they seem to fit. The merest glance at the contradictory and confused collocations of Tiepolo's early works is enough to reveal how imperfect the historiographic reconstruction of his youthful career is.

Therefore all one can do is return to the original source, Da Canal, to establish at least a few definite dates and around these arrange the other works that critics have attributed to the same period. Substantially, Da Canal locates six "large shards" for us: two dated works – the *Apostles* in

[7] *Letters from Italy* (...) *by an English woman*, London 1776, III, p. 274, quoted by F. Haskell (1980, p. 274, n. 1)

[8] K. Pomian (1989, pp. 259-260).

[9] See of course F. Haskell (1980) and K. Pomian (1989).

[10] *Vita di Gregorio Lazzarini scritta da Vincenzo Da Canal P.V.* (1732) *Pubblicata la prima volta nelle nozze Da Mula-Lavagnoli*, ed. G. Moschini, in Vinegia, Palese, 1809.

[11] V. Da Canal (1732, pp. XXXI-XXXII). My italics.

[12] The date 1719 was read by Morassi in 1934, and has since disappeared.

the Ospedaletto, which he attributes to Tiepolo at the age of nineteen, and the *Pharaoh Submerged*, painted by Tiepolo at the age of twenty – and four undated works (at least according to Da Canal) but probably not too distant in time: the *portraits* and the *pictures* for Doge Cornaro, the *Sala* frescoed in Palazzo Baglioni at San Cassiano, the *St. Lucy in Glory* at Vascon and the *fresco* in the church of Maria Assunta at Biadene. Still restricting ourselves to Da Canal, we can add a seventh "shard", which the writer cites a little later but mentions as "one of his first creations": "A *sala in Ca' Zenobio* divided into various stories"[13]. The biographer states that Tiepolo was born in 1697 and not the previous year, and thus when he says "aged nineteen" for the *Apostles* at the Ospedaletto he means 1716, which we must obviously interpret as 1715; similarly, the *Pharaoh Submerged* which Da Canal assigns to Tiepolo aged twenty must be understood as belonging to 1716.

Other little pieces of data have been provided by various scholars, whose research has managed to fill some of the gaps in our knowledge of Tiepolo's career between the second and third decade of the century. Mariuz and Pavanello (1985) have established 1716 and 1719 as the *post quem* and *ante quem* for the work in Biadene, which Da Canal claimed as Giambattista's "first fresco". The same scholars (1985) have ascertained that the fresco Da Canal says was carried out for Palazzo Baglioni at San Cassiano (but in Abbot Moschini's transcription of 1809, it must be noted) was in fact done in the Villa Baglioni in Massanzago, at some point before 1724 (figs. 4, 5). Moretti (1973; 1985) managed to pin down the *Martyrdom of St. Bartholomew* in San Stae to the year 1722 (fig. 7), and the small canvas with the *St. Dominic in Glory* at the Accademia in Venice to before 1723 (fig. 8). Moretti also unearthed the documents that enable us to date the *Madonna del Carmelo* in the Brera between 1721 and 1727, while Barcham (1989) has narrowed this period to around 1722. Finally Moretti (1984-85) and at the same time Aikema (1985) have discovered the *St. Lucy in Glory* of Vascon, which Da Canal referred to, and read the date 1722 on it. Thus there are no more than about ten works that can be assigned with any certainty to these years; another sixty or so, however, have been attributed to the same period.

As has happened in other cases where documentary evidence is scanty, an insidious mechanism has been set in motion. Starting from the corroborated works, critics have proposed other paintings as being by Tiepolo, without the support of any documentary proof or even circumstantial evidence, but merely on the basis of presumed similarities in style; this new corpus – a mixture of certainties and interesting hypotheses – has then become a pole of attraction, drawing yet more works into its field of influence. Finally, with the consent of the critics, this highly conjectural catalogue has in turn become the basis for comprehensive interpretations of the works of the young Tiepolo. In other words, critical literature on the subject has behaved rather like an accordion, alternating periods of generous expansion and excessive openness with moments of restrictive tightness, when attempts are made to take stock of the data in order to establish "once and for all" the nature of Tiepolo's early poetics. This is what happens in bibliography when, after decades of individual and limited contributions, the need is felt for a systematic monography.

But as the level of 'conceptuality' in Giambattista Tiepolo's youthful corpus is dangerously high, it is best to start from the facts.

The apprenticeship with Gregorio Lazzarini

Having to make a virtue of necessity, Giambattista thus embarked on an artistic career and from 1710 worked as an apprentice with Gregorio Lazzarini (1655-1730), who "lived and kept his studio at San Pietro di Castello"[14]. It is fairly clear that this arrangement was not only to be explained by the fact that the painter's studio was just a few minutes' walk from the Corte di San

[13] V. Da Canal (1732, p. XXXIV).

[14] G.M. Urbani de Gheltof (1879, pp 4-5). The idea that the young Tiepolo was obliged to undertake this career finds support in a document which Federico Montecuccoli degli Erri discovered and generously made known to us. This is a deed executed before a notary in which Giambattista's mother, Orsetta, a widow for ten years and now "in dire need", recounts that she has pledged some of her belongings (of modest value) with the goldsmith Giambattista Moscheni "at the sign of the Seven sisters". Whatever the outcome of the case Orsetta brought against Moscheni, it is worth noting that the document bears the date 22 November 1709, and that just a few months later Giambattista "had to" start his apprenticeship with Gregorio Lazzarini (ASV, *Notarile, Atti, Bellan Giacomo, Estragiudiziali*, b. 1864).

Domenico. The choice had fallen on the painter who "then enjoyed the most noble fame" in the city[15] and whose *atelier* seemed in many ways the most promising, even in a city so well-supplied with places where a young man could embark upon a profitable apprenticeship. Lazzarini's studio enjoyed connections with a host of important local and international patrons, and it was the well-established practice of Italian studios that the *magister* would pass these connections onto his most talented pupils.

In 1694 Lazzarini had been officially enrolled in the list of painters *"di Stato"* thanks to a commission to paint six canvases for the triumphal arch built in honor of Francesco Morosini il Peloponnesiaco in the Sala dello Scrutinio of the Palazzo Ducale. In 1698, with Antonio Molinari and maybe Antonio Bellucci, he had painted a cycle of large paintings on mythological themes for the Procurator Vittore Correr[16]. He had painted a ceiling for the new Palazzo of the Zenobio family at the Carmini, where the French painter Louis Dorigny had already done a series of frescoes and where Luca Carlevarijs enjoyed the position of *pittore di famiglia*. There had also been jobs for the Widmann family (a cycle of historical paintings on Scipio the African), then, in the 1680s, for the Labia family, who owned the largest collection in Venice of works by the great Neapolitan painter Luca Giordano[17], and again, at the beginning of the eighteenth century, several canvases for the Palazzo of the Lin family on the Grand Canal[18]. "A highly prolific painter [Lazzarini], his works were requested in great abundance above all in the Venetian palazzi and the mainland villas of the Baglioni, Barbarigo, Donà, Falier, Nani, Sagredo, Zenobio, Zorzi etc."[19]: almost all these names will turn up later as generous patrons of Giambattista Tiepolo. For the Dominicans of Santi Giovanni e Paolo, Lazzarini worked on several occasions between 1699 and 1710-1714[20]: in 1699 he delivered the *Mystic Wedding of St. Catherine*, in 1700, *St. John the Baptist Preaching*, in 1703 the *Presentation at the Temple*, in 1707 the *Plague of Serpents* and the *Punishing of Korakh, Datan and Abiram*, and finally between 1710 and 1714 — when Giambattista was already in the studio — the *Massacre of the Innocents*. Not to mention the commissions for foreign patrons that Da Canal tells us of: the Elector of Meinz, the Counts of Schönborn, the Princes of Liechtenstein and others still in Poland and France. But Tiepolo's aim was not simply to inherit the opportunities that Lazzarini's business put in his way.

Da Canal tells us that Giambattista soon left behind the style of his master and, "all spirit and fire", embraced a manner that was "rapid and resolute". We will return to these words later for their aesthetic significance; what interests us now is a simple biographical observation: Da Canal himself, who seems so keen to stress Tiepolo's precocity in picking up the fashions of contemporary painting, states that the young pupil departed "from his [Lazzarini's] diligent manner" but does *not* say that he left the studio.

When Da Canal talks of abjuration, he is referring solely to artistic choices, not to actual disagreements on a personal level, culminating in rude door-slammings. Violent emotional reactions are not in keeping with what we know of Giambattista's character; we must bear this in mind in order to avoid any pre-romantic interpretation of Da Canal's description of Tiepolo as "all spirit and fire".

Tiepolo received far more from Lazzarini than was believed until quite recently. He was not enrolled in the *Fraglia* (Guild) of Venetian painters — that is, considered an independent *maestro* — until 1717, when he was twenty-one. Da Canal himself assigns his first works (the *Apostles* in the Ospedaletto and the *Pharaoh Submerged*, respectively of 1715 and 1716) to the period when he was still under Lazzarini's tutorship. Our own opinion is that Tiepolo's apprenticeship lasted from 1710 to 1717 and that, although his career was already launched, Giambattista preferred to stay with his first master until he was of age. We can therefore imagine the young artist working serenely alongside the tolerant Lazzarini, on the one hand, absorbing the

[15] V. Da Canal (1732, p. XXXI).
[16] The three canvases, painted one each by the three artists, are now at Ca' Rezzonico, but for the attributions cf.: G. Romanelli and F. Pedrocco, *Ca' Rezzonico*, Milan 1986, pp. 41-44.
[17] F. Haskell (1980, p. 250).
[18] S. Sponza (1989, pp. 248-253).
[19] G.M. Pilo, entry on "Gregorio Lazzarini", in *La pittura del Seicento a Venezia* (1959, pp. 136-137).
[20] S. Sponza (1989, pp. 244-246). The canvases are in the Basilica of Santi Giovanni e Paolo.

profound sense of his teachings and, on the other, remaining keenly awake to all that was going on in Venetian painting in this second decade of the century.

Federico Bencovich had returned to Venice in 1710 and Giambattista Piazzetta was enrolled in the *Fraglia* of Venetian painters in 1711, immediately after his return from Bologna. Andrea Celesti had died in 1711, but between 1705 and 1707 he had carried out a cycle of luminous frescoes in Caselle d'Asolo that already looked forward to the revival of the Veronese style[21], brought about by Sebastiano Ricci, who was away from Venice during the years of Tiepolo's education, as was Giannantonio Pellegrini, Rosalba Carriera's brother-in-law. The Venetian *maestri* of the late seventeenth-century were active[22]: Antonio Bellucci, who sometimes worked alongside Antonio Molinari and Lazzarini, Louis Dorigny, with his openness to international culture, Nicolò Bambini, who at the end of the century had frescoed Villa Perocco at Vascon di Carbonera[23]. And the turn-of-the-century painters were still on the scene: Paolo Pagani, Giovanni Segala and Antonio Balestra.

But before entering the troubled question of these varied influences, we must return to the studio of the fifty-five-year-old Gregorio Lazzarini and ask ourselves – since seven years is by no means an insignificant period of time – what effect his tutorship had on Giambattista's pictorial language.

The influence of Lazzarini

Until only a few years ago criticism on Tiepolo doubted that the academic Lazzarini could have contributed much to Tiepolo's formation. Indeed, it actually became a commonplace to affirm that Tiepolo's development as an independent artist did not truly begin until he turned his back on Lazzarini's style and studio and directed his attention towards Piazzetta and Federico Bencovich, who at the beginning of the eighteenth century represented a continuation, in highly dramatic and rhetorical terms, of Venetian "tenebrismo", a tendency that had characterized the end of the sixteenth-century. Da Canal, who defined Lazzarini as "a little weak in the force of color", is cited in support of this conviction, which has been shared by a long line of critics right up to our own time. A few examples may serve. Anna Pallucchini writes that "from his apprenticeship with Lazzarini, all that the young painter gained was a training in the basic techniques"[24]. Lazzarini is called "retardataire" by Wittkower[25]. Rodolfo Pallucchini talks of a "return to classicism of an academic flavor"[26], while Levey swiftly dismisses the relationship between Lazzarini and Tiepolo, limiting it to the transmission of profitable social occasions[27].

There is no need now to revise Gregorio Lazzarini's position in historical and artistic terms: the old artist was what he was, and we cannot recreate his works just for the pleasure of turning him into an unsung hero[28]. What we must do is assess fairly his influence on the development of Tiepolo. Morassi went to the heart of the matter when he wrote that what the pupil picked up from his master was a color that was "iridescent at heart (...) and above all he learnt the skill of boldly moving complex groups of figures in vast pictorial compositions", even though he immediately goes on to state his belief that Tiepolo's conversion to the "tenebrismo" of Bencovich and Piazzetta was a moment of expressive liberation[29]. Martini sees Lazzarini as "dominated by a mannered classicism, of Bolognese and Roman derivation"[30], but, he adds, "with a color of extraordinary excellence"[31]. This fits in with Morassi's intuition, adding a further allusion to the world of Bologna and Rome, to which Giambattista's receptive talents are unlikely to have been indifferent. A good critical summary of Lazzarini's poetics has been provided recently by Sponza (1989). Following Da Canal, the author recalls the two years Lazzarini spent in the studio of the *tenebroso*, Francesco Rosa, who in turn acted as a mediator of the language of the Genoan painter, Langetti, whose tormented works are to be found in various Venetian collections, and

[21] F. Zava Boccazzi (1965).
[22] In general: R. Pallucchini (1981, pp. 363-395).
[23] F. D'Arcais (1967).
[24] A. Pallucchini (1968, p. 85).
[25] R. Wittkower (1958, p. 418).
[26] R. Pallucchini (1981, p. 363).
[27] M. Levey (1986, pp. 6-7).
[28] However, there is no critical monography on him, as S. Sponza quite rightly points out (1989).
[29] A. Morassi (1955, p. 6).
[30] E. Martini (1982, p. 3).
[31] *Ibidem*, p. 4.

3.
opposite
Portrait of Doge Marco Cornaro. Venice, private collection.

4.
Triumph of Aurora.
Massanzago (Padua),
Villa Baglioni, ceiling.

5.
Myth of Phaeton.
Massanzago (Padua),
Villa Baglioni, east wall.

of Luca Giordano, in his Ribera phase. To these must be added the still vibrant tradition of Tintoretto and, as regards the architectural settings, that of Paolo Veronese, "but in the classicist interpretation of Padovanino"[32]. With this eclectic heritage at his disposal, Lazzarini could change his style according to whether his subject was biblical, hagiographic or erotic[33]; but mostly he "seems to use the same approach, in the art of painting, that rhetoricians used in theirs: in accordance with the argument to be described or represented, the style could be sublime, middling or trifling"[34]. In short, he was a master of vast and composite culture, who succeeded in transmitting to his pupils, Tiepolo included, an admiration for the city's glorious achievements in the sixteenth century along with an interest in the tensions and the solemn, dusky tints of the *tenebrosi*; furthermore, he was able to suggest a way out from the arid shoals of seventeenth-century *tenebrismo*, or at any rate an alternative to it, through the ordered arrangement of figures in wide settings and a careful balance between figures and their surroundings; lastly, he insisted on the need to master drawing skills and to study all technical procedures with infinite patience: this was undoubtedly the "Bolognese" component in his professional make-up.

Barcham goes even further in his revaluation of Lazzarini as Tiepolo's first and, we might add, only master[35]. He actually declares it "unnecessary" to refer to Piazzetta and Bencovich in order to explain the lesson in *tenebrismo* that Tiepolo learnt while still in Lazzarini's studio; he emphasizes the importance of the Bolognese manner in Lazzarini's pedagogical rules and concludes that Tiepolo learnt from him "how a painting developed from its first drawings through to its eventual completion on canvas"[36]. Thus it was not only a training in techniques and practical skills that Lazzarini imparted to Tiepolo, but also a considerable store of artistic culture that the artist was then able to draw on at will, adopting whichever tendency the theme called for. Of course, this is not to deny the attention that Tiepolo undoubtedly paid to Piazzetta's sacred dramas or to the singular contorsions of masses and lights in Bencovich's works; but we must see this attention in terms of an inquisitive interest rather than an acritical devotion. In Lazzarini's studio Tiepolo learnt fast. He absorbed all he could from his master and at the same time observed all that the teeming city had to offer him. He looked, experimented, assimilated and rejected nothing; all that passed before him was stored up for later use. It is true that in his works for the Ospedaletto (1715) and in his *Pharaoh Submerged* (1716) he revealed a style that was already close to the "neo-*tenebrismo*" of Piazzetta and Bencovich; but at the same time he was still producing works like the *Cornaro Portraits* that were based firmly on Lazzarinian principles – and, indeed, works that were extremely forward-looking, well beyond Lazzarini but also beyond Piazzetta: wide-ranging compositions, with soft, light colors and architectural backgrounds depicted *sottinsù* (from below) in the Veronese manner. In later years, he was to produce works that looked back to Lazzarini, if the occasion called for it; and even in his maturity, when he had quite firmly adopted the neo-Veronesian style, he was still capable of returning to Piazzetta. In this sense it is certainly true that he left Lazzarini behind, but the independence he achieved was a fully conscious one: he felt perfectly free to experiment with the manners and techniques of all his contemporaries and of the artists of the past, without imitating any of them; this independence enabled him to become the most cultured painter of the eighteenth century – but the only Tiepolo of his age.

The Lazzarini manner, which Tiepolo was to reject in favor of other solutions, was defined by Da Canal: "Natural and not furious, solid and well-settled in the shadows and very different from the most recent of this century"[37]. As always when dealing with texts that are remote from our own age, we must interpret the vocabulary Da Canal used according to his own codes of meaning, and not ours.

Natural for an eighteenth-century connoisseur did not mean "similar to what the eye sees in

[32] R. Pallucchini (1981, p. 377).
[33] Lazzarini's numerous erotic paintings are all small in size and are part of the voyeuristic tradition of the sixteenth-century private studios, so that the moralistic Da Canal judges them thus: "This is highly dangerous work for an honest Christian man" (1732, p. LXXI). See also E. Martini (1982, nn. 19-23 on pp. 467-468).
[34] S. Sponza (1989, p. 245).
[35] W.L. Barcham (1989, pp. 13 foll.).
[36] *Ibidem*, p. 13.
[37] V. Da Canal (1732, p. XXV).

6.
Rape of Europa.
Venice, Gallerie
dell'Accademia.

nature", but "calm, measured, not odd or queer"; whereas Tiepolo's images are often defined by his supporters as imaginative, bizarre and overwhelmingly inventive. Thus Zanetti wrote of Tiepolo: "this skillful painter is most worthy of being listed among those who honor the Venetian school; his *most lively spirit* combined with intelligence is in fact *singular*. His distinct gift is his *readiness to invent*, and, inventing, to distinguish and resolve at the same time quantities of figures *with novel expedients*, with multiplicity, and excellent arrangements and other things..."[38].

The words, *"not furious"*, refer to the actual process of painting, or rather to the time taken to create the shapes on the surface of the canvas. Even today in Venetian dialect, the word *"furia"* is not synonymous with *"furore"* (fury) but means haste, rapidity. Lazzarini was therefore slow and deliberate, while Tiepolo worked at lightning speed, a characteristic that links him to a certain virtuoso tendency in Baroque art – one thinks of Luca Giordano, known as *"fa presto"*. It is significant that the well-known drawing with *The Life-Drawing Class* shows a sand-glass at the feet of the model: the pupils must learn to draw carefully and diligently, but they must learn to do so within the established time-limits[39]. Thus Count Tessin was to write of him in a letter sent to the King of Sweden in 1736, informing him of the outcome of his attempts to persuade Tiepolo to go to Stockholm: "He does a painting in less time than others need to mix the colors"[40].

"Solid and well-settled in the shadows" is another technical description, and at the same time an appreciation of the sobriety of his chiaroscuro, in contrast with Tiepolo who, particularly in this youthful phase, makes an almost sculptural use of lights and shadows, picked up from Piazzetta's and Bencovich's *"macchia"* painting.

In conclusion, Tiepolo's debt to Lazzarini cannot be evaluated on the technical or stylistic plane, but rather in terms of professional deontology: the young artist was taught to respect the local artistic tradition, in both its recent and more remote manifestations, without being stylistically constrained by it, and he learnt how to adapt his tone and style to the demands of the subject. This was the best apprenticeship that a young painter subjected to the rules of the old studios could have hoped for: self-discipline, a wide range of cultural reference points and total freedom of expression.

A sudden change in direction?

Let us return to Da Canal once again: "Tiepolo (...) was his [Lazzarini's] pupil although he departed from his diligent manner, since all spirit and fire he embraced a more rapid and resolute one". It is on these words that so many critics have based their idea of a sudden change in direction on Tiepolo's part around 1715: a swerve from the calm Lazzarini towards Piazzetta and Bencovich. But we do not believe that things happened in quite this way, or at least we do not accept this as the real meaning of Da Canal's words.

It is undoubtedly true that around that date, if not earlier, Tiepolo abandoned Lazzarini's manner, which was too slow, too measured and rigidly defined in closed forms. The "closed" form is typical of the academic approach, whatever the tonalities of the palette, whether light or dark. We use the term "closed form" to refer to paintings in which the images are so created that beneath the colors we can always sense (we *sense*, we do not *see*) the original drawing; the individual elements of the work are all delimited by strict outlines and do not blend into one another in the atmospheric light, nor under the reverberatory effect of the complementary colors, as happens in Paolo Veronese's works. Academic taste decreed that this was the only way to guarantee the decorum of the overall figuration: the artist passed from the original idea to the graphic plan, which was worked out to the last detail; then to the projection of this onto the surface and finally to the chromatic details – which is to say, the actual painting, which was done with unvaried brushstrokes, in long measured movements. This was an extremely slow process, whereby every

[38] A.M. Zanetti (1733, p. 62).
[39] The drawing is attributed to Tiepolo by A. Morassi (1971) with the hypothesis that it represents Piazzetta's studio.
[40] Letter of May 25th 1736 to the Court of Sweden, published by O. Siren (1902).

7.
opposite
Martyrdom of St. Bartholomew. Venice, Church of San Stae.

painting seemed to be conceived along the lines of an oration, confined within a straitjacket of rhetorical norms which resulted in a form that was heavy and stilted, but – according to conservative aesthetic taste – correct and harmonious.

Lazzarini's work is like that. But Piazzetta, who is seen as the opponent of this "diligent manner", adopted closed forms as well – so much so that his figures often seem to be contained within niche-like shells, as if they were painted sculptures[41]. Furthermore – and this is what interests us principally – he too was slow and was even accused of indolence by clients, annoyed by delays in the delivery of works. It is thus difficult to maintain that when Da Canal refers to Tiepolo's embracing a "swift and resolute" manner, he is talking about his conversion to the style of Piazzetta and Bencovich.

At a certain point in his wide-ranging investigation of Italian art between the seventeenth and eighteenth centuries, Wittkower remarks that compared with the highly finished perfection of late-seventeenth-century frescoes, Tiepolo's approach was peremptory and almost brusque: "so that in reproductions details of his frescoes often look almost like sketches"[42]. A fine intuition, but not a new one. Throughout the Baroque period there were numerous fresco-artists who worked at lightning-speed, from Pietro da Cortona to Luca Giordano, and this "sketchy" effect recognised in Tiepolo should be extended to them. In oil-painting, on the other hand, the procedures were slower and remained so in the eighteenth century as well, despite its fame as the age of the light, effervescent touch. It is no accident that Tiepolo's speed and dexterity increased at the same time that Italian and European clients began to clamor once again for frescoes, and frankly it would be hard to say which tendency came first. As has already been pointed out, it is clear that the "swift and resolute" manner Tiepolo adopted around the time of his paintings for the Ospedaletto was not an indication that he had decided to adhere to Piazzetta's technical and stylistic movement, which was almost exasperatingly slow. Rather, it showed that he had chosen a mode of operation that allowed him to pass as directly as possible from the mental formulation of the iconic idea to its actual creation on the blank surface – which is to say, he had adopted a *bozzettistico* ("sketchy") manner for the entire creative process.

Mere haste had nothing to do with it – or rather it was not simply a matter of urgently honoring contracts with an increasing number of important patrons, partly because in 1715 the great and pressing occasions were all still ahead of him. It was a pyschological inclination that expressed itself by means of a certain technique, a technique that was gradually to bring with it a style. As we will see, in some cases the notable differences between the preparatory sketches and the final results indicate that the actual execution of the work was a moment of true creation for Tiepolo and this could not but influence his stylistic rendering. But not immediately, or at any rate not without major stylistic differences. What Tiepolo was trying out on the technical level was something that the Rococo movement, represented in Venice by Sebastiano Ricci, Pellegrini and Rosalba Carriera, was working out at the very same time in radical opposition to the pathetic-chiaroscuro taste of Piazzetta and Bencovich. This applied to the strictly technical field only; from the stylistic point of view, Giambattista still appeared to be linked to Piazzetta in many works, even if not in all. His figures are made up of rocky masses, the color obeys the norms of chiaroscuro and is laid on in strictly defined blocks, even though it is already stirred by glows and tonal-shifts that throb even in the gloomiest areas of the paintings, where the darkness gleams vibrantly, in a manner that recalls Crespi.

Rococo art is characterised by dexterous virtuosity, luminous *colorismo* and rapidity in creation, and this is particularly true of Venetian Rococo, since the French version, the other pole of this international *langue*, remained closely tied to the tradition of Poussin's drawing-based classicism[43]. The closed forms of Piazzetta and Bencovich were countered by the open forms

[41] For Piazzetta see at least: A. Mariuz (1982); R. Pallucchini (ed.) (1983).
[42] R. Wittkower (1958, p. 320).
[43] Cf. C. Galli (1987-88).

8.
opposite
St. Dominic in Glory. Venice, Gallerie dell'Accademia.

9.
Queen Zenobia
Haranguing her Soldiers.
Washington, National
Gallery of Art.

10.
opposite
Detail from fig. 9.

of the Rococo artists. The images were constructed with broken lines, often only by means of the color which enabled the light to flood freely through every point of the painting; the light seems to seep into the forms and implode there, while the forms flare up into the atmosphere. The pictorial space becomes a luminous, sparkling zone, voluptuous and fragrant: it was no accident that the *deus ex machina* of this movement was Paolo Veronese and that it was to prove Tiepolo's final landfall.

The contrast between these two forms was not only limited to different circles of painters, but affected different groups of clients and patrons as well. The closed form was always the natural choice for religious commissions, which called for a certain decorum and loftiness of language; open form was to become the favorite style for privately commissioned paintings on secular subjects[44]. But it could also happen that the very same lay client might ask for Piazzetta's profoundest note in his family chapel and for Pellegrini's light touch in decorating his palazzo; similarly, a painter such as Andrea Celesti, one of the protagonists of the shift at the beginning of the century from *tenebrismo* to *chiarismo*, was perfectly happy to adopt the modes of Venetian Baroque – *tenebrismo*, that is to say – in the ducal cycle in the church of San Zaccaria (1684-88), whereas in the frescoes of Caselle d'Asolo (1705-07) he switched to the neo-Veronesian style of Sebastiano Ricci[45].

This, after all, was a polemic that went back a long way – at least to the tail-end of the seventeenth century when the debate between *tenebrosi* and *chiaristi* raged throughout Venice[46].

Tiepolo at the crossroads
Tenebrismo had held sway in Venice throughout the 1660s and 1670s, at a time when the city had just readmitted the Jesuits, had elected a series of doges strictly loyal to the Pope, and was slowly

[44] On the powers of patronage of religious organisms in Venice, cf. F. Haskell (1980, pp. 268-269).
[45] F. Zava Boccazzi (1965).
[46] R. Pallucchini (1981, pp. 363-395).

11.
Justice and Peace.
Venice, Island of San Lazzaro degli Armeni, ceiling.

but inexorably edging its way off the European political scene. At the end of the century, however, the painters Antonio Molinari (1655-1704) and Paolo Pagani (1660-1716) had attempted a moderate revision of *tenebrismo* in order to adapt to new ways of thinking: religious fervor was dying down and the patriotic ardor of the ruling class was less evident, clients were increasingly inclined to compensate for the meaningless torpor of the age with stirring allegories taken from Roman history and mythology.

In particular Molinari "seems to purify the turbid inspiration of the poetics of the '*tenebrosi*' by giving expression to that naturalistic energy which at the beginning of the eighteenth century was to foment the movement led by Piazzetta"[47]. But this compromise solution, which was worked out entirely within the bounds of an outdated artistic tendency, could hardly respond to the needs of a society in transformation.

Andrea Celesti (1637-1711) was the artist who acted as a bridge between *tenebrismo* and the new aspirations of society. In the first decade of the eighteenth century, at Villa Rinaldi in Caselle d'Asolo, he painted a secular fresco-cycle in clear colors, based on encomiastic subjects inspired by a successful *melodramma*[48]. The elegant poses of the characters caught the attention of Tiepolo; indeed, one of them – Ceres, seen from behind in the scene of Olympus – was to recur often in Giambattista's works over the course of his career.

The group of *chiaristi* includes Nicolò Bambini (1651-1739) and Antonio Bellucci (1654-1726), who both attempted to revive the dazzling example of Paolo Veronese.

A few years before Celesti, Bambini had carried out another series of frescoes on a secular, *melodramma*-based subject at the Villa Perocco at Vascon di Carbonera[49], and it was in the parish-church of Vascon in 1722 that Tiepolo was to paint his fresco with *St. Lucy in Glory*. Around 1710 Nicolò Bambini worked in the Library of the Patriarch of Aquileia, Dionisio Dolfin, in Udine[50], the same Dolfin family for whom Tiepolo would paint the pictures of Roman history in their Palazzo at San Pantalon in Venice and, immediately afterwards or at the same time, the frescoes of the Patriarchal Palace in Udine. Naturally Bambini and Tiepolo are very different artists, but Tiepolo's skill consisted in being able to make use of every stimulus that he came across without ever betraying his own personality. Undoubtedly there must have been a confrontation between Bambini and Tiepolo, and we will hear more of it later.

The other representative of the neo-Veronesian movement, Antonio Bellucci, was extremely successful outside Venice as well. He worked for the Abbey of Klosterneuburg, near Vienna. In the Viennese palazzo of Johann Adam Andreas von Liechtenstein, he painted several canvases in which the relationship between the figures and the architecture echoes the monumentality of Paolo Veronese's settings. From March 1706 he was in Düsseldorf, working for the Palatine Count and Grand Elector of Bavaria, Johann Wilhelm of Pfalz[51], for whom he painted among other things a commemorative nuptial painting, a broad canvas of an elaborate and theatrical taste showing the whole company, which Tiepolo was to recall in the celebratory frescoes of Würzburg in the 1750s.

This was the path followed by the artists at work in Venice who were born in the 1660s, Antonio Balestra (1660-1740) and Giovanni Segala (1663-1720), before the real neo-Veronesian reforms brought about by Sebastiano Ricci (1659-1734) and Giannantonio Pellegrini (1675-1741) in the first decade of the eighteenth century.

Like Bellucci, whose pupil he had been, Antonio Balestra was an untiring traveler, although within the confines of the Italian peninsula. Rome, Emilia, Naples and then Emilia again: a *petit tour* that brought him into contact with Carlo Maratta in Rome, with Correggio, Annibale Carracci and the "*incamminati*" Reni and Domenichino in Emilia, and finally, in Naples, with the Neapolitan phase of Lanfranco and with Luca Giordano and Francesco Solimena. Subsequently

[47] R. Pallucchini (1981, p. 387).
[48] *Zenobia regina dei Palmireni.*
[49] F. D'Arcais (1967).
[50] A. Rizzi (1966).
[51] The date is to be found in an unpublished letter addressed by Johann Wilhelm to the Doge of Venice, Giovanni Cornaro, on 29 March 1710, with the aim of freeing Bellucci from the fiscal obligations he was subject to, even though away from Venice; it reads: "Serenissimo Principe, this month it is now four years since Antonio Bellucci, an old citizen of Your Serenity's, came to this court in the role of a painter..." ASV, *Collegio, Lettere Principi*, file 7, paper 180r.

he was in Venice until 1719 and Tiepolo was able to profit by his anthological culture. Returning then to Verona, his birthplace, Balestra seemed to resist the Rococo that was coming to the fore in Venice and abandoned himself to "a mixture of 'Barocchetto' languor of Marattesque origin and *luminismo* that derived ultimately from Correggio, whom he had admired in Emilia"[52]. In 1705 Giovanni Segala painted a *St. Maximus in Glory* for the ceiling of the Venetian church of San Cassiano; in this work the figures stand out against a clear open sky, and they appear to be constructed in an abbreviated, almost stenographic style. This too was a technique Tiepolo would adopt in many frescoed works; this mode of sketching in hasty strokes was in fact to become his own distinctive style.

Louis Dorigny (1654-1742) played an important role in broadening the range of Venetian art, opening it to international currents. He moved from Paris, where until 1672 he had attended the school of Charles Le Brun, to Baroque Rome. He arrived in Venice in the 1670s and stayed there almost ten years. After a visit to Vienna in 1711, he went to Udine, where he painted frescoes in the Cathedral in 1715. The following year he was back in Venice, in the church of Santa Maria degli Scalzi, frescoing the Chapel of the Virgin. In the church of San Silvestro he had already painted a ceiling (now lost) with an *Apotheosis of St. Silvester*, presenting the Venetian public for the first time with a complex *mise-en-scène* of *trompe l'œil* architecture, known as *"quadratura"*, of Roman origin. In the ballroom of Palazzo Zenobio in Venice, which had just been completed by the architect Antonio Gaspari, he created another ceiling structured around *quadrature*, this time following Bolognese taste. "One could say that it was Dorigny more than Fumiani who introduced to Venice (...) the illusory-perspective problem which would later be

[52] R. Pallucchini (1981, p. 388).

12.
Sacrifice of Isaac, detail.
Venice, Ospedaletto.

adapted to Venetian taste by Sebastiano Ricci"[53]. Udine, the Scalzi church and Ca' Zenobio were all stages of Tiepolo's career by the 1720s. They offered an extra lesson in *quadrature*, which at that moment was perhaps seen in Venice as little more than a rather fantastic curiosity, but for which Tiepolo would soon feel the need to avail himself of the "specialist" skills of Gerolamo Mengozzi, known as Il Colonna. And it was here that the ways divided in the eighteenth century. One road forked towards Piazzetta and Bencovich, who in the meantime had reached maturity in their own fashion, in Bologna, following the examples of Crespi (Piazzetta) and Cignani (Bencovich). The other led towards the Rococo of Sebastiano Ricci and the more affected style of Giannantonio Pellegrini, the precious pastels of Rosalba and, later, Jacopo Amigoni (1682-1752) and Giambattista Pittoni (1687-1767).

But Giambattista Tiepolo had reached the same fork in the roads. His technique already tended towards Rococo, but his actual style was as yet ambiguous and irresolute, as is indicated by the surprising distance in style between the *Apostles* of the Ospedaletto and various other youthful works, on the one hand, and the contemporary *Portraits* for the Cornaro family on the other. It was to be some time before his technique and style came together to form a coherent poetics.

The Ospedaletto

There are no documents in the archives about the paintings placed above the lateral arches in the Venetian church of Santa Maria dei Derelitti, which was known as the Ospedaletto from the seventeenth century onwards and before that dedicated to Santa Maria Assunta. The only writing on the canvases themselves is the date "1716", legible on the book that *St. Paul* is

[53] *Ibidem*, p. 376.

holding, above the second window on the left, and a "TP" that appears at the top-left-hand corner of the margin of the book held by *St. John the Apostle* above the first altar on the left, interpreted by Franca Zava Boccazzi as T[iepolo] P[inxit]: Tiepolo painted[54]. Nor do the printed sources help us much, since what they have to say is by no means unequivocal. Da Canal (1732) mentions Tiepolo's name and says that he was nineteen when he painted here "above the niches"; but he speaks in general of *Apostles* without specifying which and how many. Anton Maria Zanetti (1733) writes that "the two Prophets" above the pulpit – where the *Sacrifice of Isaac* hangs today – are by Tiepolo, but does not say which prophets they are. Some canvases were moved during restoration works in the last century or in the cleaning operation in 1905, and so it is not easy to tell which works Zanetti is referring to – nor, indeed, whether they really were prophets. Zanetti was hardly an infallible iconographer; Nicola Grassi's Evangelists, *St. Mark* and *St. Luke*, in the penultimate space on the right, are referred to simply as "figures", though they should have been easy enough to identify, despite the dim light of the church, and the same painter's *St. Philip* and *St. James the Less*, above the third space on the right, are called "prophets", instead of apostles[55]. However, he is of assistance when he attributes to Tiepolo the *Sacrifice of Isaac*, which he identifies above the *Pool of Bethesda* by Gregorio Lazzarini in the second space on the right, between the altar with Johann Carl Loth's *Deposition* and the altar with Francesco Ruschi's *Holy Family with St. Charles Borromeo, St. Anthony the Abbot and St. Veronica*. Today Lazzarini's picture is in the last space on the right, while Tiepolo's painting above the arch is now over the pulpit in the fourth space on the right. With such flimsy documentation, the attribution to Tiepolo of other paintings above the arches, apart from that with *St. John the Apostle* signed "TP" and the one with the *Sacrifice of Isaac* attested by Zanetti, can only be based on comparisons with other works by Tiepolo in the same years. And the comparison must of course be made with works that are indisputably his – works that are signed or vouched for by documentary sources – otherwise there is a risk of building a house of cards, with a series of fragile suppositions resting on other fragile suppositions.

But first of all, let us give a description of the church. One enters it from Barbaria delle Tole; it is built on a rectangular plan, with a single aisle, and the high altar is on the short side opposite the entrance-door; the ceiling is flat. The two long sides both have three altars, alternating with empty recesses on the right and windows on the left, making a total of twelve spaces in all, six on each side. On the vertical plane, each space is crowned by a lunette. The ones above the altars are fully rounded, whereas those above the empty recesses have flattened arches. Between the twelve lunettes and the ceiling there are twelve extrados; the ones above the flattened arches are more spacious than those above the altars, the latter being linked to the ceiling by corbels which seem to divide the six extrados they are applied to (three on each side) into separate halves. The twelve extrados contain whole canvases with figures facing one another, although the ones with the dividing corbels could suggest six pairs of separate spandrels. It is among these twelve figures above the arches that Tiepolo's paintings must be sought. We can ignore the decoration of the lower band, which has been dealt with thoroughly by recent studies[56], and for the moment we can leave aside the iconographic identification of the individual figures; this has been the object of long and as yet unresolved disputes between scholars but, in this case at least, it does not seem decisive in identifying Tiepolo's work. In fact, the two texts cited in Note 56 suggest very different iconographic sequences, and we will refer to them when needed, but they both agree in their identifications of Tiepolo's pictures. Let us concentrate instead on the paintings above the arches. Scholarship is now unanimous in accepting that the *Sacrifice of Isaac* is much later than the other pictures by Tiepolo. A survey published in 1724 by the architect Domenico Rossi can help us to understand just how much later[57]. For reasons of

[54] F. Zava Boccazzi (1979).
[55] B. Aikema (1989, pp. 169-189) refers to them (as he had already done in 1982) as the prophets Ezekiel and Jeremiah.
[56] S. Sponza (1986-87); B. Aikema (1989).
[57] The document was published by M. Muraro (1975); we here quote a few passages: "... having made diligent observation whether the two little cantoria one above the other that protrude into the church itself, which occupy the columns, and deform the architecture since the above-mentioned cantoria have no equal in any other space whether it is best to remove them (...). It is my opinion that since in the church there are three empty spaces between the three altars that correspond to the three large windows on the opposite side, better form and order would result if a similar accompaniment would be made to the empty space that is next to the girls' choir, that is to say a large painted picture beneath, and above, in the vault, its half-moon window or "*gelosia*", a companion to the above-mentioned one by the choir, which serves the girls to listen to the divine service; and in this manner one façade will correspond perfectly to the other, and the architecture will not be occupied".

Arrangement of the paintings at the Ospedaletto. In italics the names of the artists, in roman the titles of the works.

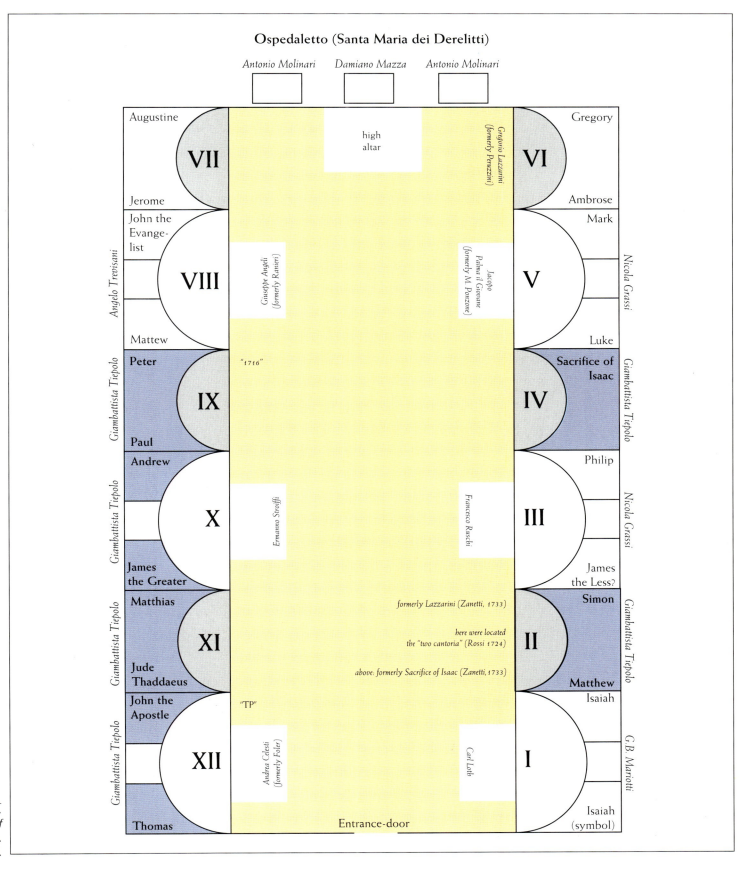

Ospedaletto (Santa Maria dei Derelitti)

Antonio Molinari   *Damiano Mazza*   *Antonio Molinari*

Augustine — **VII** — Jerome

high altar

Gregorio Lazzarini (formerly Peruzzini)   Gregory — **VI** — Ambrose

Angelo Trevisani   John the Evangelist — **VIII** — Mattew

Giuseppe Angeli (formerly Ranieri)   "1716"

Jacopo Palma il Giovane (formerly M. Ponzone)   Mark — **V** — Luke   *Nicola Grassi*

Giambattista Tiepolo   Peter — **IX** — Paul

Andrew — **X** — James the Greater   *Ermanno Stroiffi*

Francesco Ruschi   Sacrifice of Isaac — **IV** — Philip   *Giambattista Tiepolo*

Giambattista Tiepolo   Matthias — **XI** — Jude Thaddaeus

formerly Lazzarini (Zanetti, 1733)
here were located the "two cantoria" (Rossi 1724)
above: formerly Sacrifice of Isaac (Zanetti, 1733)

James the Less? — **III** — Simon   *Nicola Grassi*

Simon — **II** — Matthew   *Giambattista Tiepolo*

Giambattista Tiepolo   John the Apostle — **XII** — Thomas   "TP"

Andrea Celesti (formerly Foler)   *Carl Loth*

Isaiah — **I** — Isaiah (symbol)   *G.B. Mariotti*

Entrance-door

13.
overleaf
Power of Eloquence.
Venice, Palazzo Sandi.

14.
Detail from fig. 13.

architectural harmony, Rossi suggested removing the two small cantoria where the girls of the hospice sang and followed the Mass. He then suggested that the bare wall thus created should be dealt with in the same way as the "empty space next to the choir". This empty space (the last on the right, since the choir he referred to was up behind the high altar) still had a painting by Peruzzini on its base and a grating that corresponded to the lunette. In the space that was to be harmonized with the rest of the church, Rossi's suggestion was to fix a *"gelosia"*, or grating, like the one next to the choir, whereby the chorists could join in the services with their singing. Today, in the last recess on the right, there is a lunette with a grating, but where is the one that Rossi planned in 1724? Or rather: where were the two little cantoria which, "one above the other", occupied the pillars? They were above the second recess on the right, the lunette of which is now walled-up but which until fairly recently had a *"gelosia"*: above that second recess on the right where in 1733 Zanetti saw Lazzarini's "large picture", with Tiepolo's *Sacrifice of Isaac* above it. Therefore the architect's suggestions were put into operation between 1724, the year in which we believe Tiepolo was commissioned to paint the *Sacrifice* and delivered it, and 1730, when Lazzarini died[58].

However, if this is so, it means that between 1715, the year Da Canal says that Tiepolo began work there, and 1716, the date that can be read on the *St. Paul* and which can be considered as concluding the decoration (with the sole exception of the *Sacrifice of Isaac*), there were only eleven canvases in place. Aikema (1989) suggests that the series was complete from the beginning and that the twelfth painting was a *Triumph of David*, by Tiepolo, which was lost when the cantoria were removed and the grating was inserted in the lunette; he claims that the preparatory sketch for this is the little painting formerly in the Voss collection in Berlin and now at the Louvre. And indeed the Louvre sketch reveals an almost incandescent use of *colorismo*, with broad slashes of

[58] S. Sponza (1987) suggests 1730 for the *Pool of Bethesda*.

[59] To see just how important the delegates of the hospice considered the acoustics of the room and the quality of their female choir, one need only look through the documents published in *Arte e musica all'Ospedaletto. Schede d'archivio sull'attività musicale degli ospedali dei Derelitti e dei Mendicanti di Venezia (sec. XVI-XVIII)*, Venice 1978.

[60] Isaiah and his symbol can be recognised on the basis of a passage in the *Old Testament*, which says that a seraphim touched the prophet's mouth with a live coal which he had taken from the altar with the tongs: *Isaiah, 6, 6-7*. The picture was attributed by N. Ivanoff (1942-1954, p. 158) to Giambattista Mariotti; S. Sponza (1987) and B. Aikema (1989) agree with the attribution.

[61] The iconography of Simon with the saw, the symbol of his martyrdom, is medieval and derives from the *Legenda Aurea* by Jacopo Da Varagine. Matthew has the traditional attributes of the book and the angel who dictated it to him. B. Aikema (1989) instead sees them as the prophets Isaiah and Daniel, whose attributes are in fact identical to those of the two apostles.

[62] G.M. Pilo (1982).

[63] B. Aikema (1989) also believes them to be prophets: Ezekiel on the left and Jeremiah on the right.

[64] M. Muraro (1975), followed by S. Sponza (1987), thought that the two cantoria were here rather than in the second recess.

[65] Scholars have not yet managed to attribute this pair with any certainty; the same is true of the pair on the opposite wall; the only certainty is that the four *Doctors of the Church* are not by Tiepolo.

[66] Critics are in agreement that this pair is not by Tiepolo; recently the name of Angelo Trevisani has been put forward: cf. S. Sponza (1987, p. 224).

[67] It is a medieval tradition that James the Greater was the evangelizer of Spain and was buried in Compostela (hence the attribute of the pilgrim's shell): J. Da Varagine, *Legenda Aurea*.

red and dark scorched patches: it was thus easy to link it, at least chronologically, with the series in the Ospedaletto. A *Triumph of David*, argues Aikema, is justified iconographically by the musical purpose of the two cantoria and, unlike all the others in the series, it must have been rectangular in shape, to fit into the space between the ceiling and the higher cantorium. The idea is an interesting one but leaves some questions unanswered. Let us try to reflect on the actual position of the two cantoria. The lower one must have been halfway up, on a level with the pulpit and the windows with gratings behind the high altar; the other one, of course, must have been above the first one, on a level with the lunette, occupying it from pillar to pillar as Domenico Rossi's text tells us. But in this fashion the two cantoria, jutting out as they did, would have blocked the view of any painting placed above them, quite apart from the fact that there would have been very little space for it, unless the chorists were all huddled together in a fashion that would hardly have assisted their singing[59]. Rossi makes no mention of a rectangular painting in the lunette where he suggests inserting a grating, and yet we know that he was extremely sensitive to internal architectural harmony. And finally: where is the painting supposed to have gone? The most reasonable conclusion is that the delegates of the hospice commissioned only eleven paintings in 1715-1716, some of them from Tiepolo, and they then accepted Rossi's suggestions with regard to the cantoria and the grating, which meant that in 1724 they then had to order the final *soprarco* painting, the *Sacrifice of Isaac*, from Tiepolo, whose standing as a painter had risen notably in the meantime.

Let us now study in rapid succession the iconography of the pictures above the arches. Let us start from the first altar on the right as one enters and proceed anti-clockwise (see the plan on p. 37):

I. Above the altar with Loth's painting: the *Prophet Isaiah* on the left, the *Symbol of the Prophet Isaiah borne by a Seraph* on the right[60].

I. Above the second recess: the apostles *Simon the Zealot* on the left and *Matthew the Evangelist* on the right[61]. It was here that Zanetti saw the *Sacrifice of Isaac* by Tiepolo in 1733, and it was from here that Rossi had the two cantoria removed in 1724.

III. Above the altar with Ruschi's painting: the apostle *Philip* on the left and *James the Less* on the right[62], described as "prophets" by Zanetti who attributes them to Nicola Grassi[63].

IV. Above the pulpit: the *Sacrifice of Isaac* which Zanetti saw above Lazzarini's *Pool of Bethesda* in the second recess on the right; here, instead, Zanetti had seen: "Above the pulpit the two Prophets are by Giovan Battista Tiepolo"; it remains unclear who the two prophets (or apostles) were that he mentions[64].

V. Above Matteo Ponzone's painting, later lost and substituted by the *Annunciation* by Jacopo Palma il Giovane, Zanetti records: "The two figures in the corners above are by Nicola Grassi"; they are the evangelists *Mark* on the left and *Luke* on the right.

VI. In the final recess on the right is Lazzarini's *Pool of Bethesda*, which substitutes a painting by Peruzzini, now lost. Above the two doctors of the church, *Gregory* on the left and *Ambrose* on the right.

VII. In the first recess on the left of the high altar, above the window, the doctors of the church, *Augustine* on the right and *Jerome* on the left[65].

VIII. Above Giuseppe Angeli's painting, the evangelists *John* on the right and *Matthew* on the left[66].

IX. Above the window in the middle, the apostles *Peter* on the right and *Paul* on the left, with the date 1716 on the volume of the *Epistles*.

X. Above the altar with the picture by Ermanno Stroiffi, the apostles *Andrew* on the right and *James the Greater* on the left[67].

XI. Above the first window by the entrance, there is a pair that has not been definitely

identified as yet. According to Sandro Sponza, they are the apostles *Mathias* on the right and *Jude Thaddaeus* on the left; according to Bernard Aikema *Jude Thaddaeus* on the right and *Thomas* on the left[68].

XII. Finally, above the painting by Andrea Celesti on the first altar on the left, the apostles *John* on the right, with the initials "TP" on the book, and *Thomas* on the left[69].

This brings us to the crucial point: which are the canvases painted by Tiepolo and what do they tell us about his style, given that according to the sources they are his "opera prima"?

Tiepolo's signature on the *Sacrifice of Isaac* is undisputed, since it is attested by Anton Maria Zanetti. The trouble is that the painting is outside the time limits to be of any help as a touchstone in considering the other pictures in the Ospedaletto; this remains true even if in 1724 Tiepolo tried to "predate" his own style in order to blend in as far as possible with the works painted almost ten years earlier and thus avoid any jarring effects that his clients would not have appreciated. The only other works that are definitely proven are the figure of *John the Apostle*, initialled "TP", and that of *Thomas the Apostle*, since it is extremely unlikely that the same canvas would have been created by two different painters; nothing else is certain. We therefore have to leave the Ospedaletto and seek some kind of support among other works that we know from documentary sources to have been painted around the same time.

The sketch with the *Pharaoh Submerged*, which was mentioned by Da Canal (1732) and was perhaps exhibited at the Fair of San Rocco in August 1716 with a view to a decorative cycle for the church of Santi Cosma e Damiano on the Giudecca[70], is on a completely different scale from the figures of the Ospedaletto, which in their isolation have a biblical monumentality; thus it is difficult to compare it with these. Nonetheless, several similarities can be noted, particularly in the anatomy and in the faces, with the figures above the arches. The eyes of the people in the *Pharaoh Submerged* are painted with a single dab of the tip of the brush: a dark spot which is disturbing in its effect. Often on the oval of the faces there appears a dark area, as of a shadow cast by a nearby body, and the hair is wild and unkempt, as in Federico Bencovich's *Sacrifice of Iphigenia* at Pommersfelden. The arrangement of the figures, with Moses perched high on a rocky spur and the other characters distributed on various levels sloping downwards, recalls the skillful scenic composition of Gregorio Lazzarini's painting with the *Punishing of Korakh, Datan and Abiram* for Santi Giovanni e Paolo, of 1707. In the shape of the heads one notes a geometric simplification that makes no concessions to naturalism, drawing instead on the lofty abstraction of Piazzetta's faces, while the strained gestures of the bodies recall the "sick soul" of Federico Bencovich[71]. These are all morphological elements that we find in the painting of the *Apostles John and Thomas*, in that of *Ss. Peter and Paul* and that of *Ss. Simon and Matthew* on the opposite wall. In this last picture, furthermore, the angel accompanying *Matthew the Evangelist* (or the *Prophet Daniel*) faces us three-quarters on and is of a flaring pink complexion, due to the surfacing of the Armenian bolus which Tiepolo adopted in preparing the canvas, as Piazzetta used to do[72]. But one also notes a reddish haze in the bubble of space encircling his face. The same glow, as if the figure were standing in front of a brazier, can be seen in some background figures in Lazzarini's *Bacchantes*, now at Ca' Rezzonico but painted for the Procurator of St. Mark's, Vittore Correr; it also reappears in the female faces of the presumed *Hagar* in the Rasini collection in Milan, dated 1719.

The other two paintings that we believe are to be attributed to Tiepolo, obviously leaving aside the *Sacrifice of Isaac*, which we will return to later, are those in the tenth and eleventh space on the left, with the pairs *Andrew and James the Less* and *Mathias and Jude Thaddaeus*.

It is indirectly due to Wart Arslan (1936) that these two paintings are no longer simply studied in terms of the young Tiepolo giving himself over wholly to the pathetic-chiaroscuro manner

[68] S. Sponza (1987, p. 229 and n. 53) maintains that these are the apostles that Zanetti mistook for prophets in the fourth recess on the right, while in this position hung the painting with *Simon* and *Matthew*. F. Zava Boccazzi (1979, pp. 167-170) and B. Aikema (1989, pp. 174-175 and nn. 203-205) believe that, in place of the *Sacrifice of Isaac*, there was the canvas with *Simon* and *Matthew*, whereas the pair we are talking about, although they interpret them differently, have never been moved.

[69] According to B. Aikema (1989) *John the Apostle* on the right and *Mathias* on the left.

[70] W.L. Barcham (1989, pp. 15 foll.).

[71] E. Martini (1982, p. 44).

[72] A. Mariuz (1982, p. 75).

15.
opposite
Apotheosis of St. Luigi
Gonzaga, detail. London,
Courtauld Institute.

of Piazzetta and Federico Bencovich. Arslan suggests Pittoni and Diziani as possible authors of the two *soprarchi* and Franca Zava Boccazzi (1974, 1979) attributes them both to Pittoni. An intelligent mistake, in our opinion, since it opens the road to the idea that in this phase Tiepolo owed something to artists other than just Piazzetta and Bencovich. Egidio Martini (1974), after discovering the *Cornaro Portraits* which had been believed lost till then, attributes the five canvases of the Ospedaletto under discussion to Giambattista and suggests that Pittoni and Diziani were reference-points for Tiepolo in an attempt to explore new chromatic possibilities. Martini speaks of "blueish reflections that are to be found in the shadows, reflections that are typical in Tiepolo's youthful works but which are absent in all of Pittoni's"[73].

Other works documented by the sources – the *Cornaro Portraits*, the *Assumption* in Biadene and the frescoes for the Baglioni family – testify to the great range of Tiepolo's explorations so early in his career.

The Cornaro Portraits and other works

"He was the painter for the Doge Cornaro at San Polo, in whose rich home (...) he presided over the distribution of paintings, as well as making several *sovra-porte* with *portraits* and *pictures* of good taste." This famous note of Da Canal's (1732) offers us a good deal of important information about Tiepolo.

First of all we note his privileged contact, as a painter *"di casa"*, for the reigning doge, Giovanni II Corner of the San Polo branch. His portrait in the Doge's Palace had been painted by Gregorio Lazzarini[74] and we must therefore deduce that this was the key that opened the door of Palazzo Corner in San Polo to Giambattista. Doge Giovanni II was elected in 1709 and he governed until 1722; therefore the *Portraits* mentioned by Da Canal must have been painted a few years before that date. But the source also tells us that Tiepolo assumed the unusual role of supervisor of the family's paintings, an indication that the hobby of collecting, in certain privileged circles at least, was undergoing a transformation; specialists were now called in to supervise the arrangement of the pictures in the home, and clearly it was all the better if they were artists by profession[75].

Although the "pictures of good taste" that Da Canal refers to are still unknown, we owe to Martini (1974) the publication of the two portraits of Giovanni II Corner and of Marco Cornaro, now in private Venetian collections, and their dating around 1716. Although the two faces appear somewhat different in stylistic treatment – that of Doge Giovanni II is more lively and animated, the other more plastic and well-rounded – it is equally true that both reveal a solemn conception of the relationship between the figure and the architectural setting: this is partly Lazzarini's influence, but it also shows us how Tiepolo was already opening up to the wide schemes of the great Rococo decorators. The fragrant, luminous color of the two *sovrapporte*, as Martini quite rightly points out, testifies to the fact that "before 1722, which is to say before the dark, neo-Caravaggesque and Piazzettesque *Martyrdom of St. Bartholomew*, Tiepolo painted in clear, almost radiant tones, in the wake of Sebastiano Ricci or Pellegrini"[76]. In consequence, the scholar conjectures that the young Tiepolo passed through a Ricci stage before his encounter with Piazzetta and Bencovich. However, on the basis of the chronological evidence, we prefer to imagine that these two tendencies overlapped with one another in Tiepolo's formation and that he experimented with both in order to understand them – or rather, to take possession of them, like a bird of prey, ductile and receptive but not eclectic.

In the course of the previous generation, seventeenth-century Venetian painting had split into two opposed tendencies: Rococo on the one hand and neo-Baroque realism with a strong emotional involvement on the other – which is to say, Ricci *versus* Piazzetta. Tiepolo made a

16.
Fall of the Rebel Angels.
Udine, Patriarchal
Palace.

[73] E. Martini (1982, p. 508).
[74] A. Da Mosto, *I dogi di Venezia nella vita pubblica e privata*, Milan 1966, p. 569.
[75] On similar cases in Venice and Paris: F. Haskell (1980, p. 260) and K. Pomian (1989, pp. 202-203).
[76] E. Martini (1982, p. 509).

17.
opposite
Detail from fig. 16.

18.
Apparition of the Angel
to Sarah. Udine,
Patriarchal Palace.

19.
Apparition of the Angels
to Abraham. Udine,
Patriarchal Palace.

20.
opposite
Detail from fig. 19.

precocious synthesis of the two streams – or rather, he tried his hand feverishly at both of them, assimilating the lessons they offered and storing them for use at the opportune moment. This is confirmed by other undisputed works.

"At Biadene (...) in the Trevigiano, in the church of M. Assunta, built by the N.H. Procuratore Pisani, he [Tiepolo] did his first frescoed work...":[77] this is the ceiling with the *Assumption* painted for the future doge Alvise Pisani in the parish church of Biadene, recently identified by Mariuz and Pavanello and convincingly dated by them 1716. The state of conservation of the fresco borders on the illegible, particularly with regard to the color; however, it is possible to spot some specific similarities in the anatomy and the style with the works of contemporary artists belonging to artistic schools that were opposed to one another.

For example, the rather grim faces of the angels that thrust the Virgin upwards can be compared with the long-haired figure at the bottom on the right in the *Sacrifice of Iphigenia* by Federico Bencovich for Pommersfelden, while the gesture of the angel at the centre of the octagonal picture for Biadene is practically identical, though in reverse, to that in the *Glory of Angels* painted by Sebastiano Ricci in the chapel of the Virgin at the church of the Carmine in Venice[78]. Furthermore the angel's arm in Tiepolo's painting is upraised and casts a touching mask of shadow on his face, which prompts the question as to whether Tiepolo was already trying to understand that play of *contrejour* and colored shadows that are one of the secret devices behind Veronese's grand light.

There is something similar in the frescoes for the Villa of the Baglioni family in Massanzago, which Mariuz and Pavanello attribute quite rightly to Tiepolo and date 1718 (figs. 4, 5). His authorship of the frescoes can be demonstrated by the presence of several references to his own works and anticipations of later paintings. On the wall with the *Myth of Phaeton*, the figure of Bacchus resembles the *David* in the Louvre and is a mirror-image of *John the Baptist* in the Ospedaletto (fig. 2); Ceres, the female figure whose back twists away from us in an elegant, if slightly lopsided posture, was to become a recurrent figure in Tiepolo's works and looks back to *Ceres* in a fresco by Andrea Celesti at Caselle d'Asolo; the figure of Spring on the left recalls Europa in one of the mythological works at the Accademia (fig. 6); the nymph at the bottom suggests the angel in Biadene, the one with the shadowy face, modelled on Sebastiano Ricci; and this game of comparisons could go on. But alongside these "internal" references, Tiepolo reveals other influences.

It is obvious that the Baglioni family preferred to fresco their Villa at Massanzago, which they had owned since 1718, rather than their Palazzo on Rio Marin, which they only rented. Nonetheless it was in their Venetian home that they kept their collection of "moveable" artistic goods and it is highly probable that Giambattista saw them for himself when he made his first contact with the family: the Baglioni family's art collection was the richest in Venice as regards works from the Neapolitan school of the seventeenth and eighteenth centuries: Mattia Preti, Luca Giordano and Francesco Solimena[79]. We have already noted that Tiepolo had assimilated Celesti and Sebastiano Ricci, even though in this phase he had not yet absorbed from them the chromatic variability of the neo-Veronesian manner. To these influences we can add, as Zava Boccazzi argues[80], that of Giulio Carpioni in the *Nymph Holding the Reins*, in the fresco at Massanzago: a provincial taste, a mixture of classicism and paganism which allows the painter to use the classical myths to tell a sparkling and eccentric tale. Contrasting influences are Piazzetta, "in the calculated plastic modelling of the foreground figures", and Dorigny's works in Ca' Zenobio, with their "inserted scenes of contemporary life" that can be seen in the *Four Continents* at Massanzago[81]; the group with the *Myth of Phaeton* suggests Balestra and the figure of *Time* on the ceiling recalls Nicolò Bambini's works at Ca' Dolfin. This uninhibited use of

[77] V. Da Canal (1732, p. XXXII).
[78] J. Daniels (1976, p. 129 and fig. 299).
[79] F. Haskell (1980, p. 214).
[80] F. Zava Boccazzi (1979, p. 141).
[81] A. Mariuz and G. Pavanello (1985, pp. 110, 113, n. 22).

21.
Rachel Hiding the Idols.
Udine, Patriarchal
Palace.

22.
Judgement of Solomon.
Udine, Patriarchal
Palace.

heterogenous sources (as in Biadene, where he had brought together Ricci and Bencovich) reveals to us that Tiepolo was already able to make a successful fusion of opposites. This is what Zanetti seems to suggest when, after praising his inventive skills, he goes on to say: "adding to these a precise awareness of chiaroscuro [which recalls Piazzetta and Bencovich], and a highly lucid charm"[82]. "A highly lucid charm" – which is as much as to say, the path of decorative Rococo, even though, we repeat, he had not yet assimilated neo-Veronesian color.

There is however a small group of works that shows Tiepolo's interest in the Veronesian model at least in terms of composition. These are three small sketches and a large canvas, all of historical subjects and which seem to be related to Giambattista's undertaking for the Corner family of San Polo: *Tullia Driving Her Chariot over the Body of Her Father, A Warrior Before a Priest, Syfax before Scipio the African* and finally the same subject in the large work now at Baltimore. In the three small paintings we can see an almost tactile treatment of the material. The characters, so somatically similar to figures in Bencovich's works and to those in Tiepolo's own works at the Ospedaletto, do not, however, emerge from the dark background as they would do in Piazzetta or Crespi, but stand out sharply on bright, decorated semicircles, like those in Andrea Celesti's work at Bogliaco[83] or in Gregorio Lazzarini's *Massacre of the Innocents* for Santi Giovanni e Paolo, 1710-14[84]. It is perfectly true that neo-Palladian influences had frequently appeared in seventeenth-century Venetian painting, but how can one fail to see in Tiepolo's choices here a first tentative approach to Veronese's spatial solutions?[85] In *Tullia* we actually see the very same architectural portal of a villa, crowned by statues, that we find in Veronese's *Susanna and the Elders* in Vienna, from the series known as the Duke of Buckingham's[86]. This use of architecture and the adoption of a theatrical arrangement of the figures will reach full maturity in the painting in Baltimore, of the early 1720s, where the space, however, is treated with far greater solidity.

[82] A.M. Zanetti (1733, p. 62).
[83] R. Pallucchini (1981, figs. 896-897).
[84] S. Sponza (1989, p. 246).
[85] For example Veronese's *Dispute in the Temple* at the Prado and *Venus and Jupiter* in Boston.
[86] T. Pignatti and F. Pedrocco, *Veronese, Catalogo completo dei dipinti*, Florence 1991, pp. 302-304.

23.
Detail from fig. 22.

Private life and new conquests

In 1717 Giambattista Tiepolo's name appears for the first time in the *Fraglia* of Venetian painters. This means that he had left the tutorship, as well as the studio, of Gregorio Lazzarini and had become an independent *magister*. We believe that a sign of this official emancipation is to be found in the initials "AM" on the *St. Martin* at Ca' Rezzonico and which can be interpreted as *Artium Magister*[87]. Furthermore both the *St. Martin* and its companion painting *St. Blaise* are similar in their somewhat stiff somatic treatment to the *Portrait of Doge Marco Cornaro* (fig. 3) and we can thus hazard a similar date for them.

Tiepolo already had a circle of highly-placed patrons, such as the reigning doge and the Procurator of St. Mark's, Marco Alvise Pisani, and others on a slightly lower level, such as the delegates of the Ospedaletto and the new patricians, the Baglioni family.

Now that he was independent and launched on his career, he decided to set up a family as well.

On 21 November 1719 he married the sister of the painters Giannantonio and Francesco Guardi, Cecilia. From her he was to have ten children, two of whom, Giandomenico, born in 1727, and Lorenzo, born in 1736, would follow in their father's footsteps, forming a close-knit, hard-working family business, which served them as an *"accademia familiare"*. From documents unearthed by Bortolan[88], it transpires that the marriage was celebrated in secret, since Giambattista feared resistance from his own family. Indeed, Levey makes the interesting conjecture that Cecilia and Giambattista's furtive love is alluded to symbolically in the *Rape of Europa* at the Accademia (fig. 6); he suggests that the Phoenician princess carried off by Jupiter is painted in the likeness of Cecilia Guardi[89]. The association, Europa-Cecilia and Jupiter-Giambattista, is undoubtedly a presumptuous one, but we must get used to these assaults on Olympus, which were to become a feature of Tiepolo's allegorical tales. The pretty and slightly stiff doll-like figure, with her head rising proudly above the line of her shoulders, had already appeared in the role of *Spring* at Massanzago and was to recur frequently in Tiepolo's works, becoming a *type*, a model found within the family circle and raised far above the level of mere autobiographical reference.

At any rate, whether the amorous abduction really did take place or not, the new family now lived in the house of Giambattista's elder brother, Ambrogio, in the parish of Santa Ternita[90].

In this same period, along with Silvestro Manaigo and Giuseppe Camerata who had been his fellow-pupils under Gregorio Lazzarini, he supplied the drawings for *Il Gran Teatro delle pitture e prospettive di Venezia* by Domenico Lovisa, which appeared in a first edition in 1717 and a second one in 1720[91]. This elegant book, in two volumes, was one of many published in Venice during the eighteenth-century, with prints based on works by the Maestri of the sixteenth-century, destined for a market of foreign connoisseurs wanting records of Venetian painting from the golden age. For this publication, the drawings were engraved by Andrea Zucchi. Tiepolo did four drawings in all: the *Defeat of the Imperial Troops by Giorgio Cornaro and Bartolomeo d'Alviano* by Francesco Bassano, in the Sala del Maggior Consiglio of the Palazzo Ducale, the *Manna from Heaven* by Giuseppe Salviati, formerly in Santo Spirito in Isola and today at the Salute, and two works by Tintoretto, the *Beheading of St. Paul* (always erroneously described as the *Beheading of St. Christopher*), at the Madonna dell'Orto, and the *Assumption of the Virgin* for the Oratorio dei Crociferi, which since the beginning of the eighteenth-century has been at the Gesuiti[92].

In the reproduction of the Bassano painting there is a blatant allusion to the merits of the Cornaro family of San Polo, which suggests that the drawings were done around the time Tiepolo was working in their palazzo. But what is most important is the patient exercise of his hand and eye in reproducing four models of mannerist painting, which thus became an integral part of

[87] A. Cappelli, *Dizionario di abbreviature latine ed italiane*, Milan 1929, p. 15.

[88] G. Bortolan (1973).

[89] M. Levey (1986, p. 18).

[90] The church was demolished in 1832. For the other houses in Venice that the family lived in over the years to come: G.M. Urbani De Gheltof (1879, pp. 7 foll.); G. Bortolan (1973); P.L. Sohm (1986, p. 239).

[91] D. Succi (1983, pp. 230-231).

[92] For Tiepolo as a book-illustrator: F. Pedrocco (1986, pp. 64-76).

Tiepolo's cultural formation. In acquiring a source, a style, a model, Tiepolo never proceeded by external routes, by theoretical reflection or mere observation. He needed to "practise" that style and live with it temporarily, pretending that it was his own: not from any plagiaristic instinct, but, we might say, in order to let it flow upwards from his hands to his intellect. In this way he assimilated the lesson totally and it became a living layer of his "free" expressive capacity. Barcham finds specific points of correspondence to these mannerist sources in Tiepolo's *Crucifixion* for the church of San Martino in Burano, and thus chooses to date the large painting around 1719-20[93]. But with Tiepolo there is in fact no need to assume that his experience of a particular source necessarily coincided closely with the use he made of it, and our opinion is that the *Crucifixion* was painted later. As we said above, the point is that Tiepolo had the ability to grasp manually the sense of a source, and then preserve and hoard it in order to be able to make use of it at the right moment. If we may be permitted the comparison, Tiepolo was like an onion that absorbs the salts of the earth and transforms them into layers lying one on top of the other; at every moment of its existence, it is the most recently acquired layer that we see, but the true and natural essence of the onion is that of "all the layers together".

After 1721 Tiepolo made a graphic reproduction – once again for the engraver Andrea Zucchi – of Antonio Corradini's statue of *Virginity* in the church of Santa Maria del Carmelo[94]. Here again, the event in itself does not seem so important and we could record it simply as one of the many commissions that a young artist like Giambattista had to accept in order to provide for his family. However, Zucchi dedicated the print that he made of Tiepolo's drawing to Zaccaria Sagredo, whose art-collection became an occasion for new "encounters" on Tiepolo's part. Sagredo was in fact one of the few Venetian noblemen who truly appreciated contemporary painting. At the 1718-19 Fair of San Rocco he had bought Piazzetta's *Guardian Angel Altarpiece*, which had been turned down by many people[95]. He was also the greatest Venetian collector of prints and drawings – indeed, maybe the most important collector of seventeenth-century art in Europe[96]. As well as owning "all the rare and highly correct drawings of Lazzarini"[97], he also possessed several drawings by Rembrandt, as did Anton Maria Zanetti[98], and above all the most complete dossier of autograph sheets by Giovanni Benedetto Castiglione, known as il Grechetto. And thus Tiepolo caught his first glimpse of that world of fauns, magicians and cabbalists, which, translated into eighteenth-century terms, he was to make use of in his engravings.

Finally, on the subject of his graphic art, we must cite his work of 1724 for Scipione Maffei who brought him into contact with the erudite, proto-archaeological world of Verona. Tiepolo did twelve drawings, mostly engraved by Andrea Zucchi, for the volume *Verona illustrata* by Maffei, which was published in 1732 but was in fact ready by 1724. It is this that allows Marinelli to attribute the painting, *Heliodorus Pillaging the Temple*, now at the museum of Castelvecchio in Verona, to that same year[99].

Sacred and profane themes between the second and third decade of the century

Between the end of the second and the beginning of the third decade of the eighteenth century, it can be said that Tiepolo had seen and, to some degree, had taken possession of most of the artistic culture of the past and of his own time. From Veronese, via the mediation of Gregorio Lazzarini, he learnt to place his figures in artificial settings: i.e., in front of classical architecture that dignified the narrative. From the mannerist tradition he took bodies in dynamic and sometimes elegantly contorted postures. He scrutinized almost the entire range of seventeenth-century Venetian painting, using it as an unlimited repertory of visual models. He examined the frivolous *paganitas* of Giulio Carpioni and the astounding graphic works of Rembrandt and Il Grechetto. He temporarily identified himself with the current style of

[93] W.L. Barcham (1989, pp. 27-31).
[94] F. Haskell (1980, pp. 265).
[95] A. Mariuz (1982, p. 80); K. Pomian (1989, p. 258).
[96] F. Haskell (1980, p. 266).
[97] V. Da Canal (1732, p. 77).
[98] U. Ruggeri, in R. Pallucchini (ed.) (1983, p. 49).
[99] For the drawings: F. Pedrocco (1986, p. 70); for Maffei the antiquarian: K. Pomian (1989, p. 224); for the painting with *Heliodorus*: S. Marinelli (1978, pp. 217-221).

pathetic-chiaroscuro, at the same time drawing on the new possibilities of international Rococo. However, if we were to restrict ourselves to listing, work by work and detail by detail, everything that Tiepolo borrowed from the artists he studied, we would not end up with a compendium but an inventory: it would be like enumerating every separate part of the human body and then trying and pass it off as a description of an organism. The fact is that in this period of deliberate preparation Tiepolo was a ubiquitous experimenter; he was preserved from eclecticism by the fact that his talent was backed up by a strict critical detachment, which he had learnt from Lazzarini, and by an increasingly precise and even proud sense of his own, inimitable identity. It is no accident that a substantial number of works belonging to this phase have, in the past, been attributed to different artists and only now have found a firm place in the Tiepolo catalogue. They are sacred and profane subjects in which Tiepolo flaunts his technical skills, and allows those layers of pictorial culture that he had stashed away to bear fruit, and forces his sources to speak a different language from their own.

The first is the *Pool of Bethesda* in the Accademia in Venice, which, significantly, was first attributed to Piazzetta, and then to his "opposite", Sebastiano Ricci. The only surprise is that the name of Gregorio Lazzarini was never brought up; compared with the old master's own *Pool of Bethesda*[100] painted around the same time, it seems more like Lazzarini than Lazzarini himself. However, unlike his tutor, Tiepolo divides his space into various levels, thus imitating – and not only in this sense – the theatrical skill of Paolo Veronese. As for the style, one can note something of Magnasco's fineness of touch in the way the bodies are created with the tip of the brush: it was Sebastiano Ricci who imported Magnasco's methods into Venice, after meeting the Genoan Maestro in the course of his travels to Milan and Florence.

[100] Now at the Cini collection in Venice and once in the church of Sant'Angelo: W.L. Barcham (1989, p. 39, n. 66).

24.
Detail from fig. 25.

25.
opposite
Triumph of Marius.
New York, Metropolitan
Museum of Art.

Another work from this moment of simultaneous dialogue with all the sources is the presumed *Hagar* in the Rasini collection in Milan, which is also important because Morassi read the date 1719 on it[101]. One can see the firmness of Piazzetta in the plasticity of the figures and the use of dark tones; at the same time, however, Barcham notes similarities with Sebastiano Ricci in his *Dream of Esculapius*[102], to which we would add Lazzarini in his *Bacchantes*, now at Ca' Rezzonico, especially in the flushed faces of the two women interceding on behalf of Vashti (if it is Vashti) to the high priest.

A stronger leaning towards Sebastiano Ricci can be seen in some works of a secular subject, such as, for example, the four mythological works in the Venetian Accademia. To these we can add the *Three Nymphs* in a Milanese collection; although these figures emerge abruptly from the heavy dark background after the manner of Piazzetta, they glow with a fragrant and luminous pink: the same color that caresses the body of *Susanna* in Hartford, which was painted only a little later and is very similar in its anatomy to Pellegrini. The so-called *Death of Hyacinthus*, now in Geneva[103], also seems to belong to the early 1720s. In it we can spot the impudent *putto* from the *Rape of Europa*, which is one of the four mythological works now in Venice, and also the twisting female figure already noted at Massanzago[104].

There follows a series of paintings connected with the Virgin Mary, in which, given the theme, Tiepolo had little choice but to make use of Piazzettesque clichés, although they never prevent him from branching out on his own. In the *Rest on the Flight into Egypt*, in San Diego, the characters at the bottom of the picture are constructed with nervous touches in *"battere"* and *"levare"*, halfway between Magnasco and Piazzetta, but the painting also introduces for the first time an original and entirely Tiepolesque figure, one that has a whole history to itself in his catalogue: the tall angel hovering in the air with open wings. We are to hear these wings beating ever more vigorously as the theme evolves: from the *Annunciation* in St. Petersburg, in which the angel bursts into the picture, thrashing the air, to the *Education of the Virgin* in Dijon, where we can sense Tiepolo's interest in Nicolò Bambini's achievements at the Scalzi[105]. But in the droop of the head on one shoulder, as if the vertebrae of the neck were disarticulated, the painting looks forward to the *Sacrifice of Isaac* at the Ospedaletto.

Remaining in the context of religious iconography, we can cite the sketch for the *St. Dominic in Glory*, in which Tiepolo measured himself against Piazzetta's great ceiling-painting for the chapel of San Domenico at Santi Giovanni e Paolo. Piazzetta had painted crystal statues of incandescent rock, between Solimena and Crespi[106]. Tiepolo entered this competition, confident of his skills in this area – the orchestration of masses seen from below. However, the choice of the commissioning board, as Lino Moretti has shown (1985), fell on the older Maestro, and Giambattista could merely absorb this slight blow to his prestige and tell himself that Venetian circles, in particular religious ones, were not yet ready for the interpretation of space that he was then elaborating on the joyous, "pagan" model of Paolo Veronese. A confirmation of this comes from the *Madonna del Carmelo*, formerly in the chapel of the Suffragio del Carmelo at Sant'Aponal and now at the Brera, which Moretti, on the basis of documentary evidence, dates between 1721 and 1727 and which Barcham pins down to 1722, thanks to irrefutable historic and religious evidence[107]. In painting the holy group of greatest religious significance, Tiepolo prudently formed a synthesis of images that had already been seen in Venice: from Veronese, to Titian, and to Piazzetta in his *Sagredo Altarpiece* for the nearby school of the Angelo Custode[108]. However, for the angel whose outstretched arm indicates the redemptive virtues of the scapular, Tiepolo returned to his own creation, the figure that manages to be both antigravitational and superbly carnal at the same time – the angel that recurs in the paintings in San Diego, St. Petersburg and Dijon.

[101] From the iconographic point of view, the title, *The Repudiation of Hagar*, is not convincing. The two versions of Hagar's departure from Abraham recount that (a) Hagar flees pregnant with Ishmael (flees, she is not driven away); (b) Hagar is driven away *together with* Ishmael. And what we see in the Rasini painting is neither the one nor the other. Aikema, passing onto secular iconography, suggests that it is a *Sacrifice of Polyxena* since "the daughter of the King of Troy, according to Ovid, *before being sacrificed fell to the ground*" (B. Aikema, 1987, p. 452, my italics). But Ovid in the *Metamorphoses* (XIII, 447-480) presents Polyxena as a "strong and unhappy virgin, with a manly heart" who falls to the ground, it is true, but only *after* being stabbed: therefore it cannot be the Trojan heroine either, who is described by Ovid as an example of great strength of will. Aikema is right, however, when he observes that the priest is not driving away the woman lying at his feet but is ordering her to enter the building. For this reason it seems to us that the subject is a *Repudiation of Vashti* (Esther, 1-2), in which Ahasuerus summons his wife in order to show her beauty to his guests, and when she refuses to *enter* the banqueting hall, repudiates her.
[102] W.L. Barcham (1989, p. 39).
[103] There seems to be no reason for this title, since, according to Ovid's *Metamorphoses*, Hyacinthus did not commit suicide, but died from the fatal quoit hurled by the hand of Apollo.
[104] A figure that Tiepolo takes from Andrea Celesti in Caselle d'Asolo (R. Pallucchini, 1981, figs. 899-900) and maybe from one of the paintings by Jean Raux for the Giustinian Lolin family (C. Galli, 1987, pp. 260-262).
[105] R. Pallucchini (1981, fig. 1192).
[106] E. Martini (1982, p. 47 and n. 173).
[107] L. Moretti (1984-85, pp. 378-379); W.L. Barcham (1989, pp. 34-39).
[108] A. Mariuz (1982).

Different dramas

Between 1722 and 1724, Giambattista was engaged on four large-scale works on religious subjects, which partly made up for the disappointment he had suffered in the competition for the *St. Dominic in Glory* in Santi Giovanni e Paolo. They also demonstrate the very particular way the young painter had of approaching his numerous sources. These were two frescoes: *St. Lucy in Glory* in the parish church of Vascon and the *Apotheosis of St. Theresa* in the church of the Scalzi in Venice; and two canvas-paintings: the *Martyrdom of St. Bartholomew* in San Stae (fig. 7) and the *Sacrifice of Isaac* (fig. 12) at the Ospedaletto, which concluded the work he had begun there between 1715 and 1716.

As Da Canal testifies (1732): "In Vascon, a villa in the Trevigiano, [Tiepolo] painted the *Story of St. Lucy* on the ceiling of the church". Critics have talked of a Veronesian light, picked up from Pellegrini, which looks forward to the frescoes in Udine[109]. This would scarcely be surprising, given our conviction that Tiepolo tended to experiment simultaneously in various directions. The lofty oval of the saint elevated to heaven again suggests Piazzetta and his characteristic manner of distancing and raising the faces of the holy figures so as to render them remotely aloof; but the comparison with the series on Marian subjects – from San Diego to Dijon – strikes us as equally persuasive; in these works the angelic wings explore the space, fluttering and quivering one on top of the other like multi-colored fans, particularly in the *Apotheosis of St. Theresa* in the second chapel on the right in the church of the Scalzi. This is the first massed flight in Tiepolo's paintings; indeed, Morassi thinks that this is his first collaboration with the perspective painter, Gerolamo Mengozzi, known as Il Colonna[110]. Critics have insisted rightly on the complexity of this *sottinsù* work, which shows traces of both Bambini's paintings and Dorigny's fresco in the same church[111]. Furthermore, those free-falling clusters of figures could also be said to look back to the theatrical scenography of the *Tragédie à machine*, a late-Baroque phenomenon which, thanks to Giacomo Torelli, was very fashionable in France during the Regency period[112].

The effect of this new concept of space, ever freer and for this very reason increasingly subjected to conscious rules, can be sensed in the two works on canvas mentioned above: the *Martyrdom of St. Bartholomew* and the *Sacrifice of Isaac*, both painted after 1722 and before the end of 1724.

In the former, which is one of a series in the church to which nearly every important figure-painter in Venice at the time contributed, Tiepolo refers to numerous works by other artists; as usual, he uses these sources so as to make them his own and thus modify them at the very moment in which he imitates them: Titian, Tintoretto, Bernardo Strozzi, Solimena and, above all, Piazzetta, in his work, the *Martyrdom of St. James* in the same church of San Stae[113]. With regard to this comparison between Tiepolo and Piazzetta, Barcham puts forward a very interesting thesis. He remarks that in Piazzetta's work the martyr seems to rebel against his own destiny, even though the fulfilment of the sacred episode depends on it. In Tiepolo's painting, on the contrary, the saint favours his own martyrdom, almost abandoning himself to a torment rendered necessary by the tale. And yet, although Piazzetta asks the spectator for greater compassion (in the literal sense of *patire cum*) than Tiepolo, who is clearly less interested in interpreting the drama in an ethical sense, in compositional terms Piazzetta's image is closed in on itself whereas Tiepolo's is "propelled into the spectator's world"[114]. The forces at work in Piazzetta's painting have reached a standstill due to the reciprocal opposition between the martyr and his executioner, a standstill that seems to paralyze the possibility of future action, whereas in Tiepolo, the very absence of rhetorical and definitive postures lends the scene a vibrancy and tension that herald some imminent action.

Once again this exemplifies the use Tiepolo made of his sources. Increasingly aware of the

[109] B. Aikema (1987).
[110] A. Morassi (1955, p. 14); A. Mariuz and G. Pavanello (1985) have suggested that Tiepolo may have been been assisted by the Bolognese painter already at Biadene.
[111] For Nicolò Bambini, see R. Pallucchini (1981, fig. 1192); for Dorigny, E. Martini (1982).
[112] R.M. Isherwood, *Music in the Service of the King of France in the Seventeenth Century*, Ithaca and London 1973.
[113] The latest critic to sum up these sources is W.L. Barcham (1989, pp. 42 foll.).
[114] *Ibidem*, p. 53.

means at his disposal, he was perfectly happy to adopt a Piazzettesque arrangement, but only in order to celebrate a narrative system that was opposed to Piazzetta's. This is what happens in the *Sacrifice of Isaac* for the Ospedaletto. The way the figures stand out against the dark background derives from Piazzetta, but Tiepolo's figures do not resemble sculpted boulders set heavily down on the earth, but slow-flowing magma that gradually takes over the space. One of the problems he had to tackle was the painfully foreshortened position of the *sottarco* and the arrangement of the figures is not in fact wholly satisfactory. After this experience, however, he never again allowed himself to be defeated by the constrictions of the site. On the contrary, it was he who distorted the space, absorbing it into his paintings and then reprojecting it into real space so as to render this latter, by a paradoxical reversal of persective, an emanation of the painted space.

From Ca' Zenobio to Palazzo Sandi

In the first half of the 1720s, Tiepolo undertook two important jobs in the palazzi of noble Venetian families which prove how rapidly his fame as a decorative painter was spreading amongst the ruling class in the city: these were canvas-paintings for the Zenobio family at the Carmini and fresco work and canvases for Palazzo Sandi in Corte dell'Albero.

The two families had acquired their noble status only recently – the Zenobio in 1646 and the Sandi in 1685[115] – and they had started work on ennobling their respective palazzi even more recently: around the year 1700 the architect Antonio Gaspari, had completed the façade, the interior and the garden of Ca' Zenobio and between 1721 and and 1724, Domenico Rossi concluded his work for the Sandi family[116]. The families summoned Tiepolo to work in their new mansions from a desire to increase their own prestige; viceversa, Tiepolo was henceforth given carte blanche to "speak of glory". By the terms of this unofficial pact, Tiepolo's task was to invent a suitably lofty style and manner of painting, a combination of forms and contents in which the maximum of truth would be inextricably associated with the maximum of falsehood. When this aim was finally achieved, practically every absolutist regime in Europe – and we are now talking about the Europe of the Enlightenment – was to call upon Tiepolo to dispel all doubts regarding its future – in eminently mythographic terms, of course – and to justify the unhistorical basis of its power; he accomplished this by means of his frescoes, which managed a perfect synthesis of reality and unreality. It goes without saying that the formulation of this style was a gradual and partly unconscious process, not the fruit of a sudden choice, immediately acted upon. But after these two Venetian enterprises, based on a historical subject and a mythological-allegorical one, this was the direction that Tiepolo's art was to take.

Tiepolo's narrative system at Ca' Zenobio opens the scene on broad skies and situates the characters "in mid-field", which is to say, not far from the imaginary threshold of the frame. The figures are noticeably elongated and painted in vaguely declamatory poses. They thus shed a considerable part of the rude naturalness that Tiepolo had learnt from Piazzetta and take on a more ideal and tranquil appearance. Different planes gradually slope down towards the horizon, which is distant and slightly higher than the proscenium, as in a theater[117]. The details and the finishing touches seem more precious, almost affected; one need only note the shells on Aurelianus's chariot and the harnesses on the horses, the gleaming weapons and the banners. The faces are different too; they take on a classical fixity – as Tiepolo must have imagined "classical" faces to have been – even if there are some things we have seen before: the bearded centurion running towards the proscenium in the *Triumph of Aurelianus* recalls the figure of *Time* in Massanzago, and we can identify Cecilia herself in the robes of Zenobia tied to the chariot

[115] F. Miari (1891, pp. 77-78, 92).

[116] E. Bassi (1976, pp. 348-353, 428-429).

[117] The *historia* of Queen Zenobia, which by association of sound emphasises the glories of the Zenobio family, was extremely popular in Venetian theatre of the seventeenth and eighteenth centuries; cf. A. Groppo (1745, pp. 36-37, 75, 143).

of the conqueror. What emerges is a "heroic style", which rediscovers the monumentality of the sixteenth-century, with an added touch of frivolous disenchantment typical of the eighteenth-century. What Tiepolo seems to be attempting to do, in fact, is to recount the same *fabulae* of earlier times – *"le donne, i cavalier, l'arme, gli amori, le cortesie, l'audaci imprese io canto"* – but adopting a different narrative system. But in order to achieve this he first had to understand, to experiment with and thus gain possession of (following a very different path from that taken by Pellegrini and Sebastiano Ricci) the secrets of Paolo Veronese's pictorial style.

This is what Tiepolo started to do in the fresco for the Sandi family in Corte dell'Albero, raising a high song to eloquence (figs. 13, 14). On the great ceiling he unites "reddish tones (...) with the now clear-silvery tones of his new manner"[118]. Ricci and Pellegrini had attempted to reproduce the dazzling luminosity of Veronese by means of a device that was ultimately banal – using ever clearer tints. But Veronese's universal light was not produced by simply brightening his palette, but was the result of a system of "chromatic relations" based essentially on two principles applied simultaneously: colored shadows and the juxtaposition of complementary colors (but we will return to this later). That is why we referred to the "secrets" of Veronese's style. In the vast sky of Palazzo Sandi, Tiepolo does achieve a noticeable increase in general luminosity, even if this is not yet brought about by juxtaposing "pure complementary timbres". Indeed, in order to open up that great centre of light in Olympus, where he places the figures of Minerva and Mercury, he has to resort to broad circles of intense yellow against a background of thick blue. Only later would he realize that to achieve Paolo Veronese's overall light, what mattered was not the "quantitative" values of each single area of color in itself and for itself, but rather the reciprocal relations that each area of color established with the others around it. We observe too that in the very heart of this heroic poem Tiepolo allows himself to introduce almost brazenly a series of playful elements, *"scherzi"* in the musical sense of the term: in the main part of the fresco, he gives Amphion a dog; Orpheus is depicted playing the violin in the episode with Eurydice, since the lyre had been given to Amphion; and elsewhere there are boys, blindfolded cupids and so on. In short, a series of digressions which have often been explained as the product of a sceptical attitude towards allegories, Olympian fables and episodes of Greek and Roman history, typical of the eighteenth century. But in fact the reverse was true for Tiepolo. They are not impromptu *divertissements*, put there to render the story less credible, but rather fragments of living reality, familiar to everybody; Tiepolo actually considers them indispensable in order to make the stories closer to everyday life, and thus more believable. But there is something else as well.

From underneath Amphion's cloak, the lively face of a boy stares out at the spectator (fig. 14). He is the only one of the painted figures who is allowed to pierce the "fourth wall", just as at certain moments in Goldoni's plays a character addresses the audience directly, confiding his own opinion on the events being represented. In these moments of by-play, which usually concern minor characters and are generally humorous in tone, the lines are recited loudly enough to be audible to the other characters; however, by theatrical convention, no-one on stage seems to notice and the spectator has the exciting impression that he is interacting with one of the characters unbeknownst to the others – indeed, behind their backs. The section with *Amphion Building the Walls of Thebes with the Power of Music* is the first one that the spectator sees when entering the room, and thus acts as the starting point of the whole cycle. Our attention is caught at once by this direct gaze, since the boy is next to the key-figure of Amphion, dressed in his swirling dark-blue cloak. And if one observes the small face carefully, one realizes that an ashy-blue timbre hovers over it, cast by the hero's cloak: which is to say, that in the only character who irresistibly engages with the spectator, Tiepolo has painted the first colored shadow of his career.

[118] E. Martini (1964, p. 62).

In the fresco in Palazzo Sandi, which can be dated around 1724, Tiepolo has therefore seized upon the basic foundation of Paolo Veronese's light and color: the shadows are not dark gorges, as they appear in Piazzetta, but take on the atmospheric color generated by the chromatic areas nearest to them. As for the other secret, that of the reciprocal action of the complementary colors, we have to wait until his work for the Dolfin family, in both Venice and Udine, in the second half of the 1720s.

Towards Udine

Various other paintings marked different stages in his development, even if none of them is directly dated on the surface. There are also works that seem retrograde in tendency, due to the necessity of offering his patrons, particularly in Venice, what they expected of him. Tiepolo's progress towards a profound comprehension, from within, of the Veronesian style cannot be summarized in a purely mechanical fashion: it was a strategic path, not a peremptory triumphal march. Besides, we have already talked about Tiepolo's burgeoning poetics as a stratified structure which, depending on circumstances and the network of social relations, allowed one or other of the many tendencies that constituted it to emerge, sometimes even to blatantly contradictory effect.

In the *Temptations of St. Antony*, for example, the background is slate and the clouds are burnt and copper-colored; the figures stand out against it sharply as in Giuseppe Maria Crespi's painting of *Aeneas with the Sybil and Charon*, now in Vienna. But the clustered trees on the right, against the sunset, have the same impalpable greyness, like dead ashes, as the curtain of clouds between the hermit-saint and the naked tempters, while the hasty dashes with which the figures are constructed already have a fragrant and satisfactory flavour. The same pungent hedonism can be noticed in the *Venus with a Mirror* in the Gerli collection, based on Titian's erotic works. The color has not yet achieved the light glazing of his mature works, but the juxtapositions played on icy tints are increasingly fine and elegant. The *putti* seem even too highly modeled and plastic, and can be compared with the delightful *Small Angel Reading*, in a private collection in Zurich, and also with the boy almost crushed by the weight of a cloud in the *Annunciation* in Krakow. To return to the subject of Tiepolo's sudden shifts in style, it is no accident that the Krakow painting has been attributed to Piazzetta and to Bencovich, and the *Madonna and Child with Angels*, now at the Courtauld in London, reveals a pronounced influence of Piazzetta, especially in the figure of Mary, which is very similar to that of Piazzetta's *Guardian Angel Altarpiece*, formerly in the Zaccaria Sagredo collection[119]. This of course does not prevent Tiepolo, in both the Krakow *Annunciation* and the painting in London, from displaying a sharp chromatic taste that has little in common with the pathetic-chiaroscuro tendency, a taste that already heralds the triumphal neo-Veronesian style of the frescoes in Udine.

And finally, there are signs of Piazzetta's influence in the *Apotheosis of St. Luigi Gonzaga*, painted, probably for the Venetian market, around 1726, which was the year that the Jesuit saint, who died of the plague in Rome in 1591, was canonized (fig. 15). However, one only needs to observe the vari-colored jewel of the two *putti* at bottom-left and the airy opening in the background to realize how even a pious theme could be transformed by Giambattista on the eve of his departure for Udine.

Tiepolo and the Dolfin family

In the second half of the 1720s, Tiepolo was practically monopolized by the Dolfin family of the San Pantalon branch, who engaged him to work in the cathedral and the castle of Udine, in their Palazzo in Venice with a series of ten paintings on Roman history, and at the same time

119 A. Mariuz (1982, file 22).

in the new rooms in the Patriarchal Palace in Udine with a cycle of frescoes that bring his period of preparation to a triumphant conclusion.

We have no documents that testify to the role of Patriarch Dionisio Dolfin (1663-1734) in commissioning the fresco-works from Tiepolo in the "gran sala del pubblico palazzo di Udine" – which is to say in the castle, the seat of government[120]. But there seems no doubt that Dionisio Dolfin, the elected Patriarch of Aquileia since 1699 and the real *genius loci* in extending the political prestige of Udine in the Friuli, must have been personally involved in summoning Giambattista to work in the castle. He was already working for the Patriarch (or was about to do so) in the Cathedral and the Patriarchal Palace, and was working (or was about to do so) for the Patriarch's elder brothers, Daniele III (1654-1729) and Daniele IV (1656-1729), in the family's Palazzo in Venice.

The frescoes in the castle are monochrome; they are badly preserved and no longer complete. All the same Tiepolo, especially in the four pairs of small angels above the windows, chose to adopt *sottinsù* lighting, as on a theatrical stage and to provide effects of *contrejour* on the faces; thus he painted monochromes that were conceived "in color", obtaining with just one tint those polychrome shadows we have already noticed in Palazzo Sandi.

It is highly probable that for the apse fresco in the chapel of the Confraternity of the Blessed Sacrament in the Cathedral of Udine, the Patriarch Dolfin played a vigorous role as an intermediary. In this relatively confined space Tiepolo painted monochromes of Old Testament subjects on the narrow base panels and a multi-colored flight of music-playing angels emerging from a *trompe l'œil* opening at the top of the segmented vault. The monochromes at the bottom are once again in *contrejour* and appear delineated by sharp lines of white lead. Above, the colored angels in the vault of the apse glide downwards, casting shadows on the wall, which were already present in the preparatory drawing now in Frankfurt. It was the first time that Tiepolo had ever made use of such a device: the illusion that the figures are not painted on the two dimensions of the wall but emerge from it, occupying the three-dimensional space of reality. The great swarm gliding across the sky has been compared with Dorigny's fresco at the Scalzi and, indeed, at the Cathedral in Udine[121]. However, what Tiepolo inaugurated here was a game that could be defined: "Where are the figures?" In other words, he is playing at falsifying real space and, viceversa, conferring natural truth on the painted space, as we will see more clearly later on.

From 1726 until 1729 Tiepolo worked during the winter on the ten paintings of Roman history for the main hall of the *piano nobile* of Palazzo Dolfin at San Pantalon, and in the summer on the cycle of frescoes for the Patriarchal Palace in Udine[122]. Both buildings bear the signature of Domenico Rossi and had been built recently. Tiepolo was often to be called to new buildings. When families managed to climb to the top of the social ladder, the most suitable way this achievement could be celebrated was by commissioning paintings in the new style. A family's prestige was no longer measured by their collection of hanging-pictures; what was required now was the imperishable forms of fresco. Those who lived as tenants in other people's palazzi had to be content with adding to their traditional collection of "moveable" artistic goods, as we have seen with the Baglioni family in Rio Marin. But those who built their own mansion at their own expense to increase the prestige of the family – and the example of the Baglioni family in Massanzago holds true here as well – preferred something more lasting. Tiepolo's task, therefore, was not only to "speak of glory", but to do so adopting the technical and expressive medium (fresco) that was capable of immortalizing a coat-of-arms. Giambattista was to become the undisputed European master of these means, the artistic amphitryon of a new way of living in a villa.

The series of paintings he carried out between 1726 and 1729 in Palazzo Dolfin at San

[120] V. Da Canal (1732, p. XXXIII).
[121] R. Pallucchini (1981, p. 375).
[122] For technical reasons – the rapid absorption of the paint by the fresh plaster – summer is the most suitable season for fresco-painting.

Pantalon for the Patriarch's brothers, Daniele III and Daniele IV Dolfin, could be considered to constitute an exception to what has just been said. The ceiling of the room already held a large fresco in late-Baroque style and it is possible that they feared that a clashing effect might be created if Tiepolo were to paint frescoes on the walls.

The self-laudatory aim of the cycle is clear: to give a Latin foundation – the *Epitome Rerum Romanorum* by Lucius Annaeus Florus – for the devotion to their country that the two Dolfin brothers had shown in the fields of soldiership and diplomacy[123]. What is less clear is the original arrangement of the paintings, of which only the external frames now remain *in situ*. The architectural reorganization of the great room, especially on the side that gives onto the Rio di Ca' Foscari and that provides the light, was carried out at around the same time as the decoration. It is therefore probable that the clients, the architect and the painter agreed upon the entire operation at an early planning stage, in particular with regard to the sources of lighting. On these grounds, and observing the quality of lighting within each individual painting, it is possible to hypothesize the scheme shown below[124].

The standard of painting is suddenly much higher than in Palazzo Sandi. The diffused glow that pervades the various scenes is immanent because the vigour of the colors is not intrinsic to them but depends on the chromatic juxtapositions that Tiepolo attempts here for the first time. Lanzi grasped this very well: "His manner of distributing the colors is such that *in cases where other painters chose the liveliest of colors, he made use of pale and sometimes even faded tones, but then, setting them alongside colors that were pure and clear* and at the same time natural, he endowed the frescoes with such splendor, delicacy and sonority as is perhaps unmatched in painting"[125]. Lanzi is here talking about frescoes, but his intuition can also serve to explain the novelty of this cycle of canvas-

[123] A glance at the collection of papers *Segretario alle Voci* in the ASV reveals Daniele III's excellent *cursus honorum* in diplomacy, and Daniele IV's in military matters.
[124] G. Pradella (1979-80, p. 48).
[125] L. Lanzi (1795-96, t. III, epoca quarta, p. 211); my italics.
[126] If a primary color such as yellow is set alongside its dark complementary color – green, which is yellow plus blue – the light color seems even brighter and the dark one becomes even more solid. It is obvious that in Tiepolo's case the procedures were the fruit of empirical practice, based on what he saw in Paolo Veronese: it has nothing to do with the neo-impressionist theories of Seurat and Signac. But it is equally certain that when in the early 1740s Francesco Algarotti was convinced that he had indoctrinated Giambattista in the scientific contents of Newton's optics, which he did much to divulge in the eighteenth cen-

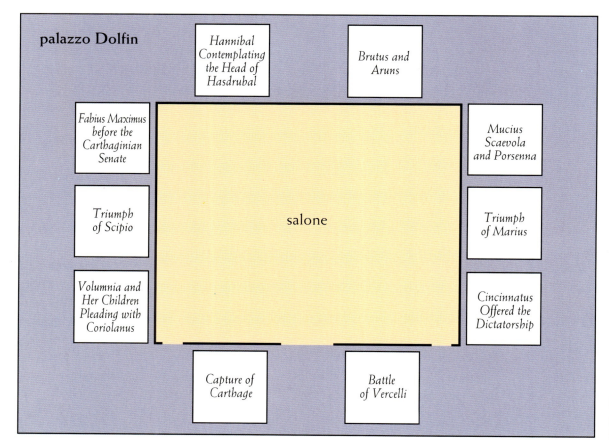

Original arrangement of paintings in the *salone* of Palazzo Dolfin.

tury, he was in fact deluding himself. PerhapsTiepolo did not understand much of his friend's learned explanations and let him believe that he owed a great deal to him. But in fact all that the Count could have passed on to him in terms of theoretical abstraction on Veronesian color, Tiepolo had already ever since the second half of the 1720s. With regard to the connections between Veronese and Tiepolo, it is worth reporting what Piai wrote about the former: "Veronese (...) set his colors alongside clear areas (...), juxtaposed in such a way as to construct the figures with color alone used to act as light and shade. Thus he illuminated a blue by placing next to it a pink-lilac, with violet veins that picked up from the blue, which thus took on the value of a shadow even though maintaining its pure timbre; and with the same procedure he set acid-orange yellow alongside the warm golden olive-green yellow, working respectively as light and shade. With this chromatic composition, in which the lights and shadows were built by means of pure color, Paolo obtained a result of maximum luminosity, because the complementary colors, when set alongside one another exalt each other, gaining prominence from the light that they themselves create": M. Piai (1974-75, pp. 301-302).

[127] M. Muraro (1970, 1989); A. Rizzi (1972); S. Johnson Jordan (1985); W.L. Barcham (1984, 1989). It was Muraro who first connected the whole question with the problem of patriarchal jurisdiction and who, on this very account, correctly insisted on the use of the term "Patriarchal Palace" and not "Archiepiscopal Palace": M. Muraro (1970, p. 62).

[128] W.L. Barcham (1989, p. 71).

[129] An exception is the Throne Room, or "Portrait Room", where, since it is a matter of portraits, the problem of reciprocity between real and painted space does not present itself.

[130] M. Muraro (1970, p. 28).

[131] A. Morassi (1955, p. 2).

paintings. He refers in fact to the different interpretation that Tiepolo gave to Veronesian light, compared with "other painters" – meaning Sebastiano Ricci and Pellegrini. For Ricci and Pellegrini it was a question of choosing "the liveliest colors". Tiepolo, however, did not only work on each single tint, which could even be "pale" and "faded" in itself. He went well beyond the masters of Venetian Rococo in his understanding of the deeper and more subtle aspect of Veronese's methods, that of the complementary colors. It is not only a question of brightening the pallet or avoiding dark preparations of the canvas, as people persisted, somewhat reductively, in thinking. It was rather the creation of a light that had no counterpart in nature, a light that was sensationally more real than reality, and was obtained by juxtaposing areas of colors that were complementary with one another[126]. This can be verified in the Patriarchal Palace in Udine, which, as we have said, was a landmark in his career and at the same time a resolution of all Tiepolo's youthful works (figs. 16-22).

As has been pointed out by those scholars who have studied the matter, the iconographic meaning of the whole enterprise in the Patriarchal Palace in Udine – including both the architectural and the decorative aspect – arises from a juridictional and religious conflict between Venice and Vienna over the Patriarchate of Aquileia and the right of Udine to inherit its prestige[127]. The decoration carried out by Tiepolo for the Patriarch Dionisio Dolfin begins on the ceiling of the staircase, which rises for three floors and culminates with the *Fall of the Rebel Angels* surrounded by eight monochromes on Old Testament subjects. The composition is taken from *Jupiter Driving out the Vices* by Paolo Veronese for the Sala del Consiglio dei Dieci in the Palazzo Ducale[128]. In Tiepolo's fresco, however, the angels break out beyond the frame with some parts of their bodies in stucco. The game of the colonization of real space by painted space, which we had already noticed in the *Flight of Angels* in the Cathedral in Udine, here reaches perfection. Tiepolo obtains a *finctio* by which some of his free-falling angels do not appear to belong to the ceiling itself but to a slightly lower layer of air, as if they were truly hurtling down into the real space of the staircase.

Thus, with a radical reversal of reality and illusion, Tiepolo transforms the volume of air over the staircase into a space that is "acted upon" by the painted representation. The same spatial sensibility, with angular visions and the painted world's appropriation of the observer's space and conditions, is found in other sites frescoed by Tiepolo with vast biblical scenes[129].

On the stylistic plane, critics have gone to great lengths to find famous precedents for Tiepolo's works for the Patriarch. Muraro sees the persistence of Lazzarini's influence, together with models such as Dorigny, Pellegrini, and Paolo Pagani[130]. Barcham mentions Pellegrini and Sebastiano Ricci, recalling that *in situ* there are also works by Nicolò Bambini and Dorigny. But over and above all of these, concludes the scholar, it is the Veronesian model that triumphs. Morassi sees Tiepolo here as going beyond the *chiarismo* of Pellegrini, Amigoni and Dorigny, drawing on an authentic "atmospheric poetry"[131]. There are obviously some borrowings, but Tiepolo by now surpasses them at the very moment in which he uses them. The most deeply felt influence is undoubtedly that of Veronese. Not however in the sense of a general brightening of the colors, but rather in the way he sets the complementary colors alongside one another in order to obtain a light that is anything but "atmospheric". Rather, it is chromatic light, achieved by paying attention to the reciprocal relations between the colors, as Tiepolo – and only Tiepolo – had spotted was Veronese's practice.

This conquest of an authentic prosody of color, which is no longer late-Baroque and not even Rococo in the manner of Sebastiano Ricci and Giannantonio Pellegrini, was one that Tiepolo was never to retreat from until almost the end of his days, inaugurating thus, if we need a formula, Tiepolesque Rococo.

The early maturity
1729-1737

The Thirties

Having assimilated – or rather, having discovered by empirical means – Paolo Veronese's color and light, Tiepolo was now reaching maturity as an artist, and his development can be seen through a series of great fresco-cycles. Nonetheless elements of chiaroscuro are still to be found in his works throughout much of the thirties, particularly in the easel-paintings; this heritage was not abandoned until his final assimilation of all the sources, Veronese included, in a unified and coherent style: Tiepolesque "classicism", as Morassi defined it, which was to reach its apogee in the early fifties in Würzburg. There are in fact some works, which we can place between the end of the twenties and the beginnning of the thirties (before his work in Milan), where technical and stylistic elements of his early experiences resurface, revealing an undiminished expressive vigor.

The *Sacrifice of Iphigenia*, now in a Venetian collection, shows figurative similarities to the frescoes in the Patriarchal Palace in Udine. Critics have rightly pointed out the thematic resemblance to the main scene of the frescoes for Villa Corner in Merlengo and to the great poetical work at the Villa Valmarana[1], not to mention an echo of Carpioni in the figure of the heroine about to be sacrificed. However – and it is Anna Pallucchini again who stresses the point – the compositional arrangement also reveals a renewed interest in Federico Bencovich.

The small canvas with *Alexander and Campaspe* (fig. 26) in Montreal is totally secular in atmosphere – and thus naturally brings to mind Veronese and Ricci. In addition, of course, there are those playful elements – the nude, the black servant, the little dog – and even proudly autobiographical references (Campaspe is thought to be Cecilia and Apelles, Giambattista) that Tiepolo uses when he wants to confer an atmosphere of quotidianity on myth (in this case it is an episode from Pliny that is thus realistically treated). However, in the great picture on the

26.
opposite
Alexander and
Campaspe in the Studio
of Apelles, detail.
Montreal, Museum of
Fine Arts. [1] A. Pallucchini (1968, n. 53).

27.
opposite
Detail from fig. 28.

28.
Scipio Granting
Massinissa his Freedom
(Scipio Freeing the
Slave). Milan, Palazzo
Casati, later Dugnani.

easel in front of Alexander's painter (a rare example of a study of an artist at work in his atelier) we can see, in the as-yet unpainted parts of the canvas, the way the surface is being prepared: and once again it is a preparation in Armenian bolus, which was Piazzetta's practice. The two large paintings leaning against the wall also belong to the Piazzetta tradition. It is true that we do not know which of Tiepolo's works they refer to, but it is not difficult to perceive livid lights, dark backgrounds and plastically rendered figures, all in keeping with the pathetic-chiaroscuro style.

The altar-painting formerly in Pirano with the *Madonna Giving the Girdle to St. Augustine between St. Monica and St. Vincent Ferrer* shows a pyramidic breadth and a compositional arrangement that both recall Ricci. Furthermore the decoration of the top step with small niches, which will recur ever more frequently in later altar-paintings and secular works, reveals Tiepolo's interest in classical decorum; the same touch appears in a drawing by Sebastiano Ricci for an engraving by Andrea Zucchi[2]. However, the position of the Virgin, thrust backwards almost in retreating perspective and surrounded by ecstatic saints, is still conceived in the style of Giambattista Piazzetta's altar-paintings. The same compositional device can be noted in the painting in Piove di Sacco, which for this very reason, even though enriched by the landscape at the bottom, can be attributed to the early thirties.

The frescoes in Palazzo Archinto and Palazzo Casati Dugnani in Milan

Thanks to a profitable network of erudite friendships – Scipione Maffei from Verona and Alberto Zumani, both in correspondence with Filippo Argelati, librarian to Count Carlo Archinto who bore the imperial insignia of the Golden Fleece – Tiepolo was summoned to Milan to decorate five rooms in Palazzo Archinto for the "felicitous nuptials" between Filippo, Carlo Archinto's

[2] It may only be a singular chronological coincidence, but Ricci's drawing, which shows *David reproached by the Prophet Nathan*, was paid for in 1728: J. Daniels (1976, cat. 440d, figs. 65-66).

eldest son, and Giulia Borromeo Grillo[3]. The frescoes, on account of the vastness of the ceilings and the usual practical constrictions of the seasons, took two years to complete.

In the spring and summer of 1730 Tiepolo painted the ceilings of three rooms: *Perseus and Andromeda, Juno, Fortune and Venus Honoring the Arms of the Archinto and Borromeo Families* and *Minerva and Nobility*. In the spring and summer of 1731 he completed the cycle with the more demanding compositions: the *Myth of Phaeton* and the *Triumph of the Arts and Sciences* (which shows the date 1731 on the only fragment that survived the devastating bombardments of Milan in 1943).

Between the two stages of these frescoes it is certain that Tiepolo was back in Venice towards the end of 1730 and for the first few months of the following year; and there was also a preliminary contact – as yet with no result – with Count Giuseppe Casati who had asked him to work in the Palazzo he had just acquired.

The two rooms with the *Triumph of the Arts and Sciences* and the *Myth of Phaeton*, both painted in 1731, are new in some ways: a sign that Tiepolo, far from Venice and with vast walls to work on, felt perfectly at ease. At Massanzago he had already tackled the theme of Phaeton and here too there are elements of chiaroscuro. As at Massanzago, the figure of Time appears, isolated and rotating in the air; he is similar to the figure of the angel at the top left in the *Triumph of St. Dominic* by Piazzetta in Santi Giovanni e Paolo – and, of course, to countless other "flying machines" created by the late-Baroque tradition. But whereas the composition in Massanzago is broken up into isolated and paratactic blocks among rocks and clouds, in Palazzo Archinto the fresco is conceived on broad and co-ordinated lines, a great sphere of air crossed by the transparent band of the Zodiac like a rainbow. One touching detail is constituted by the sunflowers at the bottom of the painting that turn towards the god Apollo. This is an allusion to a passage in Ovid's *Metamorphoses*[4]: Clytia was mercifully transformed into a sunflower after starving herself to death on account of her unreciprocated love for Apollo. Tiepolo chooses to depict the event just after the transformation and, as on other occasions, then inserts a detail from nature in order to ground the myth in reality.

For the *Triumph of the Arts and Sciences*, the last work in the series, a local *quadraturista* – maybe Stefano Orlandi, not the faithful Gerolamo Mengozzi this time – set up a framework of imposing propylaea, that recall low-German Baroque; above them hovers a great host of pre-Enlightenment allegories (Arts and Sciences) which are treated by Tiepolo as Olympian divinities. In this first enterprise outside the territories of the Serenissima, we find something new: the sky is peopled with figures who are aware of their lofty superiority, beings that observe us with serene aloofness at the same time as they apparently wish to crush us to the earth. This attitude of proud observation is one that will be developed and refined by Tiepolo (whether he is dealing with secular or sacred subjects), even to the point of haughty indifference towards the fate of man and the "history of nations". What matters, in fact, is the subtle sublimatory abstraction bestowed on the events narrated by the painting. Evoking unattainable worlds, Tiepolo will come to believe that these artificial universes, made of air, light, color and plaster, depend solely on his *vis creativa* and in the end serve to justify one, and one only, earthly virtue: his painting.

As already stated, before beginning the last two rooms for the Archinto-Borromeo wedding, Tiepolo entered into correspondence with the Milanese nobleman, Giuseppe Casati, and promised to serve him "before the end of the season" (which meant before the end of summer 1731). The agreement with Count Casati, who had become the owner of the building now known as Palazzo Dugnani only the previous year, envisaged a historical cycle centered on the figure of Scipio the African. Tiepolo honored the promise and before the end of 1731 finished the work, which included a ceiling with the *Apotheosis of Scipio*, as Levey convincingly argues[5], three great

[3] Tiepolo had other connections with Milan around 1730 or shortly before. In 1714 the Spanish War of Succession had come to an end and Milan was absorbed into the Empire. Among the various congratulatory tributes that the Milnese reserved for the Emperor was Metastasio's *La Clemenza di Tito* (M. Levey, 1988, p. 55) and a re-issue, in 1730, of the volume *Imperatorum Romanorum Numismata* by F. Mediobarbo, dedicated to Charles VI. The frontispiece was engraved by Francesco Zucchi on a drawing by Giambattista Tiepolo (F. Pedrocco, 1986, pp. 68-69) and shows the city of Milan, personified by a female figure with a turreted crown, offering the book to the marble bust of Charles VI, while the ground is bestrewn with weapons and even Time sleeps over vases brimming with coins, thus neglecting his inexorable duty. The message would appear to be that of eternal life to the Empire, since the Coliseum and Trajan's Column can be seen in the background. Recalling the anti-Austrian significance of the frescoes in the Patriarchal Palace in Udine, we could say that Tiepolo has here performed a smart volte-face. But on the eve of his departure for Spain, in what Haskell defines a "sort of statement to the press", Tiepolo made clear what he thought about an artist's relations with those in power: "Painters must try and succeed in large-scale works capable of pleasing the rich and the nobility because it is they who make the fortunes of artists and not the other sort of people, who cannot buy valuable pictures. And so the painter's spirit must always be reaching for the sublime, the heroic, the perfect": in *Nuova Veneta Gazzetta* (20 March 1762), quoted by F. Haskell (1963, p. 253 and n. 2).
[4] *Metamorphoses*, IV, 190-270.
[5] M. Levey (1986, p. 61).

29.
opposite
Day of Judgement, detail. Venice, Cassa di Risparmio.

wall-frescoes theatrically framed within *trompe l'œil* spiral cartouches and four monochromes with allegories. Despite the damage the decoration has suffered, one can see, beyond the echoes of chiaroscuro that still remain within his painting, that Tiepolo always tries to juxtapose timbres of pure color and to let multi-colored reverberations flicker in the gloom. There are several references to Paolo Veronese and also to his own work in Udine. As in Palazzo Archinto, he adds a personal touch of cool indifference. The tale may arouse admiration for the patron and for the painter who brought it into being, it may perhaps stir up envy among those who cannot afford to decorate their own residences in so splendid a fashion, but it cannot provoke any genuine impulse of the spirit for the *exempla* of the virtues that are represented.

It is a further step in the direction of that combination of artificiality and naturalness, grandiosity and coldness, that distinguishes the mature work.

A metamorphosis in religious iconography

After these two fortunate enterprises in Milan, Tiepolo returned to Rome in the late autumn of 1731. In the years that followed, he devoted himself to religious paintings mostly commissioned by Venetian parish-churches: this was a moment of reflection during which latent stylistic elements re-emerged – the influence of Piazzetta above all – but were used in a new way. The *Bronze Serpent* (figs. 30, 31) is an emphatic construction, a bold proclamation that fully matches the Biblical subjects painted by Pittoni and Sebastiano Ricci for the same church of Santi Cosma e Damiano on the Giudecca. We note the same decorative cartouches that he had used in the three theatrical scenes in Palazzo Casati, and here too they serve to mark the breaks between the episodes.

To conclude his experiments on the theme of the education of the Virgin, Tiepolo painted the altar-piece known as *della Fava* (fig. 33), for the homonymous church of the Oratoriani of San Filippo Neri, which had been finished just a few years earlier and was then being adorned with paintings. Inevitably this meant another confrontation with Piazzetta since the church contained his painting, the *Apparition of the Virgin to San Filippo Neri* and quite rightly critics have stressed this aspect, even though viewpoints on it differ greatly. There are those who denounce the inertia of the Piazzetta model in Tiepolo's work[6], those who see an attenuation of this model[7], and those who affirm an unemphatic return to it[8]. However, they all point to Tiepolo's links (whether they see them as strong or weak), with the leader of the pathetic-chiaroscuro school – which is to say, with the greatest interpreter of devotional pedagogy as it was divulgated and practised in Venice by religious institutions. However, Giambattista introduced significant variants, which once again demonstrate the interlocutory nature of his dialogue with the pictorial

30.
The Bronze Serpent.
Venice, Gallerie
dell'Accademia.

[6] A. Morassi (1955).
[7] A. Pallucchini (1968).
[8] M. Levey (1986, p. 64).

31.
Moses, detail
from fig. 30.

32.
Hagar in the Desert
Comforted by an Angel.
Venice, Scuola Grande di
San Rocco.

33.
Education of the Virgin.
Venice, Church
della Fava.

culture of his age. Piazzetta submerges his sacred figures in an unattainable third dimension, within "fiery vapors that saturate the depths"[9]. Tiepolo, on the other hand, brings the Virgin's family as close as possible to the conventional surface of the painting, to that thin lamina made of nothing that separates the painted world from reality; he sets his *dramatis personae* on a plane that seems to reach out and extend itself into that of the worshiper, or, more simply, the observer. Furthermore, the presence at the top of the painting of a group of opulent angels, almost pagan in style, in the manner of Pietro Liberi, converts the neo-Baroque religious pathos of Piazzetta into an elegance that even has a touch of the lascivious about it.

This tendency to bring the figures to the front of the stage is a compositional *topos* that recurs in other religious paintings by Tiepolo in the early thirties, such as the two canvases in the Scuola di San Rocco with *Abraham and the Angels* and *Hagar and Ishmael* (fig. 32). In both, the influence of Piazzetta can be noted, as many critics have pointed out. But the color is brilliant and the angel that appears in *Hagar and Ishmael* is closely related to the more sumptuous one in the altarpiece "della Fava". The size of the two paintings, almost on a natural scale, and the zoom-like effect of the framing, make it seem that one can almost touch the painted air and participate directly in the two events. This return to Piazzetta, together with what might be termed a moral revision of his stance, can be seen in other oil-paintings of religious subjects, all datable between 1732 and 1733. The *Adoration of the Infant Jesus*, painted for the parish church of San Giuliano in 1732 and now in St. Mark's, has the somewhat emphatic air and the typical dazed effect of Piazzetta's sacred scenes. However, the painting is greatly enlivened by the playful touch of the chubby angel at the top and the straw, which appears to be placed on the same level as our own feet.

The same tendency to involve the spectator, inviting him into the painted space, is to be found in the *Apparition of the Holy Family to St. Gaetano* (figs. 34, 35), formerly in the private chapel of the Labia family in their palazzo at San Geremia, and for a long time attributed to Giandomenico. "The foreground is chromatically ever darker", observes Anna Pallucchini acutely[10]; this causes the observer's eye to penetrate into the heart of the composition, drawing it almost magnetically into the centre of the scene, towards the points of most intense luminosity. The same effect is to be found in the painting of the *Madonna and Child with Saints* in Moscow and *St. Joseph with the Christ Child and Saints*, at the Accademia in Venice. This latter, in particular, has once again the great veils of incense in the manner of Piazzetta and an incongruous column rising towards an absent sky; but the color is lively and clear, while the polychrome squares of the floor invite us to tread on them.

From Bergamo to Rovetta

While he was carrying out the frescoes for Count Casati, in 1731, Tiepolo was contacted by the people in charge of the Luogo Pio della Pietà in Bergamo to decorate the spandrels of the dome and the two lunettes in the choir of the Colleoni Chapel. In September 1732 he was already at work, using the short time available that late in the season to paint *Charity, Faith, Justice* and *Prudence* in the four spandrels[11], and *St. Mark the Evangelist* and the *Martyrdom of St. Bartholomew* in the two lunettes. The rather low quality of the spandrels can be attributed to pressure of time, which made it necessary for him to use assistants; one of these was perhaps Giovanni Raggi, whom Tiepolo had met in the atelier of his Bergamasque friend, Vittore Ghislandi; this latter, Tassi informs us (1797), painted an unidentified portrait of Giambattista. A singular naturalistic contradiction can be noted in the frescoes, one that is not usual in Tiepolo's works.

The four walls of the spandrels are enlivened by clear clouds that expand in the sky, and yet shadows appear on this sky, particularly evident in *Faith* and *Prudence*: as if the space against which

34.
Apparition of the Holy Family to St. Gaetano (Vision of St. Gaetano). Venice, Gallerie dell'Accademia.

[9] A. Mariuz (1982, n. 42).
[10] A. Pallucchini (1968, n. 109).
[11] It was M. Levey (1986, p. 66) who identified the fourth spandrel as *Prudence*, whereas previously it had been held to be *Fortitude*. However, even with this correction, the iconographic series is still a singular mixture of theological Virtues (Faith, Hope and Charity) and cardinal Virtues (Justice, Prudence, Fortitude and Temperance).

35.
opposite
Detail from fig. 34.

the figures are depicted were at the same time a feigned void and a solid wall. In the second lunette of the choir there reappears the theme of the *Martyrdom of St. Bartholomew*, which Tiepolo had already painted at San Stae. But this work lacks the late-Baroque titanism of the earlier version; instead, there are figures of warriors with gleaming armor, to which Tiepolo would return in later years, in his works based on the poems of Ariosto and Tasso.

Having completed the spandrels and lunettes he returned to Venice; in July 1733 he was once again contacted by the authorities of the Luogo Pio in Bergamo, who were clearly satisfied with the decoration of the dome and choir and now asked him to fresco three more lunettes in the Colleoni Chapel: one on the left wall with *St. John the Baptist Preaching*, one on the back wall with the *Baptism of Christ* and one above the entrance with the *Beheading of St. John the Baptist* (figs. 38, 39). This second and more demanding commission occupied him from the end of summer to the beginning of autumn 1733. This is the date that can be read on one of the lunettes and it must be considered as marking the conclusion not only of the preparatory sketches but of the frescoes themselves. The great haste with which he worked on this occasion is testified by the fact that here the models and the frescoes are almost perfectly identical, without any of the variations that are generally found between the project and the completed work when the painter had more time at his disposal. However, this did not prevent him from reverting to his usual practice when dealing with subjects consolidated by a long iconographic tradition and inserting playful or naturalistic elements, or even snippets of esoteric culture. In *St. John the Baptist Preaching*, the tale is full of narrative digressions: the dog, the elegant decorated vase, and Cecilia nursing the infant Francesco, born in October 1732, the "Sior Pantalon" figure on the right and the enigmatic old oriental old man who, on the left, makes his first appearance among the background figures placed there by Tiepolo; the whole story, like the similar *Baptism of Christ*, is set in a "rustic atmosphere"[12] which already seems to tend towards Arcadia. On the other hand the *Beheading of St. John the Baptist* is set in a gloomy, gory interior, in which the force of the drama is skilfully played out on the contrast between the cold, even odious impassivity of the couple on the right – a Veronesian Salome, with a Grecian profile and clothes crackling with light, and a sumptuous oriental – and the emaciated dog which (in the sketch, but not in the fresco) laps at the martyr's blood.

Similar in style to the Colleoni Chapel, and more precisely to the preparatory sketches, there is a group of canvases and small models created rapidly between Bergamo and Venice and sent to various patrons. For example, the sketches of San Daniele del Friuli show a stenographic curtness that says a great deal about the virtuoso rapidity that Giambattista's hand had attained. In the manner of the *Assumption of the Virgin*, now at Ascott House, they manage to appear cursory and yet at the same time concise and perfectly finished, offering us a magnificent example of what we should now begin to define as Tiepolo's "sketchy" style. The small-scale and "stenographic" works are not only – or not necessarily – preparatory sketches, but increasingly a form of expression carried out "for its own sake" and which had many similarities with graphic art; this was an area that would be fully explored at the end of the decade with the series of *Capricci*[13].

A work that was painted in Bergamo or Venice, but in any case at the same time as the Colleoni Chapel, is the *Crucifixion* for the Cathedral in Udine. The color is laid out in compact blocks, without the variegations of the sketches for Bergamo. There is something northern about it, with its over-emphatic chromatic contrasts and the unfortunate perspective solution of Christ who, strangely reduced in size, resembles one of those crucifixes placed at crossroads on mountain-paths. The same unfortunate relationship between the urgency of the work and the formal result is to be found in the *St. Francis of Sales Crushing Heresy* commissioned from Tiepolo by the Patriarch Dionisio Dolfin for the Church of the Filippini in Udine. Apart from the skilfully

[12] *Ibidem.*
[13] T. Pignatti (1965 and 1979); D. Succi (1983, p. 359); ID. (1985, *passim*).

36.
opposite
Madonna and Child with Ss. Antony of Padua, Francis, and Louis of Toulouse, oil sketch. New York, Corsini Collection.

managed color of the robe and sash, where he appears to get the effect of whites and blacks by the use of light blues and dark blues, the painting shows clear signs of having been produced to order. Far greater freedom and frankness are evident in the small series – almost a miniature triptych – devoted to St. Jerome, which is now split up among different places. This is a typical example of Tiepolo's early "sketchy" style in the process of being perfected. It is possible that these were small models for paintings in some rustic hall in the Bergamo countryside, which were then not carried out for reasons unknown, but it is equally possible that they form a small devotional cycle perfect in itself and destined for just one patron whose name is now lost. The curt style of *St. Jerome in the Desert* and the *Communion of St. Jerome*, with the figure of the hermit-saint propped up in both cases against a ramshackle fence, contrasts somewhat with the elegant and tumultuous whirl of angels that acts as a chorus in the *Death of St. Jerome* in the Poldi Pezzoli Museum. However, all three share (and the same is true of the sketches for the Colleoni Chapel) an anguished insistence on sharp-cut drapery and lean, emaciated figures.

This rather uninspired period, which was probably due to his attempting to satisfy too many requests and also perhaps to the use of assistants, came to an end with the great painting for the high altar of the church of Ognissanti in Rovetta, near Bergamo, which shows the *Virgin in Glory, Adored by Apostles and Saints*. We know that the painting was not put in place until 1736 since the sculptor, Andrea Fantoni of Rovetta, was slow to complete the complex frame in stone. Perhaps, as a friendly incitement to speedier work (since he had completed the altar-piece by 1734[14]), Tiepolo gave him the picture of *St. Luigi Gonzaga* in 1735, which is now in London. Whatever the truth of the matter, the altar-piece in Rovetta was a fundamental stage in Tiepolo's early mature phase since it testified to his abandonment of the traditional concept of the iconography of altar-paintings and his whole-hearted adoption of the canons of an original neo-sixteenth-century style. It was certainly no accident that this should have happened away from Venice. With regard to the brilliant color, Barcham writes: "This splendor marks a new era in Tiepolo's religious oil-paintings"[15]. But what is even more striking, in our opinion, is the new concept of space and the arrangement of the protagonists. Starting from St. Peter, standing erect like a giant to the fore of the scene almost as if to impose a theatrical *attractio attentionis*, a spiral of forces is developed that passes via St. John the Baptist on the right, returns to the angel hovering in the center, turns around the great hub of the column set in the middle, touches the group of martyrs and saints placed above the dazzling cloud, and finally rises to the Virgin who, with her upward gaze, discharges all this energy towards an undetermined point outside the picture. At various points, this slow rotatory movement is intercepted by darts of sudden light that seem to energize each separate phase. In the preparatory sketch at the Poldi Pezzoli Museum one can see that the original plan was quite different, with a clear division between an earthly layer and a celestial one, lacking the extraordinary "legato" effect of the final version.

The frescoes at Villa Loschi at Biron di Monteviale

In the frescoes that Tiepolo carried out in the summer and autumn of 1734 in the Villa of Count Nicolò Loschi at Biron, outside Vicenza, many of the different threads that we have considered so far are brought together to form an indissoluble whole (figs. 41, 42).

First of all, it must be noted that he was once again summoned to work in an architectural space that had only recently been completed, as at Vascon and at Ca' Zenobio, at the Patriarchal Palace in Udine and Palazzo Dolfin at San Pantalon. At Biron di Monteviale, the Loschi family proceeded to transform an entire strip of land, finally arranging the internal spaces of the villa around the decoration that was to celebrate their virtues. It is also worth pointing out that Giambattista was asked again to exalt the nobility in terms of their ethical and social role and

[14] This is why we examine the painting before the frescoes for Villa Loschi at Biron.
[15] W.L. Barcham (1989, p. 186).

37.
Rebecca at the Well.
New York,
Corsini collection.

38.
Beheading of St. John
the Baptist. Bergamo,
Colleoni Chapel.

to add to their glory by carrying out a strictly pre-ordained iconographic program. The Loschi family had only recently been granted their noble status. It was only in September 1729 that the title of Count had been conferred on Nicolò, his relatives and his male descendants by the *Provveditori sopra Feudi*, the Venetian magistrature that took responsibility for the legitimacy of noble titles throughout the territory of Venice. Shortly afterwards the same Provveditori issued a severe proclamation against false aristocratic pretenses, which were particularly numerous in Vicenza, giving rise to the saying: *"No ga Venezia tanti gondolieri, quanti Vicenza conti e cavalieri"*[16]. At that time the élites of all the mainland cities under Venice began a general dynastic revaluation. But the Loschi did not need to do so, since the decree of 1729 was not canceled by that of 1734 and furthermore showed that the central government had also forgotten the perpetual ban that had been issued in the seventeenth century against an ancestor of the new Count Nicolò. Who, in order to goad yet further the arrogance and envy of his compatriots, conceded himself the luxury of commissioning Giambattista to paint a cycle of frescoes centered on his newly acquired nobility and the moral virtues on which it rested.

The figurative program for the Villa of the Loschi is based entirely on the *Iconologia* of Cesare Ripa, the most widely known illustrated allegorical encyclopaedia of late Mannerism, which the Count no doubt adopted on the suggestion of some man of letters consulted for the occasion[17]. But, as we have seen, with Tiepolo it is never enough merely to record his sources. He gave his patrons the guarantee of well-tried iconographic traditions, but they were rarely chosen by him. Every court, whether great or small, had its own poets and its own scholars, and it was they who suggested the allegorical themes to be painted in praise of the nobleman and his family. Giambattista's task, at least apparently, was simply to translate these notions into visual terms. It is within these none-too-wide margins that we can investigate whether such a thing as a

[16] "Venice has not so many gondoliers as Vicenza has counts and cavaliers". The whole business is carefully reconstructed in R. Menegozzo's documented work (1990, pp. 5-39).
[17] On Ripa and the success of his book: D.J. Gordon, *The Renaissance Imagination*, University of California Press (Italian edition, Milan 1987, pp. 81-111).

39.
Detail from fig. 38.

"Tiepolesque" iconography exists. The dialectics of the relations between the painter and the patron in the matter of vast fresco-cycles were almost too firmly consolidated to allow for any marked divergences. The artist, on the basis of preliminary agreements, prepared one or more sketches (in the case of Biron we only know the preparatory drawings), among which the patron chose those that best suited his self-glorificatory intentions; finally the painter set to work. It was at this stage that Tiepolo effected his own re-elaboration of the themes that had been agreed upon, transforming into a coherent pictorial account what had been imposed as a mere gallery of literary conceits. We will therefore explore the scenes frescoed at Biron in order to comprehend the imperceptible but all-important discrepancy between the source chosen by Count Loschi and the transliteration created by Giambattista Tiepolo.

The encomiastic poem begins on the landing, where the monumental staircase divides into two flights. On the walls Tiepolo painted the *trompe l'œil* statues of *Merit* and *Nobility*; overhead, on the ceiling above the staircase, *Time Unveiling Truth and Driving away Envy*. The significance is clear: after the tribulations that the family coat-of-arms had had to endure during the seventeenth-century, Time has at last thrown light on Truth, confounded Envy and revealed to the world the Merit and thus the Nobility of the Loschi family. Since this was the prologue, Tiepolo did not dare to stray from the source; the most he did was to elongate the figures with respect to the squat types to be found in the illustrations to Ripa's book. On the walls of the two flights that ascend to the piano nobile we find *Vigilance Triumphing over Sleep* and *Innocence Driving away Deceit*. In the former, Vigilance is taken faithfully from Ripa with the attributes of the cock and the torch, but Sleep shows some significant variations. Ripa had described him as "a corpulent and heavy man, lying on a bed of poppies with a vine loaded with mature grapes that will cast a shadow on him"; Tiepolo, however, depicts him as a young winged god, serene in

40.
Alms of St. John.
San Daniele del Friuli
(Udine), Cathedral.

aspect, close to a Virgilian detail of a vine shaken by pagan sprites. In the other fresco he reproduces all the canonical attributes, even in the choice of colors; however, he creates a sort of comical scene, with Innocence sitting on a classical altar, her feet trampling on Deceit, who is taunted by a small and exaggeratedly furious sprite.

In general, when the illustrations for Ripa's allegories involve more than one figure – two "moral opposites" or several characters – the figures are crowded together so that the ethical qualities they embody emerge more clearly by contrast. Tiepolo's procedure is quite different and one that Ripa almost certainly would not have approved of; he makes the whole scene lighter and airier, translating it into terms of theatrical dynamics, since the protagonists for him are not the abstract, pedantic and static conceits of a tediously edifying moral, but real characters in the theatrical and narrative sense of the term. Therefore they must act, not simply show themselves. This is clearest in the *salone di rappresentanza*. On the ceiling he reproduces Ripa's allegories almost without variations, but on the walls he seems to be re-reading the source according to his own personal taste. *Pride and Humility*, which Ripa had not given a setting, are placed in an Arcadian landscape, which is diaphanous and cold. In *Liberality Distributing Gifts*, instead of the crowd of miserly beggars proposed by Ripa, Tiepolo offers us three chubby and festive sprites, and on the right, in the guise of a pageboy, his son Giandomenico, born in 1727. Even more delightful and revealing is his tampering in *Marital Concord*. Ripa wrote: "A man on the right of a woman, both dressed in purple and with one gold chain linking the necks of both and the said chain must have as a pendant a heart which is supported by one hand of both the man and woman"; the engraving accompanying the text shows the couple standing side by side, almost soldered together like Siamese twins. Tiepolo separates and distances the two figures; he has the wife sitting down and is thus obliged to leave the husband holding the heart by himself, bending down slightly towards his wife. In other words, he creates something like a duet from an eighteenth-century opera, with a *cicisbeo* paying homage to his lady.

In the last analysis, the explanatory scenes chosen by Count Loschi did not prevent Giambattista from exercizing his own imaginative autonomy and depicting a way of enjoying life in a villa that managed to be both new and old at the same time.

Between Venice and the European market

After his work at Villa Loschi, Tiepolo returned to Venice and for a while devoted himself to a series of sketches, only a few of which correspond to completed works on a larger scale. Given the far from florid state of the economy at that time, this may have been due to a dwindling of the internal market. However, it is also true that everywhere, and not only in Venice, the current tendency, in accordance with Rococo principles, was for artistic objects that were both small in size and complete in themselves; such objects were sought after not only by wealthy collectors but also by connoisseurs whose interest was to add another signature to their collection. The lack of local demand, however, was compensated for by a number of requests that came for Tiepolo from outside the world of Venice.

The great number of paintings representing St. Roch that he painted around the middle of the thirties (fig. 43) were all connected to his activity in the field of sketching, if not actually part of it. To our current state of knowledge there are twenty-two of these works. They respond to the devotional circuit of the brothers of the Scuola di San Rocco and the fact that no two of them are the same demonstrates the artist's skill in elaborating a theme around just one note – creating continual variations with the barest of ingredients.

This period of stasis was interrupted by a commission – once again from outside Venice – to paint the *Immaculate Conception* in the Church of Aracoeli in Vicenza, probably not long after

41.
Vigilance Triumphing
over Sleep.
Biron (Vicenza), Villa
Loschi Zileri dal Verme.

42.
Liberality Distributing
Gifts. Biron (Vicenza),
Villa Loschi
Zileri dal Verme.

the frescoes at Villa Loschi. The altar on the opposite side of the church contained *The Ecstasy of St. Francis* by Piazzetta, painted according to Mariuz in 1729[18]. As usual, Tiepolo gave free rein to his emulative bent and confronted the older Maestro directly, placing a monumental statue at the centre of his work. All around it, however, he arranged a whirling array of putti, in *contrejour* under the airy cloak of the Virgin and transparent in the light at the top right. The sketch in Amiens shows even more clearly the breadth and openness of Tiepolo's concept of space; it is also impalpable and light in its strokes, as opposed to the more compact and tightly-constructed effect of the final version. The same plastic solidity can be noted in the *Madonna of the Rosary* in Cape Town, signed and dated 1735. The light and color are calm and they endow the forms with a solemnity that heralds the steady composure of the next decade. Similarly, in the small *Danae* in Stockholm (figs. 46, 47), there is a clear, still light that comes from two different directions: from the Palladian scene glimpsed in the background and an imaginary source directly opposite. The mythological scene is narrated in a playful tone: a realistic little dog is leaping up at the eagle, the symbol of Zeus; the old woman from the *Beheading of St. John the Baptist* in the Colleoni chapel reappears in the guise of a procuress; Cupid does his generous best to satisfy the spectator's voyeuristic impulses[19]. It was this mingling of seriousness and facetiousness that attracted collectors and amateurs, as well as the numerous diplomatic legations that European courts sent throughout the continent to seek out artistic talents and prestigious works for their dynastic collections. Count Tessin, while he schemed and trafficked to promote his master's ambitious decorative projects, did not neglect to put aside a considerable hoard of valuable and well-chosen small works for his own personal collection.

The free treatment of myths, stories and religious themes is another of the robust threads that links Tiepolo to Veronese – or rather to a neo-sixteenth-century *paganitas* which, in Giambattista's hand, and especially in his oil-paintings, loses a little of its earnest Renaissance heroism and becomes more cordial and effervescent, more confidential and amused. This change in tone can be seen in *Moses Saved from the Waters*, in Edinburgh, which is a version of the painting by Veronese that hung in Palazzo Grimani until 1747 and which then joined the collection of August III in Dresden, thanks to the good offices of Count Francesco Algarotti[20]. This latter, like Count Tessin, skilfully exercised the new profession of a mediator of artistic goods for the European sovereigns[21]. Using similar methods to Count Tessin, Algarotti managed to become the owner of a small copy of Veronese's work, asking Tiepolo himself for it. The wide canvas now in Edinburgh could be taken for one of those reproductions of works by the Maestri of the Golden Century that eighteenth-century painters were constantly carrying out at the behest of contemporary collectors: the larger versions ended up in the royal collections, those on a smaller scale were reserved for the professional experts who operated in the market on behalf of third parties. However, the fact that Tiepolo made a number of significant alterations would seem to disprove this hypothesis. Rather than a reproduction for connoisseurs, in which he would have suppressed his own personality in favor of Veronese, the artist may have produced a replica for himself; or alternatively, given the fact that the painting, if we add the missing part now conserved in Turin, seems too large to have been carried out for purely personal satisfaction, he may have been offering some Venetian patron who was envious of the Grimani his own free interpretation of Veronese.

In the second half of the thirties, commissions began to pour in from the places outside Venice that had first made him famous: Milan and Udine. Immediately after the *Martyrdom of St. Agatha* for the Buzzaccarini Chapel in the Basilica of Saint Antony in Padua, Giambattista was summoned to carry out some fresco-work in Sant'Ambrogio in Milan: the walls of the chapel of San Vittore and the ceiling of the adjoining sacristy. Photographs of the ceiling, which was

[18] A. Mariuz (1982, n. 49).
[19] This was Count Tessin, the envoy of the King of Sweden in Venice.
[20] M. Levey (1986, pp. 77-80).
[21] Often the noble titles that these mediators bore had been granted for their merits as collectors.

43.
St. Roch Standing.
Bergamo,
private collection.

destroyed in an air-raid in 1943, reveal a snow-white St. Bernard raised by a complex arrangement of angels above the theological Virtues and against the background of a stormy sky. At the bottom, across the fresco, can be seen the pastoral staff, the symbol of episcopal power, which, however, performs a different function in terms of the composition. In the lower band of his paintings, Tiepolo often places boards, poles, branches, rods, or travelers' staffs, lying on the ground as if by chance[22]. However, they are not there by accident. They serve Tiepolo as a measure of depth – or rather, to suggest the first step between the space of reality and that of the depicted scene, and thus to let us perceive the exact perspective of the latter.

Having returned to Venice, Tiepolo was summoned by the Patriarch of Aquileia, Daniele Dolfin, who had succeeded Dionisio[23], to paint three large canvases for churches in Udine: the *Guardian Angel, Ss. Hermagoras and Fortunatus*, and, a little later, the *Holy Trinity*. Given the importance of his patron, Giambattista could not refuse and he complied with the request very quickly, maybe with the help of some collaborator. The works do not seem to be very passionately inspired: the guardian angel who hovers in mid-air is rather too precisely sculpted by the light; the two saints are conditioned by devotional typologies of the sixteenth century[24]; the Trinity is arranged rather listlessly, following an iconographic tradition that goes back to Italian and Flemish art of the fifteenth-century[25]. The only elements in which we can recognise the real expressive verve of Tiepolo are the rocky landscapes that form the background to all three paintings, bathed in an extremely pure atmospheric light.

Once again making use of his circle of patrons, who had helped him in his youth, Tiepolo obtained an order for a wholly Venetian work: *St. Augustine, St. Louis of France, St. John the Evangelist and St. Magnus*, formerly in one of the two Cornaro Chapels in San Salvador and later destroyed or removed, it is not known when or how. The final version, testified by a copy by Kuen (who was in Venice in 1746), shows that the Cornaro family aspired to something more prestigious and wide-ranging than Tiepolo's original proposal, in his well-balanced but rather too meditative "first idea", formerly in the Chiesa collection. Tiepolo then took a hint from Sebastiano Ricci's altar-piece with *St. Procolus, Bishop of Verona and St. Fermus and Rusticus*, which he had had occasion to see in the southern transept of the Cathedral of Bergamo[26], and partly from the same painter's *St. Pius, St. Thomas of Aquinas and St. Peter the Martyr*, which had hung above the first altar on the left in the Venetian church of the Gesuati since 1734[27]. Tiepolo had adopted Ricci's schemes when painting altarpieces for churches outside Venice, for example in Rovetta,

44.
Triumph of Zephyr and Flora. Venice, Ca' Rezzonico.

[22] Just to mention the first that come to mind, such objects are to be found in *The Rape of Europa* in the Accademia of Venice, in *Rachel Hiding the Idols* at the Patriarchal Palace in Udine, in the *Beheading of St. John the Baptist* in Bergamo, in the scene with *Vigilance Triumphing over Sleep* at Villa Loschi; many others can be seen in his later works as well.

[23] It is clear that, for the special interests that the Serenissima had in the Friuli, the office of the Patriarch of Aquileia became practically a feudal prerogative of the Dolfin family, first Dionisio, then Daniele: both faithful patrons of Giambattista.

[24] For example, by the vast canvases of Bonifacio de' Pitati for the Camerlenghi in Venice.

[25] For example, the *Trinity* by Masaccio in Santa Maria Novella in Florence and the small sculpture that stands over the fire-place in the painting of *St. Barbara* by Robert Campin at the Prado.

[26] Painted in 1704: J. Daniels (1976, cat. 32, p. 9, fig. 30).

[27] *Ibidem*, cat. 452, p. 129, fig. 302 and cat. 87, p. 27, fig. 301 (the sketch).

45.
opposite
Detail from fig. 44.

46.
Detail from fig. 47.

since he rightly held that local taste was not yet prepared to accept in religious subjects the neo-sixteenth-century revival that was being carried ahead by Rococo painters. However, in the case of the Cornaro family at least, he was mistaken. He was more than happy to make up for his error of judgement with the sketch now at the National Gallery in London, in which he opens a breach in the wall at the back and sets out his characters with a bold effect of *sottinsù* which, henceforth, was to be a recurring device in his altarpieces.

Meanwhile the circles in which he was known expanded enormously with the first requests from the German-speaking world. It was in fact the Prince Elector of Cologne, Clement August, who ordered an enormous canvas for the high altar of the church of Notre Dame in Nymphenburg (completed around 1738) with *St. Clement the Pope Adoring the Trinity*. Tiepolo's début in Bavaria was marred by a slight accident: a misunderstanding over the exact measurements of the altar obliged him to reduce drastically the solemn composition of the sketch, which had been conceived along the lines of a Vatican ritual. And thus he had to compress the space between the figures, to abolish part of the architectural apparatus and to transform the processional staff, which in the sketch had conferred a sense of immensity on the encounter between the earthly and unearthly, into a sort of tiresome pitchfork, which served to separate Pope Clement from the sacred figures who suddenly seem higher and further away. However, the orchestration of the colors is still extraordinary, and they succeed in giving rhythm to the expansion of space.

The second large-scale canvas for Germany, the *Martyrdom of St. Sebastian*, was commissioned from Tiepolo by a monastic religious order, the Augustinians of Diessen in Bavaria. Here too the artist adopted a scheme on Ricci's lines, adding however a sense of color that was entirely his own: a peaceful and serene chromaticism, which constituted one further step, maybe the last, towards the classical imperturbability of his next phase.

47.
Danae. Stockholm,
Universitet
Konsthistoriska
Institutionen.

The great decorative cycles
1737-1750

Finally, Venice

Some time before accepting the two commissions for the canvases later sent to Germany, Tiepolo signed an important contract with the Dominicans. This religious order was particularly prominent in Venice because of its patronage of costly and ambitious artistic projects. As the order was not particularly well-endowed, it financed these through the generosity of wealthy members of the congregation or funds collected from its parishioners. The contract provided for the fresco decoration of the ceiling and other surfaces of the church of Santa Maria del Rosario, or the Gesuati, on the Zattere, which had been completely restructured in the mid-1720s by the architect Giorgio Massari. Barcham makes a logical and convincing analysis of this cycle which partly corrects Niero's reading[1]. The iconography of the frescoes generally depicts the elevation of the ritual of the Rosary to an official feast of the universal Church, following the decision of Pope Clement XI in 1714.

We should also recall that at the same time there was a renewed surge of enthusiasm for the Marian cult, which the Dominicans spread extensively. There was also the close identification between the Virgin Mary and Venice[2], which had been accepted State rhetoric ever since the construction of the votive church of Santa Maria della Salute. However, its generalized and fairly conventional iconography also conceals another interpretation exclusive to the Dominican order. Barcham points out that it was not dominated by, as Niero wrote, a "subtle anti-Quietist polemic"[3] but rather, "a Dominican rebuttal not to Quietism but to Jansenism"[4], inspired by the bitter disagreement which had sprung up between the reformed Dominican congregation at the Zattere and Jacques Hyacinth Serry, a Dominican theology professor at the Studio of Padua who was also a suspected Jansenist.

This argument took place during Massari's reconstruction, just before Tiepolo's work in the

[1] A. Niero (1979); W.L. Barcham (1989, pp. 109-137).
[2] 'Linking Venetian patriotism with Judeo-Christian narrative, Catholic devotions, Roman traditions, and Dominican spirituality': W.L. Barcham (1989, p. 114).
[3] A. Niero (1979, p. 78).
[4] W.L. Barcham (1989, p.130).

48.
opposite
Institution of the Rosary, detail. Venice, Church of the Gesuati.

49.
Ascent of Mount Calvary.
Venice, Church of
Sant'Alvise.

church. The Venetian government had tolerated clandestine preaching of the Port-Royal doctrine in the Benedictine monastery of Santa Giustina in Padua, where Serry was a guest, despite the destruction of the French convent by order of Louis XIV in 1709, and Clement XI's bull of 1713, *Unigenitus*, a rebuttal to the Jansenist proposals contained in the *Réflexions morales* by Pasquier Quesnel. In his turn, Serry had published works denouncing the idolatrous excesses of the Marian cult[5]. This clash, which reveals the debate between the doctrine of grace and freedom of conscience as regards faith, was resolved in 1724 when the Dominican Vincenzo Maria Orsini was elected Pope, taking the name Benedict XIII. The new pope made Clement's 1713 bull his own, and placed the whole Dominican order at its defense. "Begun at the very moment of Serry's death, Tiepolo's grand painting cycle represents the Dominicans' rebuttal to their 'Jansenist' theologian in Padua"[6].

Tiepolo's frescoes therefore are heavily conditioned by theological, iconographical, and finally political factors due to the issue of Papal authority, an extremely delicate question in terms of Veneto jurisdiction. It is highly unlikely that an anti-theological character like Tiepolo participated much in the hidden subtleties of the polemic – the interlocutory embarrassment of the retouched *bozzetti* is eloquent testimony. The play of reciprocal references woven between the polychrome scenes of the ceiling and the monochrome pieces artfully arranged in other parts of the church is neither his invention nor the result of an agreement between Tiepolo and Massari. Barcham actually suggests that the primary text for the central scene with the *Institution of the Rosary* could be *Le glorie di Maria*, a weighty treatise written between 1730 and 1740 by Alfonso de' Liguori, against the enlightened Catholicism of Ludovico Antonio Muratori[7] – a work which was much more the reading matter of educated committed monks than artists.

Having taken care of the doctrinal obligations so important to his patrons, Tiepolo instead

[5] *Ibidem*, p. 132.
[6] *Ibidem*, p. 135.
[7] *Ibidem*, p. 136. The work was later printed in Naples in 1750.

50.
opposite
Detail from fig. 49.

had to solve the formal working-out of these contents, which involved a confrontation with the whole development of Venetian painting from the sixteenth to the eighteenth centuries. The composition is not entirely original: those *sottinsù* had already been seen in Veronese's work for the State iconography of the Palazzo Ducale, in Tintoretto's work for Santi Giovanni e Paolo, and much later, in Sebastiano Ricci's oil series in San Marziale. Nor must the application of such large scale fresco technique, finally seen in Venice, have been much of a novelty either. However, the framing device of the frescoes is simple to the point of anti-Baroque brevity, heralding a new development which supports the understanding of the narration, as well as intensifies the light from the opposed opening system devised by Massari.

Tiepolo does not use only the two dimensions of the ceiling, or rather he does not use them as if they were merely simple wall surfaces. The halberdier suspended over the large painted cornice, and the Albigensian heretic actually thrown outside the stucco frame in the *Institution of the Rosary* indicate that Tiepolo, as in the *Rebel Angels* in the Patriarchate of Udine, is illusionistically appropriating the entire volume of air that dizzily descends from the roof to the ground. But he introduces his most significant innovations in the use of color. For the first time in Venice, and for the first time in Tiepolo's painting as well, we see an iridescent chromatic fabric without intensely colored zones, an extremely light assemblage dominated by the unnatural and almost weightless value of white, obtained, just as in the engravings he began around this time, by leaving walls uncovered – the art of removal rather than addition.

The huge canvases commissioned for the church of Sant'Alvise at the same time as the *Rosary* frescoes (figs. 49, 50) represent a re-assessment of the paintings of Titian and Tintoretto, and the work of the sixteenth-century masters who had influenced his youth when he was Gregorio Lazzarini's pupil. In the move from fresco to oil technique, some of the discoveries glimpsed in the Gesuati are lost. In the canvas triptych we do not find that diaphanous color, the spaces reserved for the dazzling white, the spatial exchange between reality and representation; figures lose the classic proportional balance that they had in the Dominican ceiling and are stretched out (see the bearded thief in the central painting) or contorted (note the arched back of the torturer dragging the cross) in a version of Venetian Mannerism. Tiepolo is clearly much more at ease letting his bodies fly through the endless skies than he is organizing them on earth. However, in the central canvas we note the rotating movement of the spiral that starts in the axis along the cross, which stops on the red spot of Christ, and rears up towards the top of that shining silver horse. Of course there are also those customary details that we have learned never to consider merely decorative, such as the spectators clustered in the center and the beautiful group in *contrejour* at the top right, which seems taken from the etchings Tiepolo was then experimenting with.

After the Gesuati and Sant'Alvise, which heralded his triumph in his native city as well, Giambattista would not have any further need for cautious assessment of the local taste before putting forth his own proposals. From now on, finally in Venice as well, he would be the undisputed master of his own choices.

The frescoes in Palazzo Clerici and other works in Lombardy

The incessant travel forced on Tiepolo by continual requests for his work took him to Milan in 1740 to execute a commission for Marquis Giorgio Antonio Clerici, in what we may well consider one of the milestones of his maturity (fig. 51).

The occasion for the commission was Clerici's marriage to Fulvia Visconti which was to be celebrated in 1741. In preparation for the event, Clerici planned the restoration of the palace he had inherited in 1736, and, imitating what he had certainly seen in Palazzo Archinto and

51.
opposite
The Course of the Sun Chariot, detail. Milan, Palazzo Clerici.

52.
Triumph of Amphitrite,
sketch. Formerly
London, Walpole Gallery.

at the Casati, he resolved to consolidate his position in Milanese society by utilizing that Venetian who was now being discussed so enthusiastically from northern Italy to Bavaria. Thus Giorgio Antonio Clerici knew that he could trust Tiepolo to project his dynastic marriage into the grandest Olympus ever painted. But it was actually neither the time nor the place for such exhibitionist, even feudalistic, celebrations.

After the war of the Spanish Succession and the treaty of Rastadt (1714) the duchy of Milan had passed to Charles VI of Austria. At his death (1740) the Imperial crown went to his daughter Maria Theresa, who soon initiated an enlightened policy of reform in Lombardy in which she, among other things, elevated Giorgio Antonio Clerici to the rank of Imperial marshal. It was said that this was not an auspicious moment for triumphant displays modelled on the absolutist style of Louis XIV. Maria Theresa's accession to power would actually lead to the long crisis of the Austrian War of Succession (1740-48). At its conclusion Milan became, together with Naples, one of the centers of enlightenment renewal in Italy. Instead, here in Milan in the very year in which Maria Theresa was inaugurating her new reformist government, Tiepolo for the first time came up with that Apollinian cliché that he would adopt again and again to memorialize the fortunes of his patrons, a cliché which belonged to a decidedly obsolete vision of power.

With its mirrors looking out onto large windows, and its endless lowered vault, the reception hall of Palazzo Clerici is a majestic gallery, a miniature Versailles. The iconography of the frescoes portrays the exaltation of the *Course of the Sun Chariot* pulled by four horses driven by Apollo, with an attending escort of all the divinities and episodes that mythology could provide. The allegories of the Four Continents (all that were known then) are arranged deferentially round the perimeter of the vault. This was obviously not a particularly ambitious iconographical scheme, but it utilized a fairly universal mythology which gave Tiepolo yet another opportunity to flaunt that transparent color, festive yet classically detached and almost anodyne (in the Greek sense of the word, 'without pain') that he had already mastered so brilliantly in the Gesuati. It is therefore no coincidence that Tiepolo was never again commissioned to execute grand projects for the *ancien régime* in Milan, the city that had so triumphantly declared his success outside his home town of Venice. For the same reasons he did not receive any commissions from Enlightenment France, where Venetian painting had been at home until the 1720s, or England, the leader of Europe's enlightened monarchies. His other two Lombard works belong to the same year as his commission for the Palazzo Clerici.

The first is the fresco ceiling of the Palazzo Gallarati Scotti, now transferred to canvas, which depicts two allegorical figures which have been identified in various ways, the prototypes for many other similar compositions by Tiepolo. Anna Pallucchini calls them *Virtue* and *Fortitude*[8], but the two figures, which we have already seen separately in the wall scenes of Biron, do not quite correspond to the description in the iconographical manual that Tiepolo must have consulted, Cesare Ripa's *Iconologia*, which he used at Villa Loschi and would refer to for all his future allegorical representations. *Virtue* is actually portrayed correctly. Ripa describes her as a young woman with a spear in her right hand, a crown of laurel in her left, and a sun on her chest. The angle of the profile does not allow us to see the sun, which was included in the Biron scene *Virtue Crowning Honor*, but all the other attributes are there. The other figure, however, is not *Fortitude*, but *Nobility*, which had already appeared on the landing on the monumental staircase of the Villa Loschi. Ripa describes her with a spear in one hand, a miniature image of Minerva in the other, and two crowns at her feet. It is clear that Tiepolo had partially departed from his source, for in his version the spear has disappeared, and the two crowns have become one, held like a toy by a zephyr perched on a branch that also seems to support the theatrical *machina* on which *Virtue* and *Nobility* stand. The result is perhaps not very faithful to Ripa in terms of content,

[8] A. Pallucchini (1968, n. 139).

53.
Virtue and Nobility
Striking down Vice.
Venice, Palazzo
Papadopoli.

54.
Flying Putti Playing with
Doves. Venice, Palazzo
Papadopoli.

but is certainly inspired by a sense of amused elegance. By removing a spear Tiepolo avoids painting a sky bristling with lances, and moving the crown to the *putto* on the side he creates one of his characteristic deviations in narrative, enlivening the crowd of figures that thus appear less heaped up and more natural. Finally, he exchanges Ripa's sun with an exposed breast (flaunted by both the allegories) thus creating an opportunity for a purely Rococo exhibition of feminine beauty. The second Lombard work by Tiepolo in 1740 is the series of three paintings from the Villa Girola near Lake Como, once owned by the Austrian Artaria family, an allegorical cycle dedicated to the four elements (the fourth, *Fire*, is lost).

New idola tribus

Tiepolo was delayed in Milan because of two paintings he executed for the parish church of Verolanuova near Brescia, on the border between Lombardy and the Veneto (fig. 56). Count Gian Francesco Gambara, who had commissioned them for the confraternity of the Holy Sacrament, required that Tiepolo work *in loco*, perhaps because the two sketches he had produced in Venice in lower, wider dimensions showed that he had distorted the true dimensions, or possibly because of the difficulty of sending ten-meter-high canvases from Venice to Verolanuova without damage. The Old Testament subjects reveal an authentic dramatic tension which Tiepolo had demonstrated as early as his *Pharaoh Submerged* from 1716. A quarter of a century had passed, however, and the two episodes, the *Gathering of Manna* and the *Sacrifice of Melchizedek* became, respectively, a boisterous celebratory confusion and a military display. Not, of course, that Tiepolo was making some irreverent statement. He was clearly unable to resist the temptation to revive the two scenes as exotic tales, providing an excuse to indulge in strange stories and extravagant characters for the sheer sake of curiosity. A kaleidoscopic narrative vein

55.
Portrait of Antonio
Riccobono. Rovigo,
Accademia dei Concordi.

emerges, an irrepressible taste for fanciful frivolity, aimed more at eliciting surprise and wonder than devotion. Tiepolo certainly could not have felt authorized to do this by his two sources, which were Tintoretto in San Giorgio Maggiore and the Madonna dell'Orto for the composition, and Sebastiano Ricci in Santi Cosma and Damiano for the outdoor setting, punctuated by soaring trees reaching all the way up to the sky[9]. A new mentality was being born in Europe, an attitude that rejected the figurative dogmas of the late Baroque for a jaded satisfaction in the witty remark, *pruderie*, and the chorale, brought however into common experience – as in the theater of Goldoni. In other words, a pre-bourgeois attitude was taking shape.

Some Venetian works of Tiepolo's, dating from the early 1740s, display just this enjoyment in producing images that reflected everyday life, even if they were often based on allegorical subjects, as well as the subconscious creation of a new method of narration. Thus was born Tiepolo's purely original sense of drama, paradoxically at the same time his most intensely classical and formal phase was underway.

In 1741 Tiepolo painted frescoes in two parts of the Palazzo Papadopoli Arrivabene[10]. The subject of the larger ceiling was incorrectly identified as *Fortitude and Wisdom*. Instead, from a comparison with Palazzo Gallarati Scotti and Ripa, we see that it is again *Virtue and Nobility* (figs. 53, 54). The insistence with which Tiepolo returns to this theme reveals a perfecting of the ideological conviction shared by the aristocratic society which most of Tiepolo's patrons belonged to, and which he absorbed through them. This is the belief that *Nobility* is inextricably linked, by definition, to *Virtue* and vice versa. Holding hands, as in this ceiling, these two *idola tribus* defeat whatever allegorically evil or detestable forces may lurk in public or private life, such as Vice, Deceit, Envy, and Sedition.

[9] Ricci's painting however has a horizontal thrust; J. Daniels (1976, cat. 464, pp. 135-136, fig. 318).
[10] A. Morassi (1962, p. 61).

56.
opposite
The Gathering of Manna,
detail. Verolanuova
(Brescia), parish church.

Tiepolo here begins to reveal himself an authentic poet of the patrician classes, and even though the virtues triumph regularly and the vices surrender without fail in these simplified games, he always manages to introduce variants that make the tale less saccharine. In his own way he creates unusual duets and combinations of different allegories of good sentiments, distributing the attributes to the ever-present *putti* or angels, by removing – or adding – symbolic objects, in the attempt to make the event more familiar, common, and hence easy to narrate. Frozen allegories and static concepts begin to move and interact in his hands, thus becoming credible situations, clashes between personified wills in which it even seems possible to make out some plot, just as in a play, acted in costume, but rendered real and vivid by events taken from real life.

A confirmation of this contradiction between content and form in the narrative would come, however, later, in the two ceilings for the Palazzo Dolfin Manin at the Rialto (figs. 81, 82) arbitrarily linked by George Knox[11] to the *Gerusalemme Liberata*. The ceiling of one of its rooms, which is now in Pasadena, was correctly recognized as *Virtue and Nobility Defeating Ignorance*[12], and this is the third time that we meet these two allegories placed together. This time *Virtue* is painted frontally with a sun on her breast, while in compensation she has been deprived of her spear which has ended up behind *Nobility's* cloak. The other ceiling, traditionally called the *Riches of Venice*, vice versa depicts *Nobility, Temperance and Generosity* but it is no longer recognized as an autograph work after extensive restoration. As for the cycle of the *Gerusalemme liberata*, which has never been proved to come from the frescoes in Palazzo Dolfin Manin of Rialto, it is composed of four paintings today in Chicago, flanked by four vertical paintings now in the National Gallery in London. It is possible that the ovals of the satyrs of Rome and Pasadena were part of the cycle, used like ornamental panels above the doors.

This would be the first time Tiepolo turned to Italian literature for the decoration of a patrician house, instead of myths and allegories[13], but here too what counts is not the fact in itself, but rather the way in which Tiepolo describes it. The four horizontal canvases refer to specific passages in the poem by Tasso, although they are placed in somewhat disturbing Arcadian landscapes that the heroic poem itself would never have countenanced. They become instead the actual physical atmosphere of all of Tiepolo's literary passages, as if Tasso had been viewed through a filter of Metastasio[14].

In the *Apotheosis of Admiral Vettor Pisani* for the palazzo Pisani Moretta as well, Tiepolo introduced *felix puerilis aetas* – zephyrs and putti – so that he could push the various attributes to the side, attributes which would otherwise be too cumbersome for the mythical-allegorical figures in the center. This is a sort of watering-down intended to lighten part of the erudite burden of depiction in favor of the more natural scenes. Iconographical doctrines and dogmas begin to diminish, and the reasonable makes progress, even if its contents belong to the instructive abstractions of myth and allegory. Tiepolo raises despots, warriors and coats of arms up to the highest skies of moral concepts. But then he takes them down a degree, down to a melodramatic layer all his own, in which the *kitsch* of aristocratic ideology and the worldly *bonhomie* of Goldoni harmoniously merge.

Virtue and Nobility Defeating Ignorance[15] is the only non-Venetian work in this group, but it repeats the iconographic and figurative scheme which we saw earlier. Tiepolo's narrative reworking manages to capture the delicate point of contact (the area of balance, as we called it earlier) between a society moving towards its twilight, but which makes itself out to be eternal and is described as such by Tiepolo, and a mentality that is just beginning to gain definition and, perhaps, awareness. Thus there re-emerges the contradiction between a narrative system already close to Goldoni's pre-bourgeois system, and the contents of the narrative, still linked to the heroic

[11] G. Knox (1978).

[12] Ripa describes the allegory of Ignorance as an opulent woman, blind and bejewelled, girdled by a crown of poppies and escorted by a 'a Bat or Nightjar' (C. Ripa, *Iconologia*, 'Ignorance'), which allows us to identify the figure in the lower part of the fresco at Palazzo Papadopoli as *Ignorance* and not *Vice*.

[13] On Tiepolo and Tasso see: R. Guerrini, in *Torquato Tasso...* (1985, pp. 345-60).

[14] It seems that the two similar paintings (once in the Wrightsman Collection, New York, and now in Milan, private collection) should be omitted.

[15] *Ignorance* and not *Error* or *Perfidy* as they are occasionally identified as even today.

57.
opposite
Invention of the Cross (Exaltation of the True Cross and St. Helena). Venice, Gallerie dell'Accademia.

58.
The Family of Darius
before Alexander.
Montecchio Maggiore
(Vicenza), Villa
Cordellina.

59.
opposite
Detail from fig. 58.

world of myth. However, as the unconscious confrontation with Goldoni was kept from the poems, myths and allegories, so too, but in the opposite way, was Tiepolo's conscious reception of Metastasio. This was a reception which went only halfway – he availed himself of the contents, but not the structure, of the message.

Francesco Algarotti

The first half of the 1740s was very important for Tiepolo. His fame spread to increasingly illustrious patrons, both in Venice where he enjoyed great esteem, and in northern Italy and even in some parts of southern Germany, though there he was still considered just one of the many artists that the market placed at the disposal of the Court. But it is truly in these years that his name, his most refined technique and his inimitable narrative imagination flourished unchallenged due to a new development. In May 1743 Count Francesco Algarotti (Venice 1712 – Pisa 1764) returned to Venice as an intermediary and artistic consultant of the Prince Elector of Saxony and King of Poland, Augustus III, of the Wettin dynasty[16].

After the death of his father Augustus II the Strong (1733) and the war of the Polish succession concluded with the peace of Vienna (1738), Augustus III intended to dedicate himself entirely to the task of transforming Dresden, the capital of Saxony, into a European city. He delegated the affairs of state to his prime minister, the powerful Baron Heinrich von Brühl. Situated on the Elbe river, the city was restructured and rebuilt as a new Venice of the North, and the Royal Art Collection was especially restocked and refurbished following a prospective policy of decisive importance. Though the entire project cannot be credited to him alone, it was so important that it transformed Dresden into the most important artistic center on the continent.

Thus in 1742 Augustus III invited the young Francesco Algarotti to court. He had already been made a count by Frederick II of Prussia[17] and Augustus III conferred on him the military assignment of war advisor. The title was purely nominal, because the 'campaign' that the Prince Elector had in mind for Algarotti, as a Venetian and former pupil of Carlo Lodoli, art connoisseur and collector, and a member of the most exclusive European intellectual elite and a scientific popularizer[18], was a mission to Venice to buy paintings by sixteenth-century masters. These were considered the only works that, according to a widespread and deeply-rooted conviction of the time, would confer immediate international prestige on a dynastic collection[19]. Algarotti managed to alter at least partially this rather one-dimensional plan, and encouraged research in other areas as well. He especially urged the purchase of works by contemporary painters whom he commissioned directly for historical subjects. He allotted his themes to each painter according to what he believed most congenial to his style (but we will return later to Algarotti as art critic – his differentiation of subjects according to style).

Algarotti had a good first-hand knowledge of contemporary Roman, Bolognese and French painting, but strangely enough, he had little personal acquaintance with the art of his own hometown of Venice. His only indirect source of information seems to have been his brother Bonomo who remained in Venice while Francesco had been traveling through the courts and salons of half of Europe[20]. Francesco's idea was to take advantage of the extraordinary opportunity offered by Augustus II and Brühl to create the first modern museum, meaning a center for the historical documentation of the movements and developments in art, even if rather severely limited to paintings of *historia*[21]. This explains the inclusion of contemporary artists and the division of commissions, taking account of the style of the artists for the works to be sent to Dresden.

We learn all this from Algarotti's outline, the *Progetto per ridurre a compimento il Regio Museo di*

[16] On Algarotti see D. Mion (1980-81) and especially F. Haskell (1980, ch. XIV, pp. 347-360), with an annotated bibliography; on the Saxony Wettin, see A. Walther, 'Bernardo Bellotto a Dresda', in *Bernardo Bellotto. Le Vedute di Dresda. Dipinti e incisioni dai Musei di Dresda*, catalogue, Vicenza 1986, pp. 31-56.

[17] After his assignment in Saxony expired in 1746, Algarotti returned to Prussia where he was nominated a Knight of the Order of Merit, while his title of count was also extended to his descendants (D. Mion, 1980-81, p. 28).

[18] In 1737 Algarotti had already published *Newtonianismo per le dame* (published in Naples), it was received with some suspicion in Venice and later retitled *Dialoghi sopra l'ottica newtoniana*). He had already raced through an ambitious Grand Tour at an early age which took him from Rome, Bologna and Padua on to Paris where he met Voltaire, and later went to Prussia, England, Saint Petersburg and again to Berlin where he was a guest at the court of Frederick the Great of Prussia (1740-42).

[19] Augustus III's father, Augustus II, may have actually been an even more enlightened collector than his son, for he also bought works by contemporary painters (F. Haskell, 1980, pp. 293-294); however, with Augustus III and Algarotti, the conception of the museum changed radically. No longer a dynastic treasure meant to glorify its rulers, it became a documentation center of different periods and schools with a decisively modern slant.

[20] *Ibidem*, pp. 356-357, n. 1.

[21] Francesco Algarotti also cherished a more personal goal, of which he often reminded his patrons – he wanted to become the director and conservator of the gallery he was establishing along such enlightened and modern lines. He was to be disappointed. Despite his insistence, the position was conferred upon the prime minister's cultured confidant, Baron Carl Heinrich

60.
opposite
The Continence of Scipio. Montecchio Maggiore (Vicenza), Villa Cordellina.

Dresda[22] ('Project to establish the Dresden Royal Museum'), which he prepared when he was still in Dresden and which he submitted for the approval of Augustus III before leaving for Venice. According to Algarotti's project, he recruited Pittoni, Piazzetta, Tiepolo and Balestra, all artists connected with Venice. From Bologna he asked Donato Creti and Ercole Lelli, from Naples Franceschiello (Francesco de Mura) and Solimena, from Rome Mancini and Pannini and even two painters from France, Boucher, the leading figure of the Rococo of Louis XV, and Louis-Michel Van Loo[23]. The list blends Algarotti's competence, sense of service, and personal expertise with his own personal predilections and interests as a collector and dealer, for he knew he would be able, while ordering important paintings for the Prince Elector, to keep the sketches for his Venetian collection in order to use them for exchange. Augustus II, however, altered the '*Project*'. While maintaining his order for the purchase of Old Masters, he decided to commission only Venetian artists, whom he knew and appreciated because of his frequent visits there in his youth[24], and he added Jacopo Amigoni and Francesco Zuccarelli to Algarotti's list.

With a completely original critical sensibility for those days, in what amounted to a true anticipation of modern historiography, Francesco Algarotti decided that all the individual subjects to be commissioned from contemporary artists, stubbornly retaining the same historical themes for all[25], must be congenial to the characteristic style and language of each artist. For example, he thought of offering Pittoni a commission for a *Crassus Invading the Temple of Jerusalem* since he 'is singular in the dressing of priests, and adorns most pleasingly his compositions with architectural elements'[26]. From Piazzetta, instead, who had some time earlier provided him with a frontispiece for his *Newtonianismo per le dame*, Algarotti commissioned a *Caesar as a Young Man in a Grotto in Famagosta*, a dramatic and even anti-classical subject, but particularly well-suited to Piazzetta, who is described as a 'great draughtsman and good colorist but not elegant in his forms and physiognomies'[27].

Algarotti was less informed about Tiepolo than the others. During the years of his greatest success Algarotti had been living outside of Venice, and it seems that his brother Bonomo had not gone out of his way to find new talents such as his. In the *Progetto* he presented to Augustus III, Francesco planned for 'Tiepoletto, witty painter of sketches (...) Gideon's night victory, by light of torches concealed inside terracotta pots'[28], which rather incredibly was his verdict for a Giambattista much closer to Piazzetta, or Magnasco, or the early Tiepolo, but was certainly not fit for the mature Tiepolo of the 1740s. But when Algarotti reached Venice and finally saw his latest work for himself, a dramatic change ensued.

Leaving aside the old paintings purchased by Francesco Algarotti on the Venetian market for the collection of Augustus III[29], we will concentrate on the paintings commissioned from Tiepolo by Algarotti.

The first must have been the *Victory of Gideon* mentioned in Algarotti's *Progetto* before his trip to Venice. Once he had seen his recent work, however, he realized by his own admission that in Tiepolo he had discovered another Veronese, an artist capable of not only satisfying the classical tastes of the Prince Elector, but one who could convince him that there existed living artists whose paintings were worthy to hang alongside the Old Masters of sixteenth-century classicism. He abandoned, however, the nocturnal theme he had proposed in Dresden, which was inappropriate for the style he had so quickly discerned in Tiepolo, and fell back, rather significantly, on a lighter, almost frivolous subject, *Timotheus or the Effects of Music*. He also sent Brühl a letter describing the project in the same summer of 1743[30]. In Algarotti's words, the scene was to be set in a 'latticed room (...) arranged however so that it has little to do with Greek elegance, and represents what existed long ago in Asia (...) depicting verdure and gardens of that charm and freshness that are imagined in the felicitous climes of the Orient'[31]. As for the

von Heinecken, and this disappointment was the major reason for his return to the service of Frederick II of Prussia.
[22] F. Algarotti (1764, VIII, pp. 351-388).
[23] *Ibidem*, pp. 366-370.
[24] Since he could no longer leave Dresden and Warsaw purely for pleasure, between 1739 and early 1740 he sent his son to Venice, the hereditary prince Frederick Christian, partly so that he could make his own Grand Tour, but mostly so that he could add to his own collection of Venetian art; cf. M. Gemin (1982).
[25] Even in assigning the measurements and dimensions of the paintings, it is significant that Algarotti chose a rectangular horizontal format which he called 'alla pussina', Poussin's style of heroic classicism (F. Algarotti, 1764, VIII, p. 365).
[26] *Ibidem*, p. 366. The painting is lost but the sketch, today in the Accademia of Venice, was once in Algarotti collection, as we learn from the valuable *Catalogo* compiled by G.A. Selva (1776) on the death of Francesco's brother, Bonomo.
[27] F. Algarotti (1764, VIII, p. 366). Both painting and sketch are now lost.
[28] *Ibidem*, p. 367.
[29] Tiepolo actively assisted Algarotti in his acquisitions of Old Masters, exploiting his own acquaintance with the old patrician families of Venice who were in the midst of selling off parts of their collections. He was the mediator for Algarotti for the Zaccaria Sagredo collection, which was being divided up just at that time on the death of Zaccaria. He also helped him with the Dolfin family to buy what was then believed to be an extremely valuable Holbein *Madonna*, and he again assisted him in buying from the Cornaro (H. Posse, 1931). The Count thanked Tiepolo, who had by then become a friend, with expensive gifts which he later listed among his expenses when he presented his accounts in Dresden.

61.
opposite
The Virgin Giving the Scapular to the Blessed Simon Stock.
Venice, Scuola Grande dei Carmini.

62.
An Angel Showing the
Scapular to the Souls in
Purgatory.
Venice, Scuola Grande
dei Carmini.

63.
An Angel Saving a
Workman Devoted to
the Virgin.
Venice, Scuola Grande
dei Carmini.

dramatis personae, he adds that 'Alexander, touched by the sweet song of Timotheus, abandons himself to the lap of Thaïs who is sweetly watching him and demonstrating with her shimmering lascivious eyes a living image of the tenderness of the song of Timotheus'[32]. Clearly Algarotti feels absolute faith in the imaginative powers of his reborn Veronese, *his* discovery, whose virtue he extols to his somewhat recalcitrant patrons: 'the decorations and the expressions will spring easily from the fertile imagination of Sig. Gio. Batista, who with such glory to Venice has revived the grace, charm and magnificence of the great Paolo himself'[33]. These words are perhaps not particularly important in themselves, since this Timotheus was not executed either, perhaps because of its indulgence in the senses[34], but they are revealing of how Algarotti interpreted, and imagined directing, the work of Tiepolo. He imagined him painting an Arcadia exotically re-located in the Orient, with the complication of some erotic impulse aroused by music, which is not a bad critical synthesis of Tiepolo's style up to that date.

The third change of subject was finally the definite assignment, and Tiepolo actually did finish the *Caesar Contemplating Pompey's Severed Head*, although none too quickly. Unfortunately, as the sketch and painting are both lost we cannot comment on it. Certainly the setting in Egyptian Alexandria again reveals a marked predilection for the exotic, also confirmed by the subject of the second painting ordered by Algarotti for Dresden, the *Banquet of Antony and Cleopatra*, which this time was executed without any delays. Algarotti must have been under the illusion that he had opened his friend's eyes to new mysterious horizons, and sure of his para-scientific mastery of Newtonian optics, he must have felt that he would be able to impart some secrets on painting. This brings us to the sensitive question of the give-and-take relationship between Algarotti and Tiepolo.

We can certainly imagine that the two, having spent many long days together[35], must have had discussions similar to those in Algarotti's *Newtonianismo*: conversations between a Arcadian *cicisbeo*[36] with a smattering of fashionable scientific theories, and a *marchesa* animated by a 'great desire to become Newtonian'[37]. Algarotti must have done his utmost to explain to Tiepolo the light as a 'mine of the seven primary colors'[38] and shadows colored with 'those minute atoms that fly through the air, that flow from one into another ray of the image, *bordering the shadows, changing color*, that resemble shining dust or ruby, or chrysolite, or another precious stone'[39]. And the other, so as not to offend him but also in self-defense, must have listened to him with his cold but patient Venetian composure.

It is clear that Giambattista offered Francesco Algarotti his valuable assistance to ensure the success of his Venetian mission. He obtained him access to the patrician Venetian collections that he knew so well, and he effectively strengthened his position at the court in Dresden. His assistance and support must have further fed Algarotti's aspiration to become the director of the Royal Collection in Dresden, and Tiepolo must have had to make himself available to satisfy the count's not always clear instructions. He listened tolerantly to the theoretical effusions of the vacillating intellectual, caught halfway between Metastasio and Muratori, between Arcadia and the philosophy of the Enlightenment, between late Baroque conceptions and emerging Neo-classicism, and only too self-conscious thanks to his own good fortune. He even taught him how to etch, dropping his suggestions so tactfully that they made up for his incurable lack of talent.

But what could Algarotti offer to Tiepolo? Tiepolo had long ago found for himself a window on faraway worlds, demonstrated by the many Oriental references in his sacred and secular paintings, at least from the Colleoni chapel onwards. We should also remember that according to Succi[40] it was precisely in 1743 that Tiepolo's great etching period began. That was the year in which the exotic *Capricci* was printed, followed a few years later by the even

[30] The description is part of a very detailed report, known as the *Argomenti*, in which Algarotti gives an account of all the subjects he had commissioned from contemporary Venetian artists: cf. F. Algarotti (1764, VIII); H. Posse (1931).

[31] F. Algarotti (1764, VIII, pp. 379-381).

[32] *Ibidem*.

[33] *Ibidem*. My italics.

[34] Augustus III had to convert to Catholicism in order to be crowned king of Poland.

[35] D. Succi is responsible (1985, pp. 32-40) for identifying two prints which were signed by both Tiepolo and Algarotti during the latter's stay in Venice.

[36] Algarotti corresponded with Metastasio and was a fervent admirer; cf. E. Bonora, 'Intro-duzione', to F. Algarotti, *Dialoghi sopra l'ottica newtoniana*, Turin 1977, pp. 191-192.

[37] F. Algarotti, *Dialoghi...*, ed. cit., p. 12.

[38] *Ibidem*, p. 54.

[39] *Ibidem*, p. 71. My italics.

[40] D. Succi (1983 and 1985).

64.
Faith, Hope and Charity.
Venice, Scuola Grande
dei Carmini.

65.
Prudence, Sincerity and
Temperance. Venice,
Scuola Grande dei
Carmini.

66.
Fortitude and Justice.
Venice, Scuola Grande
dei Carmini.

67.
Patience, Innocence and
Chastity. Venice, Scuola
Grande dei Carmini.

68.
opposite
Detail from fig. 67.

more enigmatic *Scherzi di fantasia*. Moreover, from the mid-1720s Tiepolo had a direct encounter with classicism through the antique findings reproduced in Scipione Maffei's *Verona illustrata*, not to mention his access to the choicest patrician collections of antiquities. As for the accuracy of his sixteenth-century references (the attention lavished on the costume and the reconstruction of atmospheres and settings that seemed to mean so much to Algarotti), Tiepolo had in Venice – in its collections, churches, public and private palazzi – a much wider sampling of models than Algarotti could ever have given him by his suggestions, which were in any case usually limited to vague exhortations to look at Veronese. As for the scientific theorizing regarding color and light, out of politeness to 'Signor Contino' Tiepolo had listened to his abstruse conjectures, but knew in his heart that light and Veronesian colors were not academic subjects, but something that he had discovered through laboring on his painting, day after day – a far cry from optic prisms and primary colors.

Thus Tiepolo received much less than he gave. There was, however, one aspect in which Tiepolo came out the winner, seen in the other two works (in addition to *Caesar* and the *Banquet*) commissioned by Algarotti in the summer of 1743, to offer as a sort of bribe to the prime minister who seemed the major obstacle to his nomination as superintendent of the emerging Royal Collection[41]. These were *Maecenas Presenting the Arts to Augustus* which also ended up in the collection of Catherine II of Russia in 1769, with which Algarotti flattered Brühl in his portrayal as a friend of Augustus, and the *Triumph of Flora* which is today in San Francisco (fig. 70)[42]. These works were painted along with those for Augustus III, but Count Algarotti took a different interest in them, not only because his longed-for conquest depended on Brühl, but because these were paintings destined for a private individual, and not the Royal Collection.

[41] However, the *Banquet of Cleopatra* today in Melbourne (whose sketch Algarotti kept for himself and is now in the Cognacq-Jay) ended up mysteriously in Brühl's collection rather than in Augustus III's gallery, and was later auctioned in Amsterdam in 1765 to the Tsarina Catherine II of Russia (M. Santifaller, 1972, p. 148).
[42] Even though Algarotti requested that Tiepolo insert dedicatory messages to the prime minister in both works, the *Triumph of Flora* did not remain for long in Brühl's collection. He passed it on to his secretary, the Baron von Heinecken, who in turn sold it in 1765: cf. M. Levey, Tiepolo's *'Empire of Flora'* (1957, pp. 89-91).

69.
Rinaldo Abandoning Armida. Chicago, Art Institute.

70.
opposite
Triumph of Flora, detail. San Francisco, M.H. de Young Memorial Museum.

71.
Virtue and Nobility
Defeating Ignorance.
Venice, Ca' Rezzonico.

Thus the classical, historical, Veronesian tone of the 'official' paintings gave way to a different taste, moving towards those French models that Algarotti had admired from the very beginning of his *Progetto* for Augustus III, and which constitute perhaps the only influence, as fleeting as it may have been, of Algarotti on Tiepolo. However, when the Count commissioned Tiepolo for paintings for his own collection, (and he certainly must have instructed him on what he wanted)[43], his voyeuristic, decidedly Francophile taste fit for the private study stands out – a clear case of private vices and public virtues.

Conceding something to the special French-spirited classicism suggested by Algarotti, Tiepolo did not realize that a dangerous abyss was opening before him. In a way, he was almost working towards his own ruin. The spread of the Neoclassical reaction championed by Mengs in the second half of the century had serious consequences for his reputation, especially at the extremely delicate moment which was approaching at the court of Spain.

Virtues secular and sacred

An unusual aspect of Tiepolo's commissions in Dresden is that although the city had recently experienced an exciting architectural flowering[44], he was commissioned only for works on canvas and not to paint frescoes for all those new residences. One reason must have been that Algarotti, while he was planning the orders for commissions from contemporary artists, was thinking not only as an art collector but as a dealer as well, and thus preferred small-format, easily-transportable works. Algarotti also was dreaming of directing a Royal Collection that was closer in spirit to a modern art gallery than to a frescoed Roman palazzo, in which his role as superintendent might have been superfluous. But another cause must have also been the power of the Protestant tradition in Saxony, in spite of Augustus III's conversion to Catholicism

[43] See for example *Diana and Acteon*, today in Zurich: M. Levey, *Two Paintings by Tiepolo from the Algarotti collection* (1960, pp. 250-257).
[44] A. Walther (1986. pp 57-65).

72.
opposite
Detail from fig. 71.

in order to become the King of Poland. This deeply-felt and severely 'an-iconical' tradition[45] did not possess highly codified models of representation, and prohibited 'scandalous and idolatrous' large-scale decorations, which were instead so popular in Catholic Europe.

Tiepolo was to return to these large-scale cycles in the summer of 1743, when he was busy with the Dresden canvases. He was commissioned by a lawyer from Vicenza, who was also active in Venetian legal circles, Carlo Cordellina, to fresco the ceiling and walls of the ground floor of the villa that Giorgio Massari was building for him at Montecchio Maggiore near Vicenza (figs. 58-60). He seems to have worked with Algarotti on this project as well, and it has even been suggested that Algarotti selected the iconography[46]. Tiepolo gave Algarotti the sketch for the *Family of Darius before Alexander*. The statues of Apollo and Minerva already painted in *Maecenas Presenting the Arts to Augustus* ordered by Francesco from Giambattista for Brühl reappear in the *Continence of Scipio*. Algarotti himself is documented as a frequent guest in the carefree salon of the Cordellina[47], whose atmosphere was more similar to the spirit of a Goldonian *Avventure della villeggiatura* than to the sober model of work, farming and happiness characteristic of the sixteenth-century villa civilization of the Veneto.

In any case, there was nothing in this cycle that Tiepolo had not already been doing at least from the beginning of the 1730s. In the ceiling he returned to that allegorical melodrama between *Nobility* (with the miniature Minerva in hand), *Virtue* (whose laurel garland is held by a *putto*) and *Ignorance* (with the bat and poppies, following Ripa's descriptions) which we saw in the ceiling frescoes of Palazzo Gallarati Scotti in Milan, Palazzo Papadopoli in Venice, and Palazzo Caiselli in Udine, all from the early 1740s. His creation of *contrejour* zones to obtain shadows colored by a dusty consistency, which is one of the linguistic elements taken from Veronese, had already been used in Palazzo Casati in Milan and earlier still in the ceiling of

[45] R. Assunto, 'Iconismo e aniconismo' in *EUA*, coll. 159-161.
[46] B. Mazza, in *I Tiepolo e il Settecento vicentino* (1990, p. 306).
[47] R. Menegozzo (1990, p. 47 and n. 18, p. 58).

73.
Time Unveiling Truth.
New York, Haboldt
Collection.

Palazzo Sandi. It certainly cannot be a discovery made only upon advice from Count Algarotti, unless we accept that it was he who introduced Giambattista to Veronese! The training of a painter is unlike that of a theoretician, and in any case Giambattista's training had already been over for quite some time. Therefore no external or abstract suggestion was going to inspire radical reassessments. At the most he might have absorbed the counsels of his learned advisors (motivated only by the very best intentions) but in his own way and in his own time. That Tiepolo had by now achieved his own expressive liberty is confirmed by a cycle of paintings executed for the chapter hall of the *scuola* (not yet 'scuola grande') of the Carmini in Venice (figs. 61-68). He handed over the eight side panels for the ceiling by June 1743, exactly when Algarotti returned to Venice (therefore their execution preceded any possible influence that Algarotti may have had on him), while the central painting was completed and installed only in 1749[48].

There are clear references to traditional Venetian painting in the lateral scenes of the ceiling, as well as in the prescriptive elements. The Veronese of the Sala del Collegio in the Palazzo Ducale is felt in the painting's setting in a continuous gold and stucco frame which acts as a unifying element for the whole composition[49], and he looked to Ripa for his allegorical instructions[50]. But this assemblage of religious virtues is treated with the sensitive fragrance of a female sky, in which he as usual takes the doctrinal facts apart and puts them together again according to the demands of human – or rather, theatrical – verisimilitude. The *Theological virtues* (from left, *Hope, Charity* and *Faith*) are painted together, while the four *Cardinal Virtues* are instead separated in two pairs placed in different lunettes. The figures of *Prudence* and *Temperance* are located in the upper left lunette and are accompanied by *Sincerity*, since Ripa demanded that she have a dove in her left hand[51], and *Justice* and *Fortitude* are in the side corner, accompanied by the sun.

In the last panel, dated 1744, Tiepolo works a small miracle of iconographic breakdown. The three allegories, which have been identified in various ways over the years, are *Patience* (an old woman, as recommended by Ripa), *Innocence* (with a lamb) and *Chastity* (with a sieve). Tiepolo, however, added a cross to *Patience*, which is generally attributed to *Obedience*, and places her in the background (ironically reluctant to paint an ugly woman at center stage). Finally he gives her a garland of thorns that Ripa instead assigns to *Penitence*, although he makes a plump little angel hovering above the scene hold it. *Innocence*, portrayed with a lamb, wears a robe of ash-gray, portrayed treading on the symbols of earthly power (thus superimposing Ripa's attributes of *Humility* over those of *Innocence*). Only the *Chastity* is not tampered with, even if she is stripped of the belt reading *Castigo corpus meum* which she has in Ripa.

In this transliteration of fragmented allegories in this complex game of compositional and narrative imbedding – a game shared by the members of the confraternity, who unanimously voted in support of Tiepolo's membership – Giambattista put forward all his stylistic and technical powers. To confirm this, we need only compare that lively sunny ceiling, now that the cycle has been restored, with the lifeless seventeenth- and eighteenth-century paintings that line the walls, although they are signed by Antonio Zanchi and Gregorio Lazzarini.

These eight paintings with a mixtilinear frame that almost seem to court the large rectangular canvas in the center, the *Virgin Giving the Scapular to the Blessed Simon Stock*, display beautifully-conceived arpeggios of complementary colors, in pallid tones which are intensified and sparkling because of their reciprocity, hot and cold colored shadows following the chromatic model that determines the crackling Veronesian transformations, but brought to a white heat and simultaneously refined by a distribution of grander, more solemn rhythms. It is here in this work from 1749, with that proud expression of that indolent matronly Virgin,

[48] A. Niero (1976-77).
[49] Carpoforo Mazzetti chose the framing with Tiepolo's consent (1740) who clearly was allowed to dictate the decorative elements of the room in which it would be hung: A. Niero (1991, p. 17).
[50] A. Niero (1976-77); but for iconographical corrections see also W.L. Barcham (1989, p. 149), emended by A. Niero (1991, pp. 36-45).
[51] Not by *Innocence* as Niero believes (1976-77), whom Ripa assigns a lamb, nor by *Purity* as Barcham claims (1989, p. 149), as accepted by Niero (1991, p. 41).

that we feel that Tiepolo is ready for the frozen splendor of Würzburg. What he manages to do in the Carmini is transfer to oil painting from the world of frescoes the reckless sense of composition, the natural grace of narrative and the muted blaze of luminous color.

Other decorative work from the 1740s

These were years of intense activity. Algarotti was pressing for paintings to send to the court at Dresden, as were the members of the Scuola dei Carmini for their cycle. Born in 1727, his son Giandomenico was not yet old enough to help his father in any significant way on his immense number of commissions, although he must occasionally have given him some sort of assistance[52], and Lorenzo was not even ten yet. Yet Tiepolo continued to take on other ambitious projects from patrons who all knew each other and were spreading word of his extraordinary ability and highly professional attitude. This is the case, for example, of the monochrome frescoes for Palazzo Marchesini in Vicenza. His patron, Giorgio Marchesini, had been raised to nobility in 1724, five years earlier than Nicolò Loschi, whose daughter Cecilia Maria he had married in 1739. This must have been the reason for Tiepolo's return to Vicenza[53].

The choice of the rational but cold clarity of *grisailles*, instead of the decorative enjoyment of the polychrome work for which Tiepolo was justly famous, indicates that Giorgio Marchesini had a scientifically intellectual agenda. There is no concession to visual pleasure and attention is focused on the cerebral. This is emphasized in Rita Menegozzo's explanation of the iconographic cycle (1990). In the theory of fake isolated statues, punctuated by paintings by Gerolamo Mengozzi or 'Il Colonna', she sees an ill-concealed exaltation of Masonic ideals, which are indeed confirmed by biographical details in Marchesini's life[54]. Some of these allegories, however, also have more traditional meanings, although it remains true that part of the society of Vicenza was opening up to the pre-Enlightenment ideas arriving from the North in the mid-eighteenth century. The so-called *Two Allegorical Figures with Obelisk* are once again from Ripa. The beautiful female figure near the pyramid is the *Glory of Princes* from Ripa's *Iconologia*, an image that Tiepolo would return to later[55]. The other figure, the warrior resting on a lion, is *Valor*, who will be seen again in the so-called *Apotheosis of Francesco Barbaro* today in Norfolk[56]. Even the presumed *Tabernacle of the Masons*[57] frescoed on the ceiling of the gallery, with a cube topped by a cross and a half-moon, is only an innocuous symbol of Mercury which is identical with the symbol of Mercury found in the right hand of the allegory of *Decorum* in Cesare Ripa.

After a new series of monochromes for the private chapel of the Sagredo family in the Venetian church of San Francesco della Vigna, which Barcham dates correctly to 1744-45[58], Tiepolo was asked, along with the faithful Gerolamo Mengozzi ('Il Colonna'), to decorate two parts of the Palazzo Barbarigo in Santa Maria del Giglio, fragments of which have been removed and are now found elsewhere (figs. 71, 72).

[52] M. Levey (1986, pp. 127-141).
[53] R. Menegozzo (1990).
[54] *Ibidem*. See also L. Olivato, "I 'Veri Amici'. Illuminati e massoni nella Vicenza del Settecento', in *I Tiepolo e il Settecento Vicentino* (1990, pp. 284-287).
[55] For example, on the continent of Asia in Würzburg. See M. Santifaller, *Die Gruppe mit der Pyramide...* (1975, pp. 193-207).
[56] C. Ripa, *Iconologia*.
[57] R. Menegozzo (1990, p. 86).
[58] W.L. Barcham (1983).

74.
Transport of the Holy House of Loreto, sketch. Venice, Gallerie dell'Accademia.

As at Biron and in the Venetian palazzo of Carlo Cordellina, here too Tiepolo painted a ceiling with a *Time Unveiling Truth*. The old winged figure (which seems to be stripping rather than revealing truth) is deprived of his allegorical equipment, the scythe and hour-glass. With Tiepolo's usual centrifugal device it ends up the irreverent plaything of the flying *putti* pushed out to the edges of the oval frames.

The ceiling of the adjacent room, transferred to canvas and now in the Ca' Rezzonico, was frescoed with *Virtue and Nobility Defeating Ignorance*. This is the usual *topos*, halfway between Enlightenment iconography and aristocratic exaltation, which appears in Tiepolo's repertoire as early as Palazzo Gallarati Scotti and was to be repeated time and time again. The union of Virtue and Nobility conquers the social problem of cultural ignorance. This is a sign that in Vicenza as in other Venetian settings, a latent vein of heterodoxy existed, though how deep or conscious we do not know. It may have been merely a fashionable topic of conversation, just as the latest fashion from Paris would have been. The eight border monochromes are taken from Ripa, but as always they have been extensively reworked by Tiepolo to adapt them to the taste of the times[59].

In the four *grisailles* with the mirrored frame many other characters appear, who disquietingly scrutinize the innocent feminine figures that symbolize the Arts. Arranged edgewise, in a graduated position one on top of the other, they appear like a mysterious horde straight out of Tiepolo's etchings, from the *Capricci*, printed in 1743, to the first *Scherzi di fantasia* on which he had started work at just this time[60].

It is also important to remember that right in the midst of this decade of extraordinary classical achievement, Tiepolo allowed episodes and dream-figures from his most anti-classical etching to filter into his frescoes – part of the universe of secret confession where the hand anticipates the mind, and the mind owes nothing to its patrons.

Giandomenico's debut

The pressure of work at Tiepolo's workshop at this time must have been so intense that it seems unlikely that one man alone could be responsible for such a massive output. However, each year that passed was important in the education of Giandomenico, whose increasing involvement in his father's work must date, on credible stylistic bases, to these years. The workshop followed a relentless schedule, but there was no drop in the quality of the work. If the elder Tiepolo was asked to produce a plan for a project and the sketch was not approved, he would immediately furnish another, often executing two or more sketches before arriving at the final decision.

This is what happened in the *Transport of the Holy House of Loreto*, the ceiling fresco of the Scalzi (fig. 74) for which two preparatory sketches were drawn, and the three paintings in the Santi Massimo e Osvaldo church in Padua. A whole series of sketches was prepared for the large major canvas of this church dedicated to its two saints, an eventful process which must have caused quite a stir in the workshop. Many of these have been retraced by critics[61]. The two sketches for the Scalzi were not really that different from each other. The altarpiece in Padua, instead, underwent radical changes in its conception, from the first plan, which we believe is that found today in Moscow, and copied in Bergamo, to the model now in Zurich, and the final version. The Bergamo copy of the first version (in Moscow) was bought by Algarotti, which confirms the fact that, while Giambattista was toiling away, and Don Cogolo was never satisfied, the Count was haunting Tiepolo's workshop in hopes of adding to his own collection.

There is, however, a rather touching detail here. The first plan for Padua bears a note on the reverse which Lavrova believes to be by Tiepolo himself[62], reading '*Regalo fatto dal padre a Gian*

[59] They have often been incorrectly identified. For example, the tondo that A. Pallucchini designates as *Astrology* (1968, n. 160 L) is *Mathematics*, which Ripa describes as having wings on the head, a compass in the right hand, a 'large ball' in the left, and 'bare feet on a base'; among the monochromes around the mixtilinear frame, that indicated as *Music* (1968, n. 160 K) is actually *Harmony*, even if musical instruments are portrayed.
[60] D. Succi (1985, p. 25).
[61] W.L. Barcham (1989, pp. 208-213).
[62] O. Lavrova (1972, pp. 126-127).

75.
Martyrdom of St. John,
Bishop of Bergamo.
Bergamo, Cathedral.

76.
opposite
Detail from fig. 75.

Domenico' ('Gift from Father to Gian Domenico'). Believing that the growth of an artist must be measured in practical lessons and not just abstractions, Giambattista gave his son the valuable example of the early conception of a work, in which he could see the process taking shape that would lead to the definitive version. And it seems that Giandomenico was not indifferent to his father's generosity. If Levey is correct, which we believe he is, Giandomenico made his debut as his father's assistant to alleviate his father's work with his important contributions to Tiepolo's *Martyrdom of St. John, Bishop of Bergamo* (figs. 75, 76)[63].

Giandomenico's efforts are also seen in the lateral figures in Mengozzi's *quadrature* in the frescoes that Giambattista executed in the summer of 1745 for the ceiling and walls of Villa Contarini alla Mira, which had been the property of the Pisani of Santa Maria Zobenigo since the seventeenth century[64]. It may seem somewhat strange to learn that Vincenzo I Sebastiano Pisani[65] wanted to celebrate the sixteenth-century glories of the Contarini family, to whom he was not even related. And it seems even stranger that, according to Pavanello's persuasive argument, the frescoes were commissioned to celebrate the marriage of Pisani to a member of the Corner family in 1745[66]. Pisani may have asked for the usual allegorical vision based on Ripa – perhaps, considering the nature of the occasion, a *Marital Concord* with a heart hanging on a golden chain like the one he had already painted for Nicolò Loschi at Biron and was repeating at just this time in the *Nuptial Allegory* at Casa Corner. Instead, however, he decided upon the re-evocation of a fragment of worldly glory from long ago (1574) connected to a coat-of-arms not his own[67], but in some way grafted on to the villa he now owned. This grand bourgeois attitude held that the sixteenth-century myth of hospitality became almost a material possession transferred along with the property – as if Pisani could cover himself with the glories associated with a place by merely acquiring the property where the myth of these glories resided. However, Giambattista seemed to believe it himself. Pleased with the result, he gave the sketch for the largest fresco (once in the Rothschild collection in Frankfurt and now in the United States) to Francesco Algarotti[68].

Giambattista's son, therefore, assisted his father in these corner figures. It was certainly a rather grand apprenticeship, beginning from the gift of his father-teacher's first conception for the project and culminating in his direct participation in fairly significant portions of the real fresco, although admittedly decorative and almost camouflaged in Mengozzi's *quadrature*, but completely integrated in the overall scheme. It is likely that Giandomenico's contributions were closely supervised by his father, who may have helped him with preparatory sketches, corrected his brushstrokes and given him some passing suggestions. However we believe that Giandomenico was given considerable freedom to encourage his own sense of initiative. Thus it is fairly easy for an expert to make out the two different hands at work here. But there is no comparison with the irritating dilettante quality seen in Algarotti's attempts in the sketches when he was learning from Giambattista. What was now blossoming under his father's interested and vigilant eye, is instead a real talent, with individual characteristics all its own, and not the ephemeral amusement of an intellectual bent on practical experiments. In Giandomenico we find, here as well as in the figures attributed to him in the *Miracle of St. Patrick of Ireland*[69], a certain tendency towards realistic portrayal, an inclination to depict facial expressions in terms of portraiture, accentuating irregularities or defects that distinguish a face portrayed from nature from one based on a generic type. There is also some slipping into folklore, which in the future would be an element differentiating Giandomenico's work from his father's.

Another important aspect of the *Miracle of St. Patrick of Ireland* and the Desenzano altarpiece with the *Last Supper* is that both were both signed in full by Tiepolo, although Giandomenico assisted him extensively. This would seem to indicate an important acceptance of his

[63] M. Levey (1986, p. 136).
[64] Ibidem, p. 139.
[65] G. Pavanello (1979) discovered the exact name of the patron who commissioned it.
[66] Ibidem, pp. 52-59.
[67] 'Social prestige now made a greater appeal than military powers', p. 255: F. Haskell (1980, p. 255).
[68] M. Levey, *Two Paintings by Tiepolo from the Algarotti Collection* (1960, pp. 250-257).
[69] M. Levey (1986, p. 136).

77.
opposite
Martyrdom of St.
Theodora. Venice,
Ca' Rezzonico.

127

78.
Meeting between Antony
and Cleopatra. Venice,
Palazzo Labia.

79.
Banquet of Antony and
Cleopatra. Venice,
Palazzo Labia.

80.
opposite
Self-portrait of
Giambattista Tiepolo,
detail from fig. 79.

contribution, a sign he had absorbed and utilized his training to the full, and had received the approval of the head of the workshop – his father.

The frescoes in Palazzo Labia

Since Giandomenico was now his full collaborator, and he was assisted by his customary *quadratura* painter Gerolamo Mengozzi or 'Il Colonna', Tiepolo also managed to complete the frescoes in the ballroom and the smaller room called the 'Room of the Mirrors' at Palazzo Labia in San Geremia in the summers of 1746 and 1747 (figs. 78-80)[70]. The question that immediately springs to mind is why in the world would he call upon the most famous lovers in the world, Antony and Cleopatra, to confer distinction on the family. At the time Tiepolo was working for them, the Labia had already been accepted within the nobility of the Veneto for exactly a century[71], so that they had no urgent need to camouflage themselves by making extravagant gestures within the ruling class. The palazzo had been built in the seventeenth century and in the late 1730s it was enlarged and its interior restored – possibly by Giorgio Massari – thus obtaining the extraordinary cubic volume of the ballroom. This is a truly theatrical space, and may have been what inspired the Labia family – especially Paolo Antonio, who in 1738 had married a noblewoman from the Emo family – to call in the greatest decorator of contemporary architecture to be found in all of Europe[72].

But there remains the question of why they chose that particular tale of the Roman solider and the Egyptian queen described by Pliny and Plutarch. It might even have been Giambattista to suggest the theme, though it does seem somewhat improbable – Algarotti had encouraged him more than once to explore exotic oriental settings, new frontiers that Enlightenment travelers longed to explore, and he himself had begun to work from the early 1740s on that subject which was still fairly unusual for Venice[73]. And of course there were always those Oriental shamans which had first appeared in the Colleoni chapel and were to turn up ever more frequently in his etchings. However, not even the melodramatic theater can have led to his choice. In 1744 the theater of San Samuele had staged a *Cesare in Egitto*[74], although this does not seem sufficient motive to have created such a stir in Venetian society as to inspire such a costly enterprise. Nor does Paolo's possible identification (Paolo 'Antonio' Labia) with the protagonist of the *historiae* seem likely, especially as his bride's name was Fiordelise Emo, and not Cleopatra.

The Roman iconography, already used by Tiepolo for Palazzo Dolfin in San Pantalon and on other occasions[75], stood side by side with the mythological and allegorical elements, to strengthen the image of a ruling class which was actually experiencing the loss of its former power, and was struggling to rise again, or at least see itself in an imaginary overhead projection. It seems inevitable that these ostentatious symbols of a power that no longer existed had to turn to the magic of theater. Angelo Maria II Labia, the brother of Paolo Antonio, had a true passion for theater, in which he had invested a fair amount of money. He had a theater built 'where little wooden figures acted, moved by invisible mechanisms'[76]. The puppet theater was inaugurated in the Carnival of 1746, a year before Tiepolo was commissioned for the project, with titles which

81.
Nobility and Virtue Striking down Ignorance. Pasadena, Norton Simon Foundation.

[70] On Labia, the palazzo and the decoration, see: T. Pignatti, F. Pedrocco, and E. Martinelli Pedrocco (1982).
[71] F. Miari (1891, pp. 53-54); F. Pedrocco, in T. Pignatti, F. Pedrocco, and E. Martinelli Pedrocco (1982, pp. 10-12).
[72] *Ibidem*, pp. 36-44.
[73] T. Pignatti, in T. Pignatti, F. Pedrocco, and E. Martinelli Pedrocco (1982, pp. 70-77).
[74] A. Groppo (1745, p. 149).
[75] For example, in the canvases for Ca' Zenobio, and the frescoes of Palazzo Casati in Milan and Villa Cordellina in Vicenza.
[76] F. Pedrocco, in T. Pignatti, F. Pedrocco, and E. Martinelli Pedrocco (1982, p. 45).

82.
opposite
Detail from fig. 81.

are eloquent testimony to the fall of furious Latin loves to the level of farce and amorous intrigue, such as the *Starnuto di Ercole* ('Hercules Sneezing') and *Aurimedonte e Timocleone*, or the *Rivali delusi* ('The Disappointed Rivals'). This must surely be the key. On the ceiling and walls of the ballroom in Palazzo Labia we witness the completely eighteenth-century metamorphosis of ethical outbursts from the world of the ancients, into erotic arabesques, and frivolous and witty performances where the consuming passions of seventeenth-century tragedies, its heart-rending soliloquies of abandon and loss in the miseries of life, give way to languor, swooning, and duets, where the betrayal and adultery that give rise to cruel vendettas, are replaced by perfumed missives read furtively in the shelter of a bush or an artificial Rococo grotto. This was a society that was not fond of sin, or rather detested regret, a society that preferred malice to evil and was happy to exchange the cumbersome extremist sentiments of the late Baroque for an *esprit de finesse*.

The iconographical program and the general composition are permeated with a theatrical spirit of illusion. The central tondo of the ceiling represents, according to Ripa, *Virtue Ascending to the Glory of Princes*. As for Virtue, Ripa writes: 'Virtue is represented by Bellerophon, the beautiful young man seated on Pegasus, with an arrow in his hand killing the Chimera'[77]. This is the only time that Pegasus appears in the *Iconologia*, Tiepolo's primary source. And what are they doing here, otherwise, Pegasus and Bellerophon? As for the lovely figure with the pyramid, Ripa describes this in the *Glory of Princes*, 'She holds with the left hand a pyramid which signifies the clear and high glory of Princes, who with magnificence make grand and sumptuous buildings, in which glory is revealed'[78].

This is therefore a literal prologue in the heavens, a delirious show of unlimited power, which alludes to the recently completed palazzo and a princely – or doge-like – destiny is predicted for the *Labia gens*. But Tiepolo paints the walls, which constitute the interpretative completion of the ceiling, with the grandest and most impressive theatrical scenes ever seen in painting. With the assistance of Mengozzi's *quadrature*, he creates a double space with the wings of the set open to reveal the company on stage, acting out two key scenes of the drama. In the *Banquet* the spectator seems invited to climb the painted stairs and approach ('like a dwarf') the table where an overtly sensual love is being celebrated (the revealed breast), as well as vindicated pride (the bet is won by Cleopatra) and the subjection of the historic conqueror, Antony, to her desires and her enthralling beauty. In the other scene, the *Meeting*, the movement is identical and reversed. Here the spectator waits for the cortege formed on the pier to descend the painted stairs and enter the space of life. Everything is resolved in the ritual of love, thus ennobled by classical evocations, but staged on the set like a prolonged courting that seems even more important than the satisfaction of the senses, like a diplomatic negotiation made of witty remarks and retorts, official gestures that scarcely conceal intentions and innuendos barely disciplined by etiquette. Tiepolo portrays himself together with Mengozzi in the realistic space of the *Banquet*: sumptuously dressed as an Oriental, brow furrowed and eyes wide open, coldly watching the imminent sacrifice of the legendary pearl.

Towards Würzburg

Tiepolo experienced difficulties before his departure for Würzburg in the autumn of 1750, difficulties which were perhaps not apparent but which must have been worrying for him.

There was above all the obvious necessity to work out an appropriate position for Giandomenico within the general structure of the workshop. He was rapidly maturing his own personal style, and could not be used indefinitely whenever Giambattista needed finishing folkloric touches, with his immediate realist, even grotesque, stamp. The problem may also have

[77] C. Ripa, *Iconologia*, 'Virtù Nella Medaglia di Lucio Vero'.
[78] *Ibidem*, 'Gloria de' Prencipi Nella medaglia d'Adriano'.

83.
Madonna with Ss.
Catherine, Rose of Lima
and Agnes of
Montepulciano. Venice,
Church of the Gesuati.

arisen for Lorenzo (born in 1736, he was still young, but already following in his father's footsteps). The fact that Giambattista ostentatiously signed works in which he had been assisted by Giandomenico, as in the altarpiece for the parish church of Noventa Vicentina (fig. 88), is particularly telling. It almost seems to indicate the desire to reassure his patrons that his works were furnished with a certificate of authenticity by the head of the workshop[79].

Then there was the problem of renewing the repertoire. Even if all that Tiepolo had acquired up to now was more than sufficient for his staid Venetian patrons, who were not fond of too much innovation, it is possible that Giambattista himself felt the need not to repeat themes *ad nauseam*. And of course his true success was determined not only by his Venetian patrons. The real risk, indeed, was not lapsing into sloppiness since his work always had a high stylistic quality, but falling into routine and transforming the workshop into a repetitive academy for lack of new inspiration, lowering that 'furore' that had raised Giambattista above all his contemporaries. Instead, in his paintings from the late 1740s Tiepolo was indulging in self-reference, repeating recent works which were particularly acclaimed or not exploited to their fullest potential and on which he still felt he had something to say. Of course we must remember that Giambattista always had this method. It is absurd to think that an artist should waste what he had achieved and cancel his traces behind him, especially a personality as concrete and shrewd as Tiepolo. But while a dialectic relation may be a good thing, it's another matter to rest on one's laurels and be too content with one's achievements[80]. This can be seen, for example, in the two large paintings in Arkangelskoye executed from two sketches in New York and London[81] which rework the grand vivid theatrical *pièces* frescoed on the walls of the ballroom of Palazzo Labia in cloyingly ceremonious terms.

A cautious reconciliation with Piazzetta even emerges, as in the first painting on the right in the church of the Gesuati (fig. 83), or literal references to Paolo Veronese, as in the *Communion of St. Lucy* for the Corner chapel in the church of the Santi Apostoli in Venice[82], and we even see a return towards Venetian seventeenth-century portraiture, especially Sebastiano Bombelli's, as in the *Portrait of a Member of the Dolfin Family, Procuratore and Generale da Mar* (fig. 84). Of course, the quality is always supreme – there is the elegantly monumental Gesuati altarpiece, the limpid and graceful Santi Apostoli altarpiece, and the solemnly grand portrait at the Querini Stampalia, somehow permeated by a vague foreboding sense of tragedy. Yet the echoes of Piazzetta in the Gesuati work are probably only there at the request of the Dominicans who may have wanted to maintain some sort of stylistic continuity with an altarpiece by Piazzetta placed two altars further down[83]. The influence of Veronese is little more than a reference and certainly not a serious reinterpretation of the great sixteenth-century master, and the *Portrait of a Member of the Dolfin Family*, one of Tiepolo's rare portraits, was almost certainly commissioned for celebratory purposes, for which a certain Baroque *pathos* must have seemed appropriate.

In addition we must also mention some fairly ambitious secular decorative schemes, dated roughly 1749 – 1750, which do not depart much, however, from what had been done earlier, either stylistically or iconographically. Unfortunately there is little that we can say about what remains of the frescoes in Villa Corner in Merlengo (Treviso) (fig. 87) which in the nineteenth century suffered a prudish bowdlerization campaign. Instead, even if they are not in their original locations, the paintings for Palazzo Barbaro in Venice have survived. In the four ornamental doorway panels of famous women Tiepolo handles a subject common for his patrons[84] but unusual for him, and he came up with a scheme of classical porcelain splendor, peopled by beautiful, cold glassy figures. The theme of the ceiling painting is interesting, today at the Metropolitan Museum of Art in New York and known by the incorrect title of *Apotheosis of Francesco Barbaro*.

[79] It is possible that as studies continue on Giandomenico it will be discovered that his father's signature on the works from these years is instead the revealing tic of a certain disquiet regarding the work's acceptance by the patrons, or a kind of counter-proof of his son's participation.
[80] We should recall that Tiepolo gave the best of himself when the undertaking seemed impossible: we need only think of the grand decorative cycles of the 1720s and the 1730s, nearly all of them executed alone for very demanding or indecisive patrons.
[81] Seen by Cochin in Palazzo della Vecchia in Vicenza, where Tiepolo would soon work: C.N. Cochin, *Voyage d'Italie*, Paris 1758.
[82] From the painting of the same subject today in the National Gallery of Washington: T. Pignatti and F. Pedrocco, *Veronese. Catalogo completo dei dipinti*, Florence 1991, n. 253, p. 318.
[83] The altarpiece with *Ss. Vincent Ferrer, Hyancinthus and Ludovico Bertrando*, from 1738-38: A. Mariuz (1982, n. 65).
[84] The Barbaro family already had five ovals of famous women by Zanchi. But in the eighteenth century the classic gallery *De claris mulieribus* was transformed into a voyeuristic series of beautiful women. The real admirer of this entirely Rococo cult was Augustus III of Saxony, who had requested Rosalba Carriera to furnish him with 'Portraits of (...) pretty women he had never known, allegories such as the Four Seasons, or the Four Continents, or the Four Elements, religious subjects like the Magdalen and the Virgin Mary. It hardly mattered as they were all equally attractive': F. Haskell (1980, p. 295).

84.
Portrait of a Member of
the Dolfin Family,
Procuratore and
Generale da Mar.
Venice, Fondazione
Querini Stampalia.

85.
Patron Saints of the
Crotta Family. Frankfurt,
Städelsches
Kunstinstitut.

86.
opposite
Detail from fig. 85.

In a state like the Venetian republic, hostile to the worship of any one individual, such a title would have been in poor taste, if not downright risky. Thus Tiepolo had to filter the exaltation of the family through allegory.

The central figure is Valor, with his traditional lion following Ripa's instructions, surrounded by the civic virtues such as Nobility and Prudence (which are a relatively original couple among Tiepolo's learned abstractions), completed by the attributes of Fame and *Abundance*. Tiepolo's last work before he left for Würzburg was probably the reception hall of the new palazzo, which the lawyer Angelo della Vecchia had had built in Vicenza by Giorgio Massari in only a year, to the astonishment of all[85]. In the lawcourts of the Veneto, Angelo della Vecchia was the rival of the other lawyer from Vicenza whom Tiepolo had worked for in 1743, Carlo Cordellina. But this was a rivalry which first took the form of emulation and later developed into friendship. He resorted to the same artistic strategies used by Cordellina to strengthen his position in the bosom of the town's nobility[86]. He was also in contact with Algarotti, because of their common interest as collectors, and with Count Giorgio Marchesini, another patron of Tiepolo's. And he already had two sketches for the Arkangelskoye paintings by Tiepolo, which reveals that a tightly woven network of acquaintances brought Giambattista back to Vicenza, where he again painted a ceiling which portrays a reigning *Valor*, surrounded by various *Virtues*[87]. In a connecting room there was also another ceiling, now in the Cini collection in Venice, which represents the *Morning Twilight* executed according to Ripa's precise instructions[88].

In conclusion, work at the bottega of Giambattista Tiepolo on the eve of his departure for Würzburg was flowing smoothly but without any real creative outbursts, moving from self-reference to re-using what he had already done and seen. Fortunately this monotony was interrupted by his invitation to paint the enormous undertaking at the Residenz, which would be enlarged in the course of the project until it reached truly majestic dimensions. It was a job that aimed at exploiting the mythographical gifts of Tiepolo, who would respond by turning out the highest quality work in his entire oeuvre. But it was also an occasion in which the Prince-Bishop of Franconia forced Tiepolo to grapple again with the impossible – just what was needed to stimulate Giambattista's creative enthusiasm and give him back a real sense of his expressive potential.

[85] R. Menegozzo (1990, pp. 61-70).

[86] F. Barbieri (1972, 1990). Actually the title of count was conferred on the lawyer Della Vecchia only in 1774 by the Empress Maria Theresa of Austria. R. Menegozzo (1990, p. 66 and n. 16 on p. 69)

[87] Just as in Palazzo Marchesini in Vicenza (cf. par. III. 6) and Palazzo Barbaro in Venice, this is an anonymous homage to the virtuous sentiments of the patron and not an apologetic individual acclamation as the incorrect title usually used suggests: *Apotheosis of Angelo della Vecchia*. The painting was rediscovered in Palazzo Isimbardi in Milan by G. Knox (1980, pp. 22-26).

[88] 'Above the head a great glittering star (...) and with the right a lit torch (...) and in the air a swallow': C. Ripa, *Iconologia*. Reflecting on Ripa's work, which also speaks of a symmetrical *Evening Twilight*, we cannot exclude the possibility that Della Vecchia's painting had a similar *pendant*, of which, however, we know nothing. There is another work by Tiepolo, once in Munich and now lost, with the same iconography even more stylistically refined. I would instead doubt that the Providence *Fame* is his own work.

87.
Sacrice of Iphigenia. Merlengo (Treviso), Villa Corner.

88.
Ss. Roch and Sebastian.
Noventa Vicentina
(Vicenza), parish church.

Würzburg
1750-1753

Negotiations and preliminaries

Between 1751 and 1753, Giambattista Tiepolo worked a transformation on the Residenz in Würzburg, and changed it into a magical world of his own, which is why we have decided to treat it in a separate chapter. Tiepolo identified perfectly with this universe, because here, in what is unquestionably his greatest work, he had to transform, with the aid of myth and allegory, two historical events from the Middle Ages, making them into a justification of the reign of his contemporary, the Grand Elector of Franconia. We will divide the stylistically unified material in two phases, simply because they deal with different themes. The first dates from December 1751 to July 1752, and includes the decoration of the ceiling and walls of the Banquet hall of the Prince-Bishop Karl Philipp von Greiffenklau, which was later renamed the *Kaisersaal* (Imperial hall) after Tiepolo had completed his work there. The second period dates from July 1752 to the departure of Tiepolo's entire workshop for Venice in October of 1753, and includes the decoration of the vaulted ceiling above the grand staircase.

Karl Philipp von Greiffenklau was elected Bishop of Würzburg on 14 April 1749, when he also, as a consequence, assumed the title of duke of Franconia. Fifty years earlier his uncle Johann Philipp had been invested with the same title and had transformed Franconia, a small region in central-eastern Germany, into one of the most prosperous grand electorates in the Empire. This political tradition had been further strengthened by the rule of Prince-Bishop Friedrich Karl von Schönborn, from 1729 to 1746. He was responsible for Franconia's non-involvement in the wars of the Austrian Succession (1740-48), and the state's vast bureaucratic administration system modeled on that of the France of Louis XIV. Like the Sun King, Friedrich Karl von Schönborn had surrounded himself with a court of more than four hundred people – a very high number for a thinly-populated state such as Franconia – every member of which accompanied the Prince-

90.
Apollo Leading Beatrice of Burgundy to the Genius of the German Nation. Würzburg, Residenz.

Bishop on his slightest move around the kingdom[1]. Just as Louis XIV had built his Versailles, he had his magnificent Residenz of Würzburg, designed by the great Bohemian architect Balthasar Neumann and inaugurated in 1744. Now that both von Schönborn and his successor Anselm Franz von Ingelheim were dead (1746 and 1749, respectively) it was up to him to supervise its interior decoration in a bid to legitimize the absolute rule of an ecclesiastic priest over this small but rich state, autonomous but still very much a part of the Holy Roman Empire, with a very small population – only two hundred thousand inhabitants, of whom fourteen thousand lived in Würzburg.

Projects had been proposed since 1735, when the Jesuits Seyfried and Gilbert had designed a program entitled *Idee non vincolanti circa la maniera in cui l'arte pittorica potrebbe essere rappresentata e ripartita nella nuova residenza principesca a Würzburg*, ('Ideas not binding on the manner in which the pictorial arts could be represented and displayed in the new Prince's residence at Würzburg') which was followed by other projects which were either severely scaled down or delayed because of the pressures exerted by the war of the Austrian Succession on the borders of Franconia. However, these other projects were limited to the stucco decoration of the *Weißer Saal* supervised by Antonio Bossi, an Italian from the northern lake district. The duty – and the honor – of decorating the Versailles of eastern Franconia thus fell to Karl Philipp von Greiffenklau. He was elected when the war of the Succession had been over for a year and the Seven Years' War (1756/1763) was still to come. It was only during this brief sunny spell of peace that he could dedicate himself again to the Residenz.

Initially the Swabian painter Johann Zick had been employed, in the summer of 1749. Later in September of the same year, the job was given to Giuseppe Visconti of Milan. Visconti seems to have been something of an unreliable braggart, given that he suggested starting work that

[1] F. Büttner and W.C. von der Mülbe (1981).

91.
opposite
Detail from fig. 90.

very winter, a somewhat inappropriate season for successful fresco painting. He signed a contract in October 1749 and a few months later he was fired for 'artistic unworthiness'. Thus it was that the Bishop von Greiffenklau decided that he had to aim higher. Through the merchant Lorenz Jakob Mehling, his subject as a native of Würzburg but by then a long-term resident of Venice, he contacted Tiepolo in the spring of 1750. He was pleasantly surprised to hear from Mehling fairly soon, in a letter discussed in the Court Council of 29 May 1750, that Tiepolo was willing to come to Würzburg – for a considerable sum. Before sending the final contract, dated 12 October 1750, the Court Council sent a map and description of the Prince-Bishop's dining hall to Venice, which was all the idea was then limited to – and it also enclosed a new program entitled *Modesti pareri per la pittura della grande sala da pranzo del principe* ('Modest opinions on the paintings for the prince's great dining hall').

As laid out by the *Modesti pareri*, Tiepolo's task was to fresco the dining hall with a *Wedding of the Emperor Frederick Barbarossa and the Princess Beatrice of Burgundy*, which had been celebrated in 1156 by the Bishop Gebhard von Henneberg; the *Investiture of Bishop Harold as Duke of Franconia* (and therefore as Imperial Grand Elector) by Barbarossa himself, which occurred in 1168; and finally to unite the two events in a ceiling depicting the *Chariot of Apollo Leading Beatrice to the Genius of Germany*. But the *Modesti pareri* had also established the decoration in a deeper sense. Tiepolo had to join two distant unrelated events in a cause-and-effect relationship, as if the wedding were the direct cause of the Emperor's recognition of the hospitality received in Würzburg, and thus the investiture of his bishop as a vassal of the Holy Roman Empire. This false historiography was to have been celebrated before the celestial flight of Apollo's chariot, justifying the existence of the temporal power of the Bishop of Würzburg over Franconia. What could have been a more congenial subject to a creator of imaginary and Utopian narrative architecture such as Tiepolo?

First phase: the Kaisersaal

Giambattista Tiepolo arrived in Würzburg on 12 December 1750, accompanied by a servant and his sons Giandomenico and Lorenzo. The contract of 12 October 1750 only specified the decoration of the dining hall, which faced out onto a vast garden at the back. Karl Philipp von Greiffenklau had not asked him to send an oil sketch from Venice, as he preferred that Tiepolo take his own bearings once he had arrived. When he reached Würzburg, Tiepolo immediately made a careful examination of the dining hall. He must have studied the source of light (from the east) and the shape of the ceiling and the walls, and then carefully checked the point of view when entering from the *Weißer Saal* (the most important entrance to the room) and finally compared this information with the contents of the *Modesti pareri* to begin to translate all these elements into painting[2].

As it was winter, they still had to wait several months before erecting the scaffolding and starting the actual work. There still remained quite a few decisions to be made. The first problem to face was the unusual shape of the room. This is a rectangle with rounded corners and an extremely high cupola ceiling placed on pendentive niches on the long sides and on slightly concave triangular vaults on the two shorter sides. When Tiepolo began work the space reserved for frescoing was severely limited, and had equally severe decorations in the form of the complex and elegant Rococo cornices designed by Antonio Bossi[3]. There, on the two inconvenient triangular walls already partially occupied by Bossi's stuccoes, he had to paint the *Wedding* and the *Investiture* facing each other, and on the ceiling the great flight of the chariot of Apollo towards the throne of the Genius of Germany[4] (fig. 90). But moving within narrow or predetermined spaces was certainly the last of Giambattista's worries – wasn't he *the* painter of

[2] All the documents related to the Würzburg project were transcribed and published by M.H. von Freeden and C. Lamb (1956).

[3] Some of the cornices were already there, but not all of them. Bossi, who had lived at the Court since the 1730s, immediately put himself at Tiepolo's disposal, aware of the fact that the work should have Tiepolo as its only designer and creator.

[4] Actually, the *Modesti pareri* sent him in Venice seemed to locate the throne centrally. This would have placed the chariot of the sun in a static and possibly marginal position. Removing the throne from the center and leaving the entire sky for the gleaming chariot was one of the most important alterations made by Giambattista for the program suggested by the Würzburg court.

new architecture? He was used to reinventing spaces, and altering geometric features of interiors using the centrifugal force that spread out into the interior from his own paintings.

Initially Tiepolo may have thought that he had to compromise with the shape of the two triangular vaults, and pack in the two historic episodes. He did not yet know what sort of leeway his patrons would allow him in making decisions, nor had he yet taken the mental measurements of the entire setting. The two preparatory oil sketches executed for the *Wedding* and the *Investiture,* today in Boston and New York respectively, have an imposed vertical orientation, as if they had to begin and end within the confines of the cornices. Then Tiepolo must have stumbled upon an ingenious strategy which made the best possible use of Bossi's stuccoes. He constructed the episodes like normal theater scenes, with the curtain not yet completely drawn – painstakingly arranged and gilded to look just like a proscenium arch stage double curtain – that the two stucco *putti* are raising like stage hands. This is how the scenes can be painted in a horizontally amplified composition, which is confirmed by the second sketch for the *Wedding* (London) and then by the final version of the fresco itself. If we put the various versions of the *Wedding,* in sequence, from the Boston to the London studies, concluding with the fresco, we realize that this is a process of horizontal expansion, a quest for ever-increasing space.

One important aspect of the four sketches for the *Kaisersaal* is that their figures are proportionally much larger than their depiction in the final version. In addition to serving as notes for the cartoons, which we will look at shortly, the sketches were especially useful as negotiating tools to be used with the patron, to assure him that all the figures he had requested were indeed there, arranged as he had ordered them. Tiepolo seems to have moved the figures one by one towards the observer to highlight them and bring them up for discussion. This is why they appear on a larger scale in the sketches than they actually are on the walls. It also explains why the sketches themselves seem a bit crowded, with a somewhat blocked and almost suffocating internal rhythm.

Tiepolo must have had to respond to the overall problem of the distribution of individual elements with a calculation that was entirely mental, as we defined it earlier. This was an evaluation process that Tiepolo had found necessary ever since the frescoes for the Udine Patriarchate – an evaluation of illusionist placement of figures, of *all* the figures, both individually and placed together in a reciprocal relationship within the overall context. In other words, he had to answer that question once again – where were the figures to be placed? Painted on a wall or hovering in real space? The Prince-Bishop trusted Tiepolo to produce work of an extremely high standard, but expected nothing more than painting, however magnificent. Tiepolo, however, did something more – he created a true representation in that it actually participates in the real concrete space of the room itself. However, to make this 'artistic illusion' real, he had to select an impressive and unified observation point, which would be that of the entrance of the *Weißer Saal* , and using this as a basis to place all the figures of the three frescoes in proportion with the physiological measurements of the observers. This was so that those looking at the figures from below could see them as truly living beings, fellow humans placed in a sky that had to seem the natural sky above the hall. These were not to be meta-physical characters plunked down in alien spaces. Therefore it is the space and the concrete measurements of the figures which determine the homogeneity of the characters painted up above. Tiepolo thus rediscovered a sort of classical Renaissance anthropocentrism, on the threshold of the disenchanted and predominantly skeptical age of the Enlightenment.

There was finally the problem of the setting and costumes. The two historical episodes to be painted on the vaults had taken place in the twelfth century, but was it really necessary to portray them with painstaking historical accuracy. Couldn't they be transformed and placed in

92.
Detail from fig. 93.

a different past? Tiepolo chose the sixteenth century, because this allowed him to locate everything within that mythical Venice he had learned to celebrate as the Utopian location *par excellence*. And of course, he could use portray clothes and costumes that he, by then, knew better than anyone else.

Once the winter of 1750-51 was over, all was finally ready. Tiepolo took his decisions, altering in significant points the original program instructions handed down by the Court in Franconia. He also finished up both his practical and theoretical preparatory work. On 17 April 1751 he received a visit from Karl Philipp von Greiffenklau, who had come to him 'to see the drawing of the room to be painted, now begun by the painter Tiepolo'[5]. The sketches must have been ready, and the 'drawing of the room' mentioned is almost certainly a preparatory cartoon on a one-to-one scale[6]. Once he received the approval of Karl Philipp, who was very pleased by what he saw, Tiepolo attacked the ceiling. He had to begin from the top to make sure that the scaffolding would not damage the walls which had already been painted. He finished the fresco straight away, in only two months, helped in the minor borders by his sons and the local painter Urlaub. On 8 July 1751, the feast of Saint Kilian, patron saint of Würzburg, von Greiffenklau organized a banquet in the *Weißer Saal* and after the meal he went with his guests to the adjoining room to witness the unveiling of the finished ceiling. The movement runs from south to north (from right to left in respect to the entrance of the *Weißer Saal*) and must act as an intermediary between the *Wedding* and the *Investiture*. The allegory of Virtue appears on the right edge, accompanied by her attributes taken from Ripa, with the crown of laurel and the scepter. There follows a great cloud that overflows beyond the perimeter of Bossi's cornice, which is thronged with assorted divinities of good omen: the Ceres of Franconia with the sheaf of corn and the bridal torch; under her there is a Venus with Cupid, and a Bacchus recalling Massanzago,

[5] F. Büttner and W. C. von der Mülbe (1981, p. 39).
[6] The Court documents report a few days after 17 April that 'The painter Tiepolo has today begun painting the principal room and *tracing*', *ibidem*, my italics. 'Ricalcare' or 'trace' means to pass directly over the cartoons with a metallic point. The cartoons were prepared on the ground and then lifted up on the walls.

93.
opposite
Wedding of Barbarossa with Beatrice of Burgundy. Würzburg, Residenz.

GIO. BTTA. TIEPOLO 1752

94.
Investiture of Bishop
Harold as Duke of
Franconia. Würzburg,
Residenz.

possibly executed by Giandomenico, in light of the obvious anatomical mistakes. The central part of the sky, that the *Modesti pareri* dictated should be occupied by the throne, is instead crossed by the chariot of Apollo dressed as the *Phoebus orientalis* that leads Burgundy to the Genius of Germany and not to Frederick Barbarossa as was long believed (fig. 89). This 'refers to the consequences derived, for both the Empire and Franconia, from the wedding of the Emperor celebrated at Würzburg'[7]. The chariot is pulled by four extraordinary horses of different colors, portrayed *sottinsù*, symbolizing the four stages of the day (fig. 91). Burgundy, brought as her dowry to the Genius of Germany, has the features of princess Beatrice and is held by the hand of Concordia, while the nuptial god Hymen hovers on the horizon. To the left above the wall where the *Investiture* would be painted the next year rises the throne of the Genius Germaniae presided over by the allegory of Fame. To the left of the throne, kneeling and holding a shield before him, is the Genius of Franconia, to whose right is placed a putto holding the sword of temporal power over the Grand Electorate. The red and white banner is the emblem of Franconia. On the right of the throne, near the steps, the figure mantled in shimmering white and with the slightly greenish face in *contrejour* is the allegory of Faith following Ripa's iconography. Under the throne, the old man embracing the nymph is the river Main. Both the figures protrude from the cornice and each has a leg modeled in stucco, imitating the painting, to portray the illusion of an invasion of real space. This is what Karl Philipp von Greiffenklau saw with his guests on 8 July 1751.

Immediately after completing this Tiepolo moved on to the two walls, and began work on the *Wedding* (figs. 92, 93) which he finished in the autumn of 1751, while Franz Ignaz Roth continued with the gilding of Bossi's stuccoes on the already completed ceiling[8].

In his staging of the scene Tiepolo took into consideration the sources of light in the

[7] *Ibidem*, p. 75.
[8] Roth's contract is dated 21 July 1751.

95.
opposite
Detail from fig. 94.

room, just as he had done ever since the Ca' Dolfin paintings in San Pantalon. In other words, he worked so that the artificial light of the fresco coincided perfectly with the natural light streaming in from the windows, which are located to the left when looking at the *Wedding*. While he continued to think vertically the scene was fairly hemmed in and crowded, and the characters were forced to squeeze themselves into the narrow margins of the scene (compare, for example, the Boston and London sketches). Later, when he finally fell upon the idea of horizontal orientation which made use of the theatrical dynamism of Bossi's stucco theater curtains, he began to fresco and all went well. To the left, kneeling in an amaranth cloak, is the father of the bride, Rainald von Burgund, with an escort of pages in green. On the altar, the Bishop Gebhard of Henneberg, portrayed with the face of Karl Philipp von Greiffenklau, is making a gesture of blessing – an extraordinary example of the power of pictorial superimposition. Next come the bride and bridegroom genuflecting on the steps before the altar. The face of Frederick Barbarossa is taken from the *St. James the Greater* of 1749-50, with slightly bulbous eyes and red hair. This three-quarter view is almost baulked and dominated by Beatrice. She, a real 'ice-princess bride'[9], is a typically haughty Tiepolo beauty, who seems to look down on the world from above, although she kneels. She has an unforgettable profile like those found on the classic medallions of antiquity, and a dress with a long shimmering blue train, borne by two elegant pages. Lower down, stretched out on the steps, is a court dwarf like that found in the *Banquet of Cleopatra* in the Palazzo Labia. Here too – note the staff hanging on open space – this figure functions as a *trait d'union* between painterly artifice and the real space of the room. On the vertical of the dwarf rises a figure with a sword unsheathed on his shoulder, and a severely inquisitive gaze which seems to admonish the court of onlookers, none of whom seem very interested in the royal couple. This is the Grand Marshall of the Empire, placed as prescribed by the ceremony under the Imperial coat of arms with the two-headed eagle, followed by the standard embroidered with the slogan SPQR, alluding to the Holy Roman Empire. His counterpart, the Grand Marshall of Franconia, whom we have already seen at the throne of the *Genius Germaniae* on the ceiling, stands to the extreme right, with a sheathed sword slung over his shoulder. Among the two high court officials there are a pair of characters with cardinals' hats, who are the papal nunzios dictated in the *Modesti pareri*, together with others wearing ermine hats, identified as Prince Electors of the Empire[10]. Above, in the diaphanous *contrejour* shadow, an orchestra and a singer lean over from an alabaster loggia.

Once the *Wedding* was finished, the winter of 1751-52 forced a break, during which Tiepolo executed several oil paintings which will be discussed in the following paragraph. Once good weather had returned, between May and June 1752, Tiepolo completed and signed the *Investiture* (figs. 94, 95) on the wall opposite the *Wedding*.

The light here arrives from the right, as if the fresco were receiving it directly from the windows that look out onto the park. In the center, on a throne decorated with a shell and flanked by the gilded statues of Hercules (Strength) and Minerva (Wisdom) is Frederick Barbarossa crowned with laurel and dressed in ermine and damask. He grasps the Imperial scepter, which he offers to the touch of feudal submission of Bishop Harold, behind whom stand two pages wearing cloaks and the Grand Electoral crown, symbols of the spiritual and temporal powers over Franconia which the Bishop has just received. To the left, silhouetted against a Palladian arcade, the Imperial Chancellor reads the parchment of investiture, followed by two Grand Electors of the Empire and the Grand Marshall of Franconia with a sheathed sword. On the opposite side reappears the Grand Imperial Marshall with the sword unsheathed on his shoulder. Around stand halberdiers, dressed as Roman soldiers, and two Turks wearing turbans, perhaps alluding to the location of the duchy of Franconia, placed on the eastern borders of the

[9] M. Levey (1986, p. 185).
[10] F. Büttner and W.C. von der Mülbe (1981, p. 51).

96.
Olympus and the
Continents. Würzburg,
Residenz.

97.
America,
detail from fig. 96.

Holy Roman Empire. The lower left bears the signature GIO. BTTA. TIEPOLO 1752, and to the right a magnificent dog occupies roughly the same position as the dwarf in the *Wedding* and has the same function of *enjambment* with the actual physical space of the room.

In the inversion of the traditional respect paid to political and religious dignity in the *Wedding* – for here it is the Prince Bishop who kneels – we can make out the general significance and coordination of the three frescoes, which force historical reality into an ideological version very different from reality. Grateful to Würzburg for having hosted the wedding of the Princess Beatrice (the right wall upon entering) which obtained from the Empire the rich provinces of Burgundy and Provence (ceiling) the Emperor Frederick Barbarossa elevates the Bishop of Würzburg, and with him, Franconia, to the level of vital elements on the eastern border of the Holy Roman Empire (left wall). Therefore the goal and overall meaning is not only to designate the Residenz as the 'outward, visible, and imposing sign of the Prince Bishop as a ruler'[11] but also (and especially) to illustrate 'the relationship of mutual dependency between the Church and the Empire'[12]. This is the response of the Prince-Bishop Karl Philipp von Greiffenklau and his great poet Giambattista Tiepolo to the growing symptoms of European crisis of the *ancien regime* founded on the feudal hierarchy.

From now on the documents of the Court Council of Würzburg refer to the former dining hall as the *Kaisersaal*.

Second phase: the frescoes of the grand staircase

While Tiepolo was finishing the *Kaisersaal*, Karl Philipp von Greiffenklau was slowly coming to the conclusion that Tiepolo should also be employed for the decoration of the immense ceiling that soars above the grand staircase[13]. The contract with Giambattista was signed 29 July

[11] M. Levey (1986, p. 182).
[12] F. Büttner and W.C. von der Mülbe (1981, p. 86).
[13] The ceiling and the staircase were the work of the great architect Balthasar Neumann, executed in 1743. He had long fought to keep the ceiling one single immense surface, and he had won in the end.

98.
opposite
America,
detail from fig. 96.

1752, after he had finished the *Kaisersaal*, but it had already been under discussion in the Court Council since June of the same year. In fact, since an oil sketch, called 'scico' in the records, was mentioned in the session of 30 June 1752 as being ready since 21 April 1752[14], it certainly must have been under discussion even earlier. It is unthinkable that Tiepolo would have wasted his time on such a large detailed sketch, even if fairly different from the final version, unless he already had a fairly firm promise for the job.

The imposing staircase climbs in one single flight from the reception hall to the first landing, where it then divides into two parallel flights that ascend to the piano nobile, where an ample gallery turns around the stairwell just under Tiepolo's frescoes. The vision of the ceiling therefore occurs *in itinere*, and Giambattista as usual saw to the management of the perception of observers. Climbing the first ramp one has a complete view of the north side of the ceiling and a partial view of its center. Then, once the landing is reached at the level of an imaginary mezzanine, where the stairway is divided in two flights, one is obliged to turn on oneself, when suddenly, impressively, the entire ceiling and the perimeter above the trabeation is seen.

Presumably immediately after signing the contract, Tiepolo began work, starting from the center of the immense ceiling and slowly descending to the four sides of the edge. He may not have been very far advanced on his work when he stopped for the winter break (1752-53) given that he had started only at the very end of the summer, and the preparation of the scaffolding over the vast void of the stairwell must have been fairly difficult. It is certain that when he took up work again in the summer of 1753[15], he must have made a running start, because he was able to sign it – proof that the work was considered completed – at the end of September on the bottom of the western wall with the depiction of Asia. In the meantime, Balthasar Neumann had died on 19 August 1753.

The iconography of the very large fresco (roughly 580 square meters) portrays Apollo, Olympus and the Four Continents of the Earth (fig. 96). The depiction of the Four Continents spreads out immediately above the trabeation where the entire ceiling is laid out. On a pictorial plane its movement is uninterrupted all along the boundary. Each continent occupies a single side and is counterpointed on the corners by Antonio Bossi's stucco figures, so that both appear continuous from a pictorial point of view but are interrupted by the rhythm of the narrative. Each of them thus has its own center, which are allegorical personifications of each continent taken from Ripa. These personifications have a pivotal function, in the sense that they appear to us both as the narrative focus of each sector, and indicators of movement in the overall ceiling composition.

In the sketch (now in New York at the Metropolitan) the theme agreed on was 'the rising of the sun over the world'[16], a theme which would partly change the significance of the final rendering. The single fragments which make up this union of Olympus with the earthly world are not only allegories provided by Ripa, but are also derived from other cultures. They are drawn from travelers' accounts, extremely popular in the sixteenth and seventeenth centuries, interpretations of ethnography and natural history[17]; and finally, Tiepolo's own

99.
Detail from fig. 96.

[14] This is the sketch now in the Metropolitan Museum of Art in New York, in the Wrightsman Collection.
[15] Antonio Bossi's contract for his stucco ceiling decorations was drafted in the spring of the same year.
[16] F. Büttner and W.C. von der Mülbe (1981, p. 106).
[17] For example, see the ostrich followed by the ape on the Africa side, which is a copy executed by Giandomenico Tiepolo from an engraving by Stefano della Bella: J. Byam Shaw (1962, p. 81).

100.
Africa,
detail from fig. 96.

boundless imagination, which had turned Palazzo Clerici into a 'kind of pagan-Catholic cosmorama'[18]. Ripa's world of iconography, as usual constructed on isolated allegories, is taken apart and rebuilt in a lushly irrepressible narration. Reality and metaphorical representation merge in an inimitable universe – the world of Tiepolo, in which allegory is rejuvenated by slices of reality, lightened and ennobled by injections of allegory. However, in respect to the long tradition of the Baroque that favored allegory to represent the totality of the cosmos and its individual parts, Giambattista managed to bring symbols to earth and transform them into ethnographic examples, which we will see later in a detailed examination of the Four Continents. Thus even while he indulged in an exaggerated use of metaphor, Tiepolo also seemed to be feeling the invincible pressure of the *Encyclopédie*.

Climbing the first staircase up to the landing, America is the first continent we encounter (figs. 97, 98) along with a part of the sky focused on Apollo. Starting our reading from the left-hand corner, we see natives, soldiers and animals as they were described in accounts of the New World written by European explorers, which were extremely widespread and popular in eighteenth-century Europe. Next is a man with a cornucopia, symbol of the wealth to be found on the other side of the Atlantic, and then a young man seen in *contrejour* with a multicolored vase and a cup[19]. Next is the sturdy personification of America, which according to Ripa stands over a crocodile and has decapitated heads at its feet[20]. Under the man with the crocodile on his shoulders we see a European who has slipped on the trabeation, 'perhaps accidentally when he was doing his research, which is now collected in the big folder he carries with him'[21]. With a broad gesture America points to the left, where Africa begins after Bossi's stuccoes (figs. 99, 100). The black continent starts on the left, with merchants and caravan drovers dressed in exotic caftans amongst bales of merchandise. There is a camel seen from behind followed by the amusing incidental episode with the ape and the ostrich[22]. Then the personification of Africa appears, seated on an enormous camel, ebony-fleshed with stunning bluish highlights, attended by a Moor with a smoking censor[23]. This personification too invites us to look to the right, where Europe is found[24]. Just before the south-east corner, with his feet planted on the large cornice and a sheaf of papyrus in his arms, appears a white-haired old man – the river Nile.

On the opposite long side, Tiepolo painted Asia (fig. 101) which begins from the junction with America and must be read from right to left. We immediately encounter the group with the woman and the pyramid which we have seen many times before – Ripa's *Glory of Princes*[25]. Although the artist creates a certain confusion with the attributes suggested by Ripa, he treats Asia with great respect, for the Savior was born in that lap of the world, along with the first monarchies born, and therefore the first forms of associated life – as well as the arts, the sciences and according to Vitruvius, architecture too[26]. It is therefore the third continent, on an ascending scale, of a European-centered hierarchy culminating on the south wall with Europe (figs. 102-104). Tiepolo left his signature here, to the side of a block of stone carved with the Armenian alphabet, possibly the symbol of the birth of writing. The felled statue of the goddess Nature appears nearby[27]. It seems significant that Giambattista painted this symbol of *natura naturans*, or pagan pantheism, as an object neglected by the two pilgrims who instead head towards the crosses of Golgotha. A little further ahead, continuing to the left, there are two figures prostrating themselves before the personification of Asia – on an African elephant – surveyed by magicians and wise men who seem to have migrated from the world of Tiepolo's etchings. Like all his other incarnations of the continents, this too points the way to Europe, apotheosis of human progress. In spite of all Asia's merits, amply demonstrated by Giambattista who may have had in mind the teachings of Francesco Algarotti, it remains forever a ferocious corner of the world, as it was then believed, demonstrated by the mangled bodies lying at her feet, and

[18] A. Morassi (1955, p. 26).

[19] Probably full of 'cioccolatte', as Goldoni might have said. The best chocolate actually came from South America.

[20] These are proof, as Ripa recounts, of the existence of cannibalism in those areas, recalled perhaps in that ferocious group to the extreme right, with a piece of flesh threaded on a skewer.

[21] F. Büttner and W.C. von der Mülbe (1981, p. 112).

[22] Cf. note 17.

[23] Ripa actually assigned the camel and the incense to Asia, which is on the opposite side. But with these two continents, Tiepolo remixes all that he is offered by his seventeenth-century source, inverting the attributes.

[24] This is the function that we earlier defined as 'pivotal': to demand the attention of the viewer only to then direct it somewhere else, towards the real conclusion of this world tour.

[25] M. Santifaller, *Die Gruppe mit der Pyramide...* (1975).

[26] F. Büttner and W.C. von der Mülbe (1981, p. 119).

[27] The image of the Goddess Nature comes from a repertory that, like that of Ripa, was very widespread in the eighteenth century: see V. Cartari, *Imagini delli dei de gl'antichi*, Venice 1556. Cartari describes her thus: 'Image of the Goddess Nature all full of breasts, to show, that the Universe takes nourishment from the hidden virtue of the same'.

101.
opposite
Asia, detail from fig. 96.

102.
Europe,
detail from fig. 96.

103.
Europe,
detail from fig. 96.

104.
Europe,
detail from fig. 96.

the cruel tiger hunt closing up the extreme left of the continent. Europe can be reached from two directions, and we approach her here accepting the conventions of Tiepolo's narrative, from two opposite extremes. On the southern corner at the border with Asia there rises a classical pediment with an open shell-shaped tympanum before which, cloaked and turned toward the spectator, is silhouetted Antonio Bossi's portrait surrounded by the tools of sculpture. At his side a lively little orchestra with instruments and singers reminds us that the civilization of Europe created music. Lower down, carefully placed on the trabeation as if on a triclinium, sitting on a cannon, is the portrait of the architect Balthasar Neumann in the uniform of an artillery colonel[28]. On the other side, at the border with Africa, we find three other portraits. The first is the painter Franz Ignaz Roth who was of such assistance to Tiepolo, when he practically offered him his services. Next is Giambattista himself, with a calm intense expression, very different from that frowning, even scandalized expression he portrayed himself with at Palazzo Labia. Here it seems that he is contemplating his achievements and is deeply pleased with the result. Finally there is the portrait of Giandomenico wearing a wig. We finally reach Europe in the center of the composition, with her shimmering robe, seated on the mythical bull – or Jove – in whose appearance he managed to rape her. She is surrounded by religious symbols (the bishop's tiara, the processional cross and the pastoral letter) and political emblems (the crown borne by the

[28] Just as Francesco Algarotti was given a military title, Neumann too was awarded a decorative title for his employment at court and Tiepolo shows this to us with his wine-red uniform with silver frogs. Perhaps when Giambattista portrayed him he had only just died (August 1753) and thus that alert sturdy dog may have some concealed significance (for the dog is a symbol of faithfulness).

105.
Detail from fig. 96.

page on the left). Tiepolo paints her as the Mistress of the earth. All the continents converge towards her, and, as we will see, from her departs the great flight to the skies of Olympia. The *sphaera mundi* lies under her, a globe which is being decorated with historical scenes, which is almost being created by Painting.

In a gilded oval above triumphs the profile of Karl Philipp von Greiffenklau, supported by Fame and crowned by Virtue (winged and with a sun at her breast). The *trait d'union* with Europe is the great red and white cloak of velvet and ermine[29], moved by the wind and cheerful putti. A griffin-dragon emerges from under the oval, alluding to the name of the reigning Prince-Bishop[30]. At the same height of the portrait, but painted to seem lower, various Olympian divinities appear: Jove and Ganymede, Saturn and Vulcan to the left, and Diana to the right. Following towards the top the major line that starts with Europe, strikes the cloak and touches the oval surrounded by the gods, we find the ethereal Mercury who, escorted by Morning Twilight with wings and a torch (Ripa) points to the rising of Apollo in the other narrative focus of the ceiling. Apollo leaves his round temple silhouetted against a radiant sun, with a little statuette in his hand (fig. 106). Above the clouds interrupted by the appearance of the god, the natural scansions of time measured out by the sun are placed all around. The Hours bear the four different colored horses (fig. 105) already seen in the *Kaisersaal* (the different phases of the day). The band of the Zodiac marks the conjunction between astral and earthly time. To the left, the Four Seasons symbolize the annual journey of the sun through the skies: the old man Winter, Summer with a sheaf of corn, Springtime with the basket of flowers and, slightly removed, Autumn dressed as Massanzago's Bacchus.

Apollo is portrayed without punitive emblems. Indeed, a winged putto underneath is placed next to Mars and Venus, holding weapons, and dragging away the wolf of War he has captured, while the statue held in the left hand of the god of Sun significantly represents *Peaceful or Clement Fortune* (Ripa). The Sun-Apollo rises and sets eternally, and his birth corresponds to von Greiffenklau's entrance attired in the dignity of the prince of Franconia, inspired, however by the *Clementia principis*. If, therefore, the *Kaisersaal* represents the 'status of the Prince-Bishop of Würzburg legitimized by history, and his relationship with the Emperor and the Empire'[31], here in the grand staircase ceiling we witness the identification of the lord of Franconia with the Sun-Apollo, and his benevolent power, a peaceful power aimed at the common good, a sun that rises 'equally for all'. Here the deeper meaning of the fresco, even if Giambattista may not have been consciously aware of it, 'anticipated Enlightenment absolutism'[32].

On 8 November 1753 Tiepolo and his workshop set out for Venice, when his work at Würzburg was over and the fresco signed. They left behind them one of the greatest fresco cycles of all time, in terms of quality as well as quantity.

Other works for Würzburg and its environs

Tiepolo had reached Würzburg in the December of 1750, but during the cold months before the spring of 1751, and before starting on the frescoes for the Prince-Bishop's dining hall, it seems highly unlikely that any other commissions would have distracted him from the preparation of this daunting undertaking. This was not because he was not justly famed, or because he needed to be tested as had happened with Visconti, but rather because the planning work for the three frescoes negotiated by contract must have been truly imposing and complex — works too challenging to allow for much distraction. None of these so-called 'winter works' (oil on canvas) which certainly date to this three-year sojourn in Germany can be dated to this early period. But during the next break, between the late autumn of 1751 and the spring of the following year, Tiepolo had already completed the ceiling and one of the two triangular walls (the

[29] These are also the colors of the flag of Franconia.
[30] In German, Greif = griffin, and Klau = claw, hence Greiffenklau would be 'griffin's claw'.
[31] F. Büttner and W.C. von der Mülbe (1981, p. 142).
[32] *Ibidem*, p. 143.

Wedding), which had been a sublime example of his skill. There was still no talk of the staircase ceiling of the reception hall, not even in terms of negotiating a price for that Venetian who was so good, but 'cost a Peru'. The winter of 1751-52 was a particularly long one, without the urgency felt again in the break of 1752-53 when the finished dining hall was renamed the *Kaisersaal*, but he was hard at work on the newly-begun staircase ceiling which must have seemed an overwhelming challenge.

The *Fall of the Rebel Angels* and the *Assumption of the Virgin* must certainly date back to this long break of 1751-52. Both were painted for the Hofkapelle of the Residenz, and they were both signed and dated in 1752. Tiepolo resorted to earlier themes in these two canvases. The first is an obvious revival, in terms of stylistic purity and chromatic transparency, of the same theme painted for the Patriarchate of Udine. The second recalls Piazzetta's *Assumption* painted for the Teutonic Order church in Sachsenhausen (1735), even if this was a Piazzetta particularly influenced by Ricci, as Mariuz convincingly argues[33]. This sense of *déjà vu* must not, however, be attributed to any lack of commitment to the project – his professional instinct and the dimensions of the works would not have permitted this. It was due, instead, to the usual reason – his complete psychological absorption in the interminable frescoes he was working on. However, to make room for his paintings in the side altars of Balthasar Neumann's chapel, there were removed 'those altar pieces that were painted only fifteen years earlier, with the same subjects, by Federico Bencovich for Friedrich Karl von Schönborn'[34]. The winter works thus became laboratories for his sons, who were almost completely led by the hand of their father. They must have served as lessons for Giandomenico, in much the same way as he had used such exercises in the workshop just before his departure for Würzburg, and may have served Lorenzo as well, who left Venice when he was fourteen and returned when he was seventeen. It has been proved that Giandomenico's assistance was extensive, and pay receipts attest to his participation in the ornamental panels over the doors of the *Kaisersaal*. It also seems reasonable to suppose that his hand is also seen in other canvases commissioned by others, such as the two matching couples *Rinaldo and Armida* and *Rinaldo Abandoning Armida* (now in Munich but originally painted for the Residenz gallery) and the *Family of Darius Before Alexander* and *Mucius Scaevola and Porsenna*[35].

These two paintings with historic themes were executed for his friend Balthasar Neumann, with a great deal of assistance from Giandomenico. In the *Rinaldo and Armida* we see the same pediment with the open tympanum revealing a glimpse of a fusarole or semicircular whorl around a column, painted by Giambattista on the right of Europe above the grand staircase[36].

The luminous *Adoration of the Magi* instead must belong to the 1752/53 winter break, which was painted by Giambattista for the church of the Benedictine monastery of Münsterschwarzach[37]. For this painting, in which there are still found echoes and borrowings from Veronese and Sebastiano Ricci, Tiepolo used as a model a print he had executed some ten years earlier in a slightly different form[38], a fairly uncommon practice at that time but fitting in light of his own self-confidence.

Finally, the German commissions include the *Death of Hyacinthus* today in the Thyssen collection. The painting seems to have been acquired originally by the Prince of Bückenburg in Venice for the castle of Stadthagen. It must therefore be considered Giambattista's first work executed (with a good deal of assistance from Giandomenico) after his return to Venice, painted to please a German patron who may have been disappointed by the Maestro's hasty departure from Würzburg. On the right of the canvas, just above the reckless Apollo, we note the same pediment with the broken tympanum that we saw in the *Europa* of the grand staircase and the *Rinaldo and Armida* in the Alte Pinakothek of Munich – a little piece of the Residenz recreated amidst the lagoons[39].

[33] A. Mariuz (1982, n. 63).

[34] F. Büttner and W.C. von der Mülbe (1981, p. 93).

[35] As for Lorenzo's possible participation in these works, we should remember that he engraved *Rinaldo Abandoning Armida* almost immediately after his father's execution of the subject: D. Succi (1988, p. 267).

[36] But this does not necessarily mean that this painting must be of a later date than the summer of 1753, when that part of the *Four Continents* was presumably painted. It might have been finished even in the 1751-52 winter, and some of its motifs, such as the pediment itself, might have been incorporated into the fresco from the painting and not vice versa.

[37] Now in the Alte Pinakothek in Munich, it is signed and dated 1753.

[38] D. Succi (1985, pp. 40-42).

[39] Whoever the German was who commissioned it, Prince Bückenburg or someone else, he had to come all the way to Venice to collect it.

106.
Detail from fig. 96.

The Venetian works after Würzburg

We have already hypothesized that the first work executed by Giambattista on his return to Venice from Würzburg was the *Death of Hyacinthus* in the Thyssen collection. This work, commissioned by a German nobleman who had to travel all the way to Venice to get his Tiepolo, may have been the result of a promise made in Germany and then honored in Venice.

At almost the same time Giambattista must have made a start on an altarpiece, the *Apparition of the Virgin to St. John Nepomuck*, for the church of San Polo, which was placed on Massari's new altar on 8 May 1754, about a week after the death of Giambattista Piazzetta[1]. The face of the saint belongs to a whole gallery of altarpieces beginning from the 1740s, in which ecstasy and martyrdom merge in a pathetic physiognomy, with protruding eyes, pale skin, and mouths twisted in suffering. This type is found in the *St. Oswald* in the Padua church of Santi Massimo e Osvaldo (1745), the *St. James the Greater* for the Spanish Embassy in London (1749-50), and later the *Martyrdom of St. Agatha* for the church of the same name in Lendinara (c. 1755-57)[2]. In this work, as in the others, an essential quality of composition and color emerges, made of strong chromatic contrasts and individual figures dramatically plunged into simplified undecorated spaces, showing very little in common with those amusing narrative frivolities, masquerading as refined games, typical of the earlier Tiepolo. This, however, does not imply that 'there began to be distinct unevenness in his large-scale oil-paintings'[3], nor a sort of 'second Piazzetta phase' after the death of Piazzetta[4], but rather reveals the establishment of a new, almost laconic way of handling religious subjects, 'anticipating the late Spanish altarpieces'[5].

At the same time, in the secular subjects that we would attribute to this period for stylistic reasons, we again encounter those allegorical compositions that from Palazzo Clerici to Würzburg experienced an evolution in the distillation of the chromatic fabric, enriching the

---

[1] The canonization of the Prague martyr took place in 1729, decreed by Pope Benedict III. During his visit to Venice in 1739-40, Frederick Christian, son of Augustus III of Saxony and Poland, gave a reliquary of the saint to the church of San Polo and went there on 16 May 1740 to hear the panegyric given by the Imperial theologian Sebastiano Paoli: M. Gemin (1982, p. 198).
[2] However, leaving aside devotional themes, it is the same physiognomy that we have seen in the face of Frederick Barbarossa in the *Wedding* for the Würzburg *Kaisersaal*.
[3] M. Levey (1986, p. 215).
[4] W.L. Barcham (1989, pp. 223-224). Piazzetta died on 29 April 1754.
[5] M. Levey (1986, p. 214).

107.
Crowning of the Immaculate Virgin Mary. Venice, Church of the Pietà.

108.
Sacrifice of Iphigenia,
detail. Vicenza, Villa
Valmarana ai Nani.

109.
opposite
Sacrifice of Iphigenia,
detail of Agamemnon.
Vicenza, Villa Valmarana
ai Nani.

110.
Diana and Aeolus.
Vicenza, Villa Valmarana
ai Nani.

[6] The painting has been entitled in different ways by those who are not aware of the hidden significance then so popular with the European *élite* up until the French Revolution, who attempted to superimpose their system of signs on that of the age of Tiepolo. The presence of the lion (on the right) was considered sufficient evidence to interpret the entire painting as an allegory of the Serenissima, the Venetian Republic.

[7] Here we see the traditional Nobility, above, then Virtue with its wings, sun and wreath of laurel. Lower down, Temperance is seen with its vase (as in the canvas mentioned earlier, location unknown) together with other virtues: there is no trace either of Aurora's chariot, or of Night.

[8] The church was known by this name because one of Venice's 'hospitals' was annexed to it. In this case it was a home and orphanage for the female choir and orchestra who were under the direction of Antonio Vivaldi until 1740. Cf. B. Aikema and D. Meijers (1989, pp. 197-214).

[9] D. Howard (1986).

[10] That Giambattista had actually painted the model on the wall is confirmed by a late etching by Giandomenico, an incidental scene, that bears on the margin the note 'Jo: Bapta Tiepolo invenit, et pin: hoc Exemplar in pariete'. D. Succi (1988, p. 244).

[11] L. Puppi (1968).

[12] P. Molmenti (1880); A. Morassi (1941).

[13] L. Puppi (1968); R. Menegozzo (1990, pp. 91-99).

[14] For Villa Cordellina, see Ch. III, par. 3; for Palazzo Marchesini, Ch. III, par. 6; for Angelo della Vecchia, Ch. III, par. 9.

[15] M. Levey (1986, p. 232) recalls that it was precisely in 1757 that Caylus published his *Tableaux tirés de l'Iliade, de l'Odyssée et de l'Enéide* and that consul Smith had a copy.

[16] R. Menegozzo (1990, p. 95).

learned repertoire, but fortunately without emphasizing the conceptual to the detriment of the formal. However, even before Würzburg, in the large painting incorrectly identified as the *Riches of Venice*[6] which originally decorated one of the ceilings of the Palazzo Dolfin Manin in Venice, Tiepolo staged allegorical figures that he had used often and were perfectly recognizable to the observers of his day: the recurrent Nobility, above with the statuette, Temperance with the amphora, Generosity with the lion at her side and the cornucopia abundantly pouring forth riches. These are all figures taken from Cesare Ripa's *Iconologia*, and could give way, in terms of contents, to combinations as instructive as they were interchangeable. For example, Nobility must temper Generosity, or vice versa, Nobility must let itself be tempered by Generosity. These combinations even involve opposite meanings, as we can see. Moving on to the later Würzburg period, the same thing happens in the presumed *Aurora Dispersing the Clouds of Night* in Boston[7]. However, in both works Tiepolo uses the allegory as a pretext for celestial conversations – in the first, a close-up, almost a whispering incidental episode, and in the second, from further away, interwoven with beautiful women, on Olympus and elsewhere.

Between the spring of 1754 and the August of 1755, Tiepolo executed an extensive series of frescoes for a recently-completed ecclesiastical building designed by Massari, Santa Maria della Visitazione, known as the Pietà[8] (fig. 107). The *Crowning of the Immaculate Virgin Mary*[9] is frescoed on the ceiling of the larger cupola, and the *Theological Virtues* are portrayed on the oval of the smaller ceiling of the chancel. The same wall bears an ash-grey monochrome with *David and the Angel*, and finally *Fortitude and Peace* is depicted in another oval. This last is lost, but there still remain traces in the small model done in a hectic style once in Munich[10]. The clear palette used in the *Theological Virtues* recalls the ceiling of the Carmini, while the slightly bewildered expression of Charity (to the left) resembles that of Painting set at the feet of Europe in the grand staircase fresco at Würzburg. Here the ceilings become strangely dark and shadowy. On closer examination, even the figure of the Virgin in the large fresco, shimmering and multicolored above the enormous blue bubble of air of the world, confirms the discussion of the San Polo altarpiece. At least in the sacred subjects, the sparkling and festive Tiepolo of the Patriarchate of Udine is giving way to a more restrained, almost thoughtful character that anticipates the intimist mood of his religious paintings in Spain.

Back in Vicenza: the Villa Valmarana and other works

These Venetian works completed, Tiepolo was again called to Vicenza, or rather to the surrounding Berici hills and the villa of Count Giustino Valmarana, together with Giandomenico and Gerolamo Mengozzi ('Il Colonna'), according to the detailed study by Lionello Puppi[11]. Antonio Morassi's correction of Molmenti's error in reading the date placed by Tiepolo in the 'Carnival hall' in the guest-rooms also tells us when he was there – 1757[12].

Giambattista arrived with ideas he had certainly agreed upon with Count Valmarana, which probably also took into account Algarotti's doctrines regarding the relationship between painting and literature. Yet they were completely original in respect to what he had done at Biron for the Loschi, to whom his new patron was related[13], for Carlo Cordellina at Montecchio Maggiore, and Cordellina's legal opponent Angelo della Vecchia, as well as for the Freemason Giorgio Marchesini, another relative of Nicolò Loschi[14]. Tiepolo had used all his learning in those earlier works, assisted by Cesare Ripa's *Iconologia* and additions or suggestions from his patrons, to glorify the social positions and ambitions of those learned lawyers and gentlemen. This time instead Tiepolo came up with a new proposal for gracious villa living, inspired by the works of classical and Renaissance poets, such as Homer, Virgil, Ariosto and Tasso[15]. Giustino Valmarana was an active 'participant in the theater life of Vicenza and the Accademia Olimpica'[16], but because

169

111.
Minerva Preventing
Achilles from Killing
Agamemnon. Vicenza,
Villa Valmarana ai Nani.

112.
Minerva and Putti.
Vicenza, Villa Valmarana
ai Nani.

of personal suffering he was also a very reserved man, reluctant to take part in the competitive imitation that was often a feature of life in Vicenza and other cities of the Veneto mainland. He decided to retire to a villa: "And the villa, of modest dimensions, was shaped by his desire for a place of peace and refuge, opening into an interior space of enchanted fables, dense with adventure because of the multitude of characters and events evoked'. All the elements joined 'to recreate in that isolated space a world in which nature is converted into artifice and artifice has the appearance of natural truth'[17].

Here we do not find the foibles and fetishes of a frivolous nobility bent on outward rhetorical displays, nor is there a use of allegories distributed in emptier and emptier skies to emphasize the magnificence of coats-of-arms or grand families who desired only to become grander, nor even (or at least not yet) the refined manifestation of a solid bourgeoisie that entertained itself with conversations on the classics based on sound philological knowledge. We find ourselves instead in an intermediate zone, in which episodes evoked by classical poems are presented to create emotional self-identification.

In other words, there is no longer identification with the inimitable heroes of history beyond the reach of ordinary mortals, nor with abstract divinities located in distant Olympus, far removed from the innocent pleasure of peaceful living, nor with virtuous symbolic allegories – and therefore even less attainable. There is instead a subtle and almost fictive pathos, a triumph of personal sensibility, which is the message which most anticipates the modern civilization as expressed by the Rococo. There is a taste for rereading those moments, reliving those scenes in the soul, perhaps a tribute to the traditions supplied by Metastasio's drama, which was then often performed in Vicenza, partially due to Giustino Valmarana, to allow these traditions to flow into one's own self, to exercize individual options perhaps not even authorized by the literary

[17] A. Mariuz (1978, p. 261).

113.
Angelica Comforting the
Wounded Medoro.
Vicenza, Villa Valmarana
ai Nani.

114.
Angelica and Medoro
Bidding Farewell to the
Peasants, detail.
Vicenza, Villa
Valmarana ai Nani.

114.
Angelica and Medoro
Bidding Farewell to the
Peasants, detail.
Vicenza, Villa
Valmarana ai Nani.

world. Thus this unfortunately brief intermediate phase of the Venetian Rococo emerged 'from the demands of an art that spoke to the heart, staging the deep passions of heroes, as opposed to an encomiastic or merely hedonistic art. It was basically a new demand for naturalness and truth'[18].

It was, in addition, an opportunity Tiepolo had long been yearning for, at least since Biron, if not even earlier. When working from Ripa's conceptual symbols, he had then translated them into situations full of verisimilitude and good-natured human secular credibility – albeit theatrical and not realistic verisimilitude. This was no simple escape to Arcadia or places of ambiguous disguise. Nor was it a distortion of nature, or a loss of human identity. On the contrary, it was instead a quest for a dimension where real life was imaginable, where it could seem simple and rich in genuine emotions barely whispered by the heart: 'on these walls (...) he evokes a world that does not refer to anything beyond itself, but indefinitely prolongs its own echo within the sphere of the sensibility'[19].

Here Tiepolo's theatricality is born, or rather, continues to develop, a theatricality touched also by jumps and starts, shivers chilled by the glimpse of the end of his own world. This is 'An operation of sublime techniques that produces dreams, to console those who have lost centuries-old beliefs and know that the deserts of history lie outside that garden of Armida'[20]. It was much better to remain on this side of the threshold of historical consciousness, and hover in the gilded suspension of the artificial creation of emotions, as inspired and expressed by art, 'seen as an extreme approach of the Rococo, where the happiness displayed in artistic fiction replaces the unlikely happiness of life'[21].

Just as in the *Kaisersaal* in Würzburg, the decoration is widely distributed, as seen in the plan above. With its episodes and divisions, the narration runs along the walls as well as the ceiling,

[18] *Ibidem*, p. 262. Here we follow the work of Adriano Mariuz, whose intuitions and conclusions we share completely, and are of great assistance in achieving a deeper understanding of Tiepolo's unusual literary-pictorial enterprise.
[19] *Ibidem*.
[20] *Ibidem*.
[21] *Ibidem*.

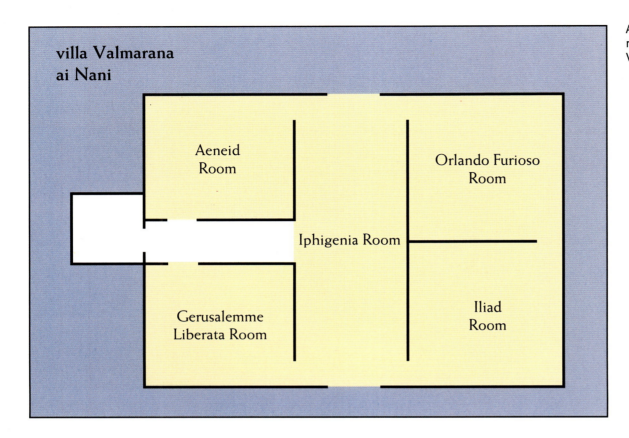

and reveals a strong tendency to position the conclusive aspects, or moral judgement of the events, on the ceilings. Each room is focused on a different plot of emotions. This diversity is felt, room by room, especially on a linguistic level, but we also find it on the level of cultural models better adapted to express those emotions, and it is finally seen in the *quadrature* which are here displayed to show those scenes to best effect. Gerolamo Mengozzi surpassed himself here. Just as Bossi did, but better, he offered his services to Giambattista and emphasized his interpretations, differentiated poem by poem, creating cornices which vary according to the narration and the different emotional impulse elicited in each of them. In Iphigenia's room (figs. 108, 109) emotions of a beautiful pathos are intertwined. Following Giambattista's precise instructions, Mengozzi created the illusion of theater wings, depicting foreshortened columns with Ionic capitals, for the entrance of the leading figures.

Other cornices, elaborately Baroque in respect to the neo-Renaissance feel of the central room, are seen in the portrayal of the *Iliad* (figs. 110-112) where the emotions become more extravagant. A more decorative mixtilinear Rococo is found in the room of the *Orlando furioso* (figs. 113-115), where the admittedly pre-Arcadian narrative plot still has a strong heroic feel. We finally arrive at the French-inspired *quadrature*, with frames barely animated by the lowered arches in the rooms of the *Aeneid* (fig. 117) and the *Gerusalemme liberata* (figs. 116, 118) where we arrive at the conclusion of this itinerary of the soul. In fact, it is actually in the *Gerusalemme liberata*, that Tiepolo inserts the only fragment taken from Ripa, the room in which the pathos of the unravelling of disappointed loves is more decidedly modern, where he allows himself to believe in the hope that these loves will be found again, and that they will see each other again, perhaps in dreams.

The ceiling scene, lost in 1944, is readable in its entirety only in photos. It has always been

115.
Cupid Blindfolded on a
Chariot Drawn by Putti.
Vicenza, Villa
Valmarana ai Nani.

defined as the *Victory of Light over Darkness*, but what meaning would a scene halfway between moralizing and meteorology have in this place? Instead, in the highest figure we recognize Virtue, with its wings, spear and laurel wreath, and the lower figure portrayed is Ignorance. Thus once again, after attempts to credit this pre-Enlightenment iconography to Vicenza and Venice itself – we need only think of the frescoes for Cordellina and the paintings for Palazzo Barbarigo – we find yet another version of the *Triumph of Virtue over Ignorance*.

All this is opposed, but in a complementary way, by the vision of Giandomenico, who here for the first time has entire walls to paint and shows the difference of his poetics from those of his father. His is a pre-realistic vision, in the sense that it neither criticizes nor mocks. It simply 'is characterized by the description of this humanity confronting a present without myths (...) It is the self-same civilization of the Venetian Rococo that shows itself in its many different aspects. The anxiety of evasion that distinguishes it together with the Enlightenment demand for observation, love of heroic fable and interest in current events'[22].

The architect Francesco Muttoni, who had built the guest-rooms and stables of the villa Valmarana, also designed Palazzo Trento in Vicenza for Ottavio Trento. Giustino Valmarana and Count Ottavio, a Venetian patrician since 1748, were first cousins. Valmarana's residence in Vicenza was right next door to the Trento residence in via San Faustino, and when the Trento family died out, the Valmarana inherited their palazzo[23]. There is certainly enough evidence to support the hypothesis that, right after the decoration of the villa Valmarana, in the late summer of 1757 or a year later, Giambattista, Giandomenico and Gerolamo Mengozzi or 'Il Colonna' were called to fresco the reception hall at Cabianca, where the Trento had their residence[24]. The grand staircase that rose from the ground floor to the piano nobile ran into the room asymmetrically and Mengozzi gave his very best in creating an illusion of equilibrium.

[22] *Ibidem*, p. 263.
[23] R. Menegozzo (1990, pp. 101-112).
[24] The principal decoration, on the ceiling, collapsed in a bombing in 1945.

117.
opposite
Armida Abducting the
Sleeping Rinaldo.
Vicenza, Villa Valmarana
ai Nani.

116.
Aeneas Presenting Cupid
in the Guise of Ascanius
to Dido. Vicenza, Villa
Valmarana ai Nani.

118.
Rinaldo Abandoning
Armida. Vicenza, Villa
Valmarana ai Nani.

Abandoning the great theater of emotions he had staged in Valmarana, Giambattista returned to allegorical representations again taken from Ripa for the ceiling. With the help of Giandomenico, he depicted the *Triumph of Truth over Error, Ignorance and Deception before the Cardinal Virtues*[25]. Giandomenico executed fake fresco statues within Mengozzi's *quadrature* on the walls. Only *Innocence* and *Faith* have survived the bombing[26].

As Mariacher[27] has proven, Tiepolo painted an altar piece in the late 1750s for the parish church of Rampazzo, near Vicenza, dedicated to the *Apotheosis of St. Gaetano of Thiene* (fig. 119)[28]. The painting was placed on the family altar, constructed by 1756, by the counts of Thiene, to emphasize their relationship with the founder of the Theatine order. In this work too we find that facial typology – the squared face and ecstatic expression – that had long been a feature of Tiepolo's painting. We can see the little church of Santa Maria Maddalena ordered by San Gaetano himself, seen at the lower left, portrayed still under construction. The same encomiastic mood is also found in the *St. Fidelis of Sigmaringen and the Blessed Giuseppe da Leonessa Crushing Heresy* which also depicts a similar church building.

Other myths, allegories and historiae

In the same season in which he completed the work at the Villa Valmarana and Palazzo Trento, Tiepolo was asked to decorate the ceilings of two rooms in the Ca' Rezzonico in Venice for the marriage of Ludovico Rezzonico and Faustina Savorgnan, celebrated in January of 1758 (fig. 122). Giorgio Massari had just finished Longhena's building, and the approaching marriage was announced with allusions to myth and allegory worthy of the two illustrious patrician families. In the first room Giambattista, aided by Giandomenico and the *quadrature* of Gerolamo Mengozzi or 'Il Colonna', revives the memory of the ceiling of the *Kaisersaal* with a *Nuptial Allegory*.

[25] *Truth* is the figure among the clouds with the disk of the sun in her hand. Under her, the blindfolded old man with the walking stick is *Error*. Further to the left lies *Ignorance*, accompanied by bats. *Deception* appears even further to the left, with the lower part of the body formed by two intertwined serpents. The *Cardinal Virtues* are placed to the sides. *Prudence* is on the right, with her mirror, and *Fortitude*, with a column, while *Temperance*, with a vase, is placed to the left, along with *Justice*, with sword and scale.
[26] R. Menegozzo (1990, p. 108).
[27] G. Mariacher (1950, pp. 153-154).
[28] Since at Rampazzo there were also properties belonging to Count Ottavio Trento (R. Menegozzo, 1990, p. 110, n. 4) it is certainly possible that he was the one to suggest the name of Tiepolo to the counts of Thiene.

178

Here he portrays bride and bridegroom in the chariot of Apollo, which stands behind them, while on the opposite side *Merit* – recognizable by the attributes dictated by Ripa's *Iconologia* – bears the standard with coats-of-arms of the two families. On the ceiling of the other room, known as the 'Throne Room' we find *Merit* again, witness to the propitious wedding, conducted by Virtue and Nobility to the temple of glory, which has a round plan[29].

The same subject, taken from Ripa along with other added allegories, was used in the tondo Giambattista frescoed for Palazzo Correr in Santa Fosca in Venice, with the indispensable aid of Giandomenico and Gerolamo Mengozzi for the *quadrature*. This was later removed, and finally destroyed in Cologne during World War II[30].

Lacking any real documentary evidence, we believe the frescoes painted by Giambattista in Villa Soderini in Nervesa della Battaglia belong to this same period. Executed with the extensive collaboration of his workshop, these were lost in 1917. On the ceiling, where the hand of Tiepolo *père* seems more extensively present, there is a completely literal interpretation of Ripa, without that perceptive narrative verisimilitude generally utilized by Tiepolo to mold the abstractions of iconography into a believable living story. Religion, in the center, carries the symbolic elephant, while Prudence, to the lower left, is accompanied by the 'deer with long antlers' prescribed by Ripa, and shows a second face on the nape of her neck. Tuscany, at the right, wears a mantle 'of red velvet lined with ermine' and underneath, the ancient Arno has 'a head circled by a garland of beech', following Ripa's instructions[31]. These are all symbols that would fit a late Baroque setting very nicely, but here they seem clumsy, awkward, and even incongruous in respect to Tiepolo's customary use of allegorical sources. The two 'historical' frescoes on the walls, with the *Entry into Florence of the Gonfaloniere Pier Soderini* and *Nicola Soderini sent as a Delegate to the Roman Senate*, reveal a realistic intensity and a graphic incisiveness in the faces of the characters that makes it doubtful that they are entirely autograph work. The presumed self-portrait of Giambattista on the right of the *Entry into Florence of the Gonfaloniere Pier Soderini*, in fact, does not really seem the face of a sixty-year-old man, even if it does show some unmistakable family features.

Farewell to the mainland

In the years immediately before his departure for Spain Tiepolo produced a number of works for patrons outside of Venice, as if he wanted to give a last farewell to the mainland dominions of the Serenissima.

He left a fairly routine, crowded, and even crude work, *St. Silvester the Pope Baptizing Constantine* in the church of San Silvestro in Folzano, near Brescia. This is a traditional altarpiece dedicated to the titular saint of the church, executed with the extensive assistance of Giandomenico, who must have considered it at least partly his, as he almost immediately used it as a subject for a lovely engraving, dated between 1759 and 1760[32].

On the basis of documentary evidence from the parish, and information furnished by a learned local contemporary of Tiepolo's, we know that the canvas had been commissioned in March of 1757, while he was preparing the frescoes in Villa Valmarana, but was obviously delivered only later – two years later, to be precise. Instead of an oil sketch, which he usually furnished for important works, here Tiepolo only produced a few pencil sketches (now in the Hague and in Venice). After all, he could totally trust Giandomenico, who had by then become nearly an alter ego – an ego with his own unmistakable personality when working on his own, but capable of teaming up for group efforts.

The magnificent signed altarpiece painted for the church of the Grazie in Este, was a work of an entirely different calibre. It was put into place at the end of 1759 (fig. 127). It was

[29] All the allegorical figures are scrupulously reproduced from Cesare Ripa's *Iconologia*. It has been written that the unraveling of the abstruse meaning of the two frescoes was solved in a short poem written for the occasion by the abbot Giuseppe Gennari. Actually the learned poet in his turn resorted to Ripa as well, whose work was extremely popular among the intellectual *élite* of the eighteenth-century.

[30] Photographs of the work reveal, at the outer edges, the *Glory of Princes* (lower down, with a pyramid) and *Prudence* (on the right, with a mirror).

[31] To the left of *Religion* we see *Virtue* and *Nobility*, and next to them an unidentified masculine figure, which we believe was painted by the workshop.

[32] D. Succi (1988, p. 198, 208).

a public commission for which Giambattista had prepared a high-quality oil sketch of fairly large dimensions. However, it is quite literally a preparatory sketch in that it has no autonomous life of its own, as instead do so many of the models Tiepolo produced, genuine finished works sought after by the most discriminating European collectors, not exercises that must await their completion in the final version. This final version, instead, seems dense with an almost unbearable pathos, without rhetoric, shot thorough by livid color, as if searching for a 'nocturnal effect which could be compared with the late works of Paolo Veronese, charged with a truly grieved sense of human involvement'[33].

Here we should note an aspect that may not seem entirely new, in respect to the first Venetian works after Würzburg[34]. In the foreground, both in the sketch as in the final altarpiece, there appears a grave paved in big sharp-edged blocks of stone, into which a coffin-bier has been thrown, whose chilling contents are revealed in the sketch. The dark and unadorned tomb, opens between us and the space represented as a inhibiting gap which prevents us from 'acting' that space, almost as if to distance us from that tragic scene. This seems confirmation of a Tiepolo who is much less inclined to request direct involvement or even amusement from the spectator, in the events which unfold in his painting. This is a Tiepolo afflicted by a thoughtful gravity that, as has been said, 'anticipates the late Spanish altarpieces'[35].

The *Adoration of the Magi* now in the Metropolitan Museum of Art, and the *Madonna and Child, with St. Catherine and St. John the Baptist,* today in the Hyde collection in Glen Falls, are similar in style to the monumental altarpiece of Este and therefore close in date as well (around 1758-59). The *Vision of Saint Anne,* signed and dated 1759 is another similar work, which is now in Dresden but was originally painted for the church of Santa Chiara, annexed to the Benedictine monastery of Cividale del Friuli. God the Father is similar to that in the large painting in Este. He too bears a symbolic *sphaera mundi* and poses with a broad declamatory gesture. The sketch[36] seems much fresher and more spontaneous than the finished work, which seems somewhat rigid probably because Giandomenico helped a great deal in the final stages. The 'view of the convent at Cividale' is an exquisite work[37], on the left. It recalls other inserted landscapes, treated with anti-naturalistic rapidity and an impressive sense of synthesis, seen in the *Apotheosis of St. Gaetano of Thiene,* in the *St. Fidelis of Sigmaringen and the Blessed Giuseppe da Leonessa Crushing Heresy,* and in the same *St. Thecla Delivering Este from the Plague* examined earlier.

Again in Friuli, commissioned by the Cardinal Daniele Dolfin, 'nephew of the old Patriarch'[38], Giambattista Tiepolo produced the frescoes and altarpiece in oil of the *Immaculate Conception* for the oratory of the Purità in Udine. The frescoes, including a ceiling with the *Assumption of the Virgin* and side walls with *Angels, Putti and Cherubs,* to which Giandomenico contributed eight *chiaroscuri* with a gold background on the walls[39], were paid for on 16 September 1759. Giambattista admittedly returned to earlier themes and treatments in this short cycle, such as the great flight of the Virgin at the center of the ceiling, borne by the glory of angels, which draws upon the central section of the Carmini, among other models. The *Immaculate Conception* is almost a copy of that done for the church of the Aracoeli in Vicenza so many years earlier. Yet the whole composition hovers in a limpid light, relatively undisturbed by chromatic contrasts, in which 'the figures lose their weight'[40].

If Giandomenico furnished extensive assistance for one of his father's works in the Folzano altarpiece, in the *Miracle of the Healed Foot* executed for the parish church of Mirano we face an extreme case of the division of labor within the workshop. In this work Tiepolo *père* provided the preparatory sketch while Tiepolo *fils* was responsible for the final execution. Not even the sketch, however, is one of Giambattista's better efforts. It is indeed rapid, flowing and fragmented, but the miraculously-healed figure is also rigid and kneeling spectators are even

[33] M. Levey (1986, pp. 222-225) speaks of references to Tintoretto and to the drawings by G.B. Castiglione for the figure of the Eternal Father; W.L. Barcham (1989, pp. 227-228) distinguishes the source for four of the episodes (the group with the girl child and the mother in the foreground, the man with his hands on his head, the man to the left holding his nose, and the group in the middle ground transporting a body in a sheet) in an etching by Marcantonio Raimondi taken from a drawing by Raphael, in that Pietro Testa that Tiepolo knew so well as early as the time of Massanzago (compare A. Mariuz and G. Pavanello, 1985) and finally in engravings taken from Poussin.
[34] See Ch. V, par. 1.
[35] M. Levey (1986, p. 214).
[36] Now in the Rijksmuseum in Amsterdam.
[37] M. Levey (1986, p. 221).
[38] M. Levey (1986, p. 244).
[39] A. Rizzi (1967, p. 45).
[40] A. Morassi (1955, p. 32).

119.
Apotheosis of St.
Gaetano of Thiene.
Rampazzo (Vicenza),
parish church.

120.
Nuptial Allegory. Venice,
Ca' Rezzonico.

carelessly rendered. For this sketch Giandomenico drew partly on his own inspiration, and partly on that of his father. We can certainly assign to him, in terms of conception as well, the curious man on the left who leans forward to see the young mutilated figure, the youth himself, and the strange picaresque individual with the odd hat that emerges from the right behind the saint, already seeming part of the series of grotesque drawings done by Giandomenico towards the end of his life, when he withdrew to the family villa in Zianigo after returning from Spain without his father and his brother Lorenzo[41]. Instead, his borrowings from Giambattista (although significantly altered) include the central Saint Anthony, whose pose and hard realistic modeling recalls the *St. Fidelis of Sigmaringen* in the Parma Nazionale, the large imploring female figure taken from a type which occurs frequently in Giambattista (from *Painting* under the continent of Europe in the grand staircase ceiling in Würzburg, to the *St. Thecla* in the Este altarpiece), and the bystanders in the background portrayed with sunken features and upturned eyes, that act as a choir for the 'miracle' as in many other collective scenes painted by the elder Tiepolo.

Giambattista was probably last invited to Vicenza, as always accompanied by Giandomenico, in the summer of 1760 to fresco three rooms in Palazzo Porto. His patron was Count Giambattista Orazio Porto, whose family's noble status – nobility of imperial provenance as it was awarded for military honors – had been recognized in Venice in 1730[42]. It is odd that critics have never connected the marriage of Orazio Porto, celebrated in January 1761, with Tiepolo's frescoes[43] which were evidently planned just before the actual event itself, as had happened in the *Nuptial Allegory* in the Ca' Rezzonico (figs. 120, 121), and with many other cases as well, as we will soon see in Palazzo Canossa in Verona.

Giambattista found himself again in the midst of the Vicenza cultural elite who were accustomed to concealing the real desire for social promotion within a veil of allegory. He

[41] A. Gealt, *Domenico Tiepolo. I disegni di Pulcinella*, Milan 1986. See also F. Pedrocco, *Giandomenico Tiepolo a Zianigo*, Treviso 1988, and *Ibidem, Disegni di Giandomenico Tiepolo*, Milan 1990.
[42] R. Menegozzo (1990, pp. 113-126): Menegozzo rightly emphasizes those warlike family virtues must refer to the iconography of the monochromes painted by Giandomenico in the room with the ceiling by Brusasorci.
[43] Not enough notice has been taken of this coincidence, even in Menegozzo's otherwise useful text, which does however comment on 'the wedding of Orazio Porto with Lavinia di Lodovico Porto' taking the information from the *Raccolta di memorie vicentine* by G. Mocenigo, a manuscript contained in the Biblioteca Bertoliana of Vicenza: *Ibidem*, p. 118 and n. 19 on p. 125.

121.
opposite
Detail from fig. 120.

willingly left Giandomenico to decorate the two smaller rooms with monochrome *historiae* illustrating the military prowess of the family and the embellishment of the barrel vault ceiling housing Veronese's paintings[44], keeping for himself the ceiling of the Salone (now in the Seattle Art Museum). In the past it was believed that the subject was personal, or the *Apotheosis of Orazio da Porto*, but the sumptuously-dressed figure seated between the clouds to the side of the lion has been correctly identified by Rita Menegozzo as the allegory of Valor based on Ripa's instructions. We would also add that Virtue is located above (with a laurel wreath) and a *putto* with the trumpet of Fame (even if Fame is not actually portrayed). Ignorance is seen to the left of Valor, which in the preparatory sketch (this too in the Seattle Art Museum) is chased away by a winged *putto*'s imperious gesture. Therefore the complete iconographic significance is the *Eternal Triumph of Valor Crowned by Virtue over Ignorance*.

The sketch for the ceiling of Palazzo Porto is one of the most extraordinary models ever executed by Giambattista. It also superbly represents the evolution of a particular phase in his late production, immediately before his journey to Spain. Here we refer to that aspect of his style that we have defined as 'bozzettistico' ('sketch-like'). This is a rapid, zigzagging synthesis, like a kind of shorthand, a dimension in which Giambattista moved magnificently since he understood that every form of representation – the model, the drawing, the etching, canvas or fresco – has its own rules and the same techniques and inspiring emotions cannot be applied to all of them.

While he is sketching out a small canvas – and it does not matter whether it is a preparatory sketch for a fresco or not – he knows that the execution must be faster than rational thought. The mind cannot supervise, or hold back the hand. Nor is the hand obliged to define details and enclose individual forms within set perimeters. Instead, the mind has the 'projective' task of the project, which abides by rational thought, and the hand instead is responsible for letting the instinct pour itself forth on canvas. Thus the hand must be able to move freely on paper or canvas without the control of any kind of 'super-ego', while at the same time the mind is thinking on a grand scale.

Therefore Tiepolo's immense frescoes, in which it seems that the logic of composition must melt away, instead appear to us founded on an inimitable harmonic statute, an authentic classical *concinnitas*, which is often incorrectly attributed to his status as late Baroque virtuoso. Everything is born in those brief moments in which the sketch is worked out, moments we imagine becoming more rapid as his ability evolves. This is what we see in the figure of Ignorance in the sketch for Palazzo Porto. This is nothing more than an indecipherable scrawl, a shorthand annotation very far removed from the polished and actually over-detailed image seen in the final version of the fresco[45]. Yet on the compositional plane everything is perfect. In the large-scale projection the forms of the figures may change radically, others may be added or omitted, and the shorthand notes of the model will have to be rendered decipherable, but the general balance and the internal rhythm of the composition will remain those of the sketch[46].

It is precisely this projectural perfection already reached by Giambattista in his sketches that permits us to compare other works which seem equally incomparable due to their apparent diversity – the sketches and the finished works. For example, it is obvious that *Time* in the sketch for the Palazzo Porto is comparable to the same character in the Boston painting *Time Unveiling Truth* (fig. 125)[47], which in its turn was taken from the Neptune in the Palazzo Ducale painting *Neptune Offering Gifts to Venice* (figs. 123, 124).

The last two large decorative cycles Tiepolo carried out on the Veneto mainland seem to be dated between 1761 and 1762. Their correct sequence can be better understood due to series

[44] A. Mariuz (1971, p. 122).

[45] And which should perhaps be attributed to Giandomenico because of a certain earthy heaviness.

[46] Provided, of course, that Tiepolo did not decide to change the spacing between the characters when he was translating the 1:1 scale cartoon sketch, which means it was the same size as the area to be frescoed. Then the conception process begins again almost from zero, with a new sketch, or new drawings. Finally, when he actually climbed the scaffolding to apply the cartoon to the wall, Tiepolo already knew exactly what he needed – in other words, he already had the fresco completed in his mind. This is because 'nothing is improvised in the fresco, but everything must be conducted by memory': C.B. Tiozzo (1986, p. 65).

[47] And not *Time Stealing Beauty* as it is still sometimes called without consulting Ripa.

122.
Nobility and Virtue
Accompanying Merit
towards the Temple of
Glory. Venice,
Ca' Rezzonico.

of letters examined here, an account of Tiepolo's last years in his native land. In a letter sent from Venice to Algarotti 10 May 1760, Tiepolo complained about an attack of 'extremely impertinent gout' which confined him to bed ,and was especially inconvenient because it prevented him from working on the sketch for the wall and ceiling frescoes of Villa Pisani in Stra[48]. In spite of the gout, the model mentioned (today in Angers) may have been executed in the same month[49].

Tiepolo must have spent the winter of 1760-61 in the long and challenging preparation of the studies, and then of the large full-scale cartoons to put into place as soon as permitted by the warmth of the spring of 1761. In a later letter to Algarotti, dated 16 March 1761[50], Tiepolo wrote: 'I find myself at present with many commitments, the biggest and greatest above all having to paint the reception hall of the Ca' Pisani in Stra, and especially two more paintings to be placed in a Church in Rome, laboring over, however, a great ceiling in canvas for the Court of Moscow'[51]. Probably the work in Villa Pisani was begun between the end of March and the beginning of April 1761, because in another letter to Francesco Algarotti of 4 April of that year, Giambattista said that he was already 'busy at Stra', but adds that 'I may have to go to Verona today to paint a room'[52]. This is a reference to the Palazzo dei Canossa in Verona, for whose decoration he had already been contacted the year before. Instead, he remained at Stra until September 1761, where he was able to finish the immense ceiling in only seventy-six days, though not the walls[53].

At the end of September Tiepolo was already in Verona working on the fresco of Palazzo Canossa, commissioned for the marriage of Matilde of Canossa to Count Giovanni Battista d'Arco[54]. On 28 September 1761 Giambattista wrote from Verona to the ambassador of Spain at the Republic of Venice, Duke de Montealegre, who among other things had put pressure on

[48] 'I will have to do the model for the room of Ca' Pisani, a work not so indifferent that it will keep me occupied for the course of three or four years': the letter is contained in the Museo Civico in Bassano del Grappa and was published by G. Fogolari (1942).
[49] C.B. Tiozzo (1986, p. 55).
[50] G. Fogolari (1942).
[51] Nothing is known of these two Roman works. As for the ceiling for the Tsarina, see D. Succi (1988, pp. 276-278). Regarding the relationship with other European courts, from a letter by A. Swayer, published by P. Molmenti (1909) and now lost, we know that Tiepolo apparently gave one of his works to Louis XV and that he was paid for it; Gradenigo tells us that the king of England commissioned him to paint a *Frederick of Prussia on Horseback Commanding a Victorious Army*, but we know nothing of this work either.
[52] A. De Vesme (1912).
[53] C.B. Tiozzo (1986, p. 58).
[54] P.L. Sohm (1983). The fres-

123.
Neptune Offering Gifts to Venice. Venice, Palazzo Ducale.

124.
opposite
Detail from fig. 123.

the Venetian government to allow Tiepolo to work in the service of the King of Spain, declaring that while he accepted the invitation, he still needed some time to put his affairs in order[55]. He finished the work on Palazzo Canossa by December, and at the height of winter returned to Stra to honor his commitment to the Pisani, whose walls may already have been painted with the *quadrature* of Pietro Visconti – who also followed him to Verona – but not with the paintings of Giambattista.

In a letter of 22 December 1761, sent either to the Venetian Tommaso Farsetti or to Algarotti[56], Tiepolo announced that he was in Stra to complete work which had been suspended. He also seemed resentful about being pressured by powers from above, to finish off business so that he could head out for Madrid: 'But unexpectedly called by 'those who command', I was ordered to start immediately'. In other words, he was given until February 1762 to complete everything and take his departure, which actually occurred 31 March 1762. This the eventful account of his last period spent in the Veneto. Let us now look briefly at the two works mentioned above.

The Verona fresco portrays a *Triumph of Hercules* in Pietro Visconti's stucco cornice[57]. The model is naturally the ceiling of the grand staircase at Würzburg which was scaled down into an oval because the room in Palazzo Canossa had a relatively low ceiling. In the Residenz, Tiepolo had permanently fixed the device of a double spatial feasibility – that moving downwards, made up of the great flight of the gods descending to earth, and that moving upwards, the physical act of the eyes of the mortals cast up to meet them[58]. The principal group is located in the center, with a chariot on which sits the demi-god escorted by allegories taken from Ripa (the *Glory of Princes*), from some of his dozen emblems, and from the band of the Zodiac with the *Temple of Glory*. Higher up there appear the figures of Fame and of Mercury spinning in the air, creating a sort of upside/down reversal of the figures to the far upper side of the oval, as if the whole thing were painted on the curved surface of a map of the world seen from above. Here again we see one of Tiepolo's many infractions of the boundary, limitations which he not only could not tolerate, but indeed, no longer observed.

The fresco is very similar to the later etching by Giandomenico, which bears the annotation 'in Petersburg' in the *Catalogo* of his graphic works[59]. This therefore refers to one of the four canvases sent by the Tiepolo workshop to the Tsarina Elisabeth Petrovna immediately before his departure for Spain. Giandomenico's etching reads 'Joannes Dominicus Tiepolo invenit pinxit et delineavit', which seem an unequivocal declaration of the paternity of the painting from which Giandomenico's etching is derived – also used in Giambattista's *Triumph of Hercules* – which he sent to Saint Petersburg together with three other ceiling canvases by his father[60].

For the *Apotheosis of the Pisani Family* in Stra (figs. 128, 129), which he predicted would take him years, Tiepolo called on his vast repertoire of symbols and imagination: civic and Christian virtues taken as usual from Ripa, Olympian gods, parts of earlier works (as in Würzburg), realistic and playful inspiration, and this time even portraits. This is the first time, as Adriano Mariuz has noted, that characters from history enter into Giambattista's grandiose skies[61]. In Würzburg the portrait of the Prince-Bishop was placed inside an oval cornice to allow him to stand with the other figures from that imaginary universe. There was no pretense that the flesh and blood Karl Philipp von Greiffenklau was actually standing above the continent of Europe, but his 'portrait' in the pictorial sense of the term. We might even say that Tiepolo seemed to believe that artists were the only representatives of reality with the right to be portrayed within pictorial fiction[62].

In these entries from *ancien régime* encyclopedias, there was always a danger that the sense of reality might disintegrate and be replaced by the pleasure of pure pictorial contemplation, or

coes were destroyed by bombing in 1945.

[55] E. Battisti (1960).

[56] P. Molmenti (1909).

[57] 'Originally from Lombardy, but who came to Venice when still very young and enrolled in the *Fraglia* of painters from 1750 to 1778': C.B. Tiozzo (1986, p. 60). Gerolamo Mengozzi or 'Il Colonna' was not employed by Tiepolo either here or in Stra, where he worked again with Visconti, nor was he used in Spain.

[58] Unlike the great Baroque skies, which are only composed vertically (which is why they are called 'sfondati', or 'bottomless'), Tiepolo reasoned in much more modern terms, considering interiors as spaces in which paintings and spectators can live together in a single theatrical environment.

[59] D. Succi (1988, p. 194).

[60] See note 51.

[61] A. Mariuz (1978, pp. 246-247).

[62] See, for example, Giambattista's numerous self-portraits, and later in Würzburg, the portrayal of a number of artists working on the Residenz – Giambattista himself, Giandomenico, Roth, Bossi and Balthasar Neumann – almost as if to say that 'we artists belong more to the eternal reality of painting than to the everyday world of history'.

125.
Time Unveiling Truth,
detail. Boston,
Museum of Fine Arts.

126.
Portrait of a Young
Woman with Domino
and Tricorne.
Washington, National
Gallery of Art.

be reduced to a mere display of learning. Instead Tiepolo always managed to keep his narratives from seeming absurd or unbelievable, maintaining the content both in form and substance. He managed this by threading those galleries of abstractions together with credible events, narrated in a completely theatrical evolution. This salvation was therefore achieved pictorially, since when Giambattista painted figures and scenes he was always recreating them, as if painting were itself a divinity capable of regenerating the universe. Nor does Stra escape the Pygmalion-like magic. The exaltation of the disarmed neutrality of the Republic of Venice, which here is celebrated through the glories of the Pisani family, takes shape with War literally pushed to the side of the composition – at the top, under the Four Continents – as well as Heresy, to the left, pursued by the dragon that it has evoked.

Reflecting on the portraits of children in the frescoes, Mariuz wrote: 'the fame of the family is entrusted not so much to the glorious enterprises of some ancestor, but rather to what the young heirs will accomplish in the future: the work corresponds, more than an apotheosis, to a party of goodwill, which offers an optimistic vision of the destinies of illustrious families,

127.
opposite
St. Thecla Delivering
Este from the Plague,
detail. Este (Padua),
Cathedral.

and implicitly, that of the Venetian Republic[63]. This corresponds to an implicit faith in an 'historic' future, and at the same time, coincides with the 'aspiration to a solar universe, a humanity liberated from the conditioning of history'[64]. This is the final limit of the myth of Venice as it was relived in the eighteenth century: allowing a nation, which is actually concretely hammered into historical time, to imagine itself silhouetted against an intangible and metaphysical atemporality.

When in September 1761 Tiepolo was still in Verona with the Canossa family, Count Felice Gazzola, the intermediary of Charles III of Spain, paid him a personal visit. He gave Tiepolo the outlines and measurements for the frescoes he was to execute in Madrid. Only afterwards was Tiepolo, after his return to Venice, able to throw himself completely into the model of the *Glory of Spain* for the Throne Room. From a letter of 13 March 1762, sent either to Tommaso Farsetti or to Algarotti[65], we learn that the sketch, now in the National Gallery in Washington, was finally ready. On 31 March 1762, with Giandomenico and Lorenzo, Giambattista left his native land. He would never see it again.

[63] A. Mariuz (1978, p. 247).
[64] *Ibidem*, p. 248.
[65] P. Molmenti (1909).

129.
Apotheosis of the Pisani
Family. Stra, Villa Pisani.

ARDVA QVÆ ET TOLLIS MONVMENTA
ET FLECTIER ÆVO
NESCIA TE CELEBRANT
CAROLE MAGNANIMVM

Tiepolo in Spain
1762-1770

The frescoes of the Royal Palace in Madrid

Strangely, members of both the Venetian and Spanish diplomatic corps had to visit Tiepolo personally to convince him to undertake the journey for Madrid[1]. For we must remember that Tiepolo had not received a single commission in Venice for two years, which his long stay on the mainland confirms. He was now offered an extraordinary opportunity to serve and glorify a power with a great past – something which by his own admission must have been a completely congenial undertaking – and under conditions that, one would think, he would have been able to arrange to his own advantage[2].

Yet Spain was obviously not Würzburg and even Giambattista, even though he was accompanied by his thirty-five-year-old eldest son and Lorenzo, already a promising portraitist of twenty-six, was no longer the same energetic artist of fifty-five that he had been when he left for Germany. Partly due to the relentless strain resulting from a life led always on the go, partly due to the infirmities of old age, forces seemed to conspire to keep him at home, where of course he still had a lot to do.

We must also remember that he was not at all sure what climate prevailed at this new court. It is true that they very much wanted him to come, but Tiepolo must have known that there were very different painters already working at the Spanish court. In any case, the insistence of 'he who commands' – or the inquisitor Marco Foscarini and the Spanish legation in Venice – conquered his reluctance. And so he left for Spain, together with his sons, a merchant from Padua, who was obviously an occasional traveling companion, and the sketch he had been working on during his last month in Venice.

The journey, which was long and partly by sea, lasted from 31 March to 4 June 1762. Slightly under the weather, he arrived in Madrid where he was a guest of Sebastiano Foscarini, the Venetian

[1] Giambattista, as was said earlier, was subjected to pressure from his own government in the person of the 'Supremo Inquisitore della Repubblica, Marco Foscarini': C.B. Tiozzo (1986, p. 60); especially E. Battisti (1960).
[2] Tiepolo was paid *ad annum*, on the same salary as the Neapolitan painter Corrado Giaquinto, who had worked at court until 1761, and Anton Raphael Mengs, who was active in the palace during Giambattista's stay.

130.
opposite
Detail from fig. 131.

131.
Glory of Spain, section
of the ceiling above the
original site of the
throne. Madrid,
Royal Palace.

ambassador at the court of Spain who was related to that same Marco Foscarini who had forced him into this adventure. The king and the court were in Aranjuez and not Madrid at the time. The Marquis of Esquilache, who together with the Duke de Montealegre and Count Gazzola, maintained relations between Madrid and Venice, asked the architect Francesco Sabatini to help the painter find housing fairly near the palace[3].

As in Würzburg, the job was originally limited to the frescoing of one ceiling of the Throne Room in the Royal Palace which had been finished by Sacchetti following the project by his maestro Filippo Juvarra. Any other painting commissions would remain unassigned until the first job was completed. In the meantime they asked him to paint a *Glory of Spain* (figs. 130-132). This was finished and signed in 1764 with the extensive assistance of Giandomenico and Lorenzo in the border figures, but the composition as a whole was scrupulously supervised by Giambattista.

Only when the first fresco was unveiled in 1764 did the king, who had finally returned to live in the palace, abandon his hesitant attitude and commission Tiepolo to do two other frescoes. Thus he moved on to the ceilings of the two smallest rooms, the Royal Guardroom (Cámara de los Alabarderos) where Tiepolo painted the *Glory of Aeneas,* and the Queen's antechamber (known as the 'Saleta de la Reina') where he painted the *Apotheosis of the Spanish Monarchy.* Both the frescoes, in which order is not known, occupied him for another two years, till the autumn of 1766.

Called to Würzburg, he had been asked to confer pictorial legitimacy on an imaginary medieval ceremony and a power that longed to be believed eternal, only a few decades after the pre-Enlightenment controversies of Ludovico Muratori and Pietro Giannone set against an historiography placed at the service of despots. He instead went to Madrid to place under divine

[3] P. Molmenti (1909). Unlike during his experience at Würzburg, Tiepolo was not a guest at court, and this was not the only difference in his treatment there.

132.
Glory of Spain, section
of the ceiling opposite
the original site of the
throne. Madrid,
Royal Palace.

protection – both sacred and profane, as we will see – an absolutist monarchy, a few decades after the publication of Giambattista Vico's *Scienza nuova* in which he decreed that the world of human actions 'was made by men'[4]. If in Würzburg Tiepolo had painted the last of the Baroque *Wunderkammern*, although transgressing all of their codes, in Madrid he took on a vast repertoire of mythology, allegory and religion. This was a true encyclopaedia of the *ancien régime* – or rather, not quite an encyclopaedia. In the mid-eighteenth century the great monument to the Goddess Reason had been published – it was perhaps the only allegory that Tiepolo wasn't aware of – and in Madrid he created his own counter-encyclopaedia, in which he gathered and revived for the last time the splendor of a universe at its twilight.

The palace was new and the Throne Room long and narrow like that in Palazzo Clerici, and its ceiling was even higher, which must have made a unified and simultaneous perception of the whole even more difficult. But while Giambattista Tiepolo must have striven, as always, for a pictorially consistent and harmonious rendering of the whole, it is probable that the king would have been satisfied with just the representation of his glories and the fact that they were being painted by that celebrated Venetian. Bourbon Spain was, according to Giorgio Spini, an 'incarnation of ecclesiastic privilege'.

Yet while Charles III had worried about founding his reign on a rigid absolutist framework during his ascent to the throne (1759), he also was beginning a system of reformist policies, at least in an economic sense, and later was even to distance Spain from the Jesuits. But the formal overall representation of his power in the new royal palace was a completely different matter. He wanted it to refer to the American colonies, religion, peace and the gods of Olympus. Tiepolo, in agreement with the court iconography that he had been sent in September of 1761, chose to set the celebration of the present Spanish monarchy in the world of imperial sixteenth-century

[4] Perhaps this is why Tiepolo's skies remain stubbornly empty in the center.

133.
St. Francis of Assisi
Receiving the Stigmata.
Madrid, Prado.

134.
opposite
Detail from fig. 133.

myth – and who better than a subject of the Serenissima could have conceived and executed such a program? In other words, he had to emphasize the current power wielded by the Bourbons through the memory of the Hapsburg Charles V.

Rising from the bottom to the top, the sketch portrays the allegory of the *Glory of Princes*, with the pyramid, flanked by other secular virtues. One new feature is that they are accompanied by three theological Virtues: the sacred and the profane. The Throne of Spain appears above, between the statues of Hercules (replaced by Minerva in the fresco) and Apollo. Next comes Fame, and in the upper right two columns are seen. These are evidently the pillars of Hercules which, in addition to the American possessions of the crown, explicitly refer to the personal motto of Charles V, 'Plus ultra'. The whole is surrounded by the four continents of the earth.

As regards the sketch, there are noticeable variations introduced in the translation into fresco, but, dealing with a closely linked project, the balance of the whole does not change much. Levey's accusation – that the fresco, in the end, 'remains perhaps more a matter of effective detail than a totally coherent, impressing whole'[5] – actually seems somewhat unfair. As mentioned earlier, it was only in 1764, once the ceiling of the Throne Room was finished, that Tiepolo received the commission to fresco two other ceilings for the Royal Guardroom and the Queen's antechamber, which kept him and his sons occupied for another two years until 1766.

Tiepolo painted the *Apotheosis of Aeneas* on the ceiling of the Royal Guardroom, prepared from the two sketches in Boston and Cambridge. The first, a beautiful work but ill-suited for translation into fresco given the crowding of the figures, was definitely turned down. The second, with much broader airier rhythms, is very close to the final version in which, from the top, appear the same Mercury from the grand staircase of Würzburg, then the group of Venus approached by the Trojan hero escorted by Virtue and Valor, while in the descending spiral whirl Time can be seen with his scythe and hourglass, and Vulcan at his forge intent on creating weapons for Aeneas. However, in spite of repeated attempts at formal and compositional correction, Levey is right when he says that the *Apotheosis of Aeneas* is 'very much a picture hung on the ceiling rather than illusionistic in the manner of his great ceilings'[6].

The *Apothesis of the Spanish Monarchy* frescoed on the ceiling of the 'Saleta' is more interesting, it too prepared from two sketches (both in New York). Tiepolo took both sketches into account for this version, extracting the best aspects of each. The final result is the central monarchical allegory on which, following Charles III's pacifist leanings, the god Apollo reigns triumphant. This is the last Apollo ever painted by Giambattista Tiepolo. In the lower left, after the four continents of the earth, and Neptune with the riches of the sea, a mighty Hercules seems to want to uproot one of the columns he placed at the mouth of the Mediterranean, as if to open the Ocean up to Spain and sound forth the sixteenth-century 'Plus ultra' of Charles V. Mars and Venus are found on the right, conversing with each other like two courtesans near the throne. Father Jove is relegated into a secluded spot, while Time, confused, withdraws to the right. Apparently Tiepolo only needed Apollo to eclipse the rest of Olympus.

Tiepolo had dealt, up to this point, almost exclusively with the King's secretary, Miguel de Múzquiz. The idea of meeting the King himself had not even been broached, even if he was receiving an excellent salary and he had been encouraged by the King's appreciation, shown by the new commissions he had been given. The king's confessor, the Franciscan Joaquín de Eleta, also still refused to see him at times, and followed Charles III about like a shadow. Possibly encouraged by Joaquín de Eleta, the King admired Anton Raphael Mengs, his *primer pintor* who succeeded Corrado Giaquinto and was working in different parts of the palace. Mengs represented that Neoclassical taste that was becoming increasingly popular at court and which, historically speaking, was diametrically opposed to the style of Giambattista. Mengs 'made

[5] M. Levey (1986, p. 262).
[6] *Ibidem*, p. 265.

135.
St. Peter of Alcántara.
Madrid, Royal Palace.

overleaf
136.
Abraham and the
Angels. Madrid, Prado.

137.
Detail from fig. 136.

a good representative of Rome, as opposed to the Venice represented by Tiepolo[7]. Here we witness two different historical and artistic eras encountering each other in the same place and at the same time, although it was not necessarily a hostile, dishonest or envious clash[8]. In spite of all this, after Tiepolo had finished the two smaller rooms, he offered his services to the Spanish king in January of the next year, as he certainly knew how to work in oil as well. It is actually odd that he had to remind the King of this himself. After some resistance in circles close to the king, Tiepolo was granted the commission for the seven Aranjuez altarpieces, finished in the summer of 1769, which we will discuss in the next section.

The seven Aranjuez paintings

Once the frescoes for the Royal Palace were finished, Tiepolo wrote to Miguel de Múzquiz in January of 1767, to offer to stay in Spain in the service of Charles III, and paint the altarpieces for the church of San Pascual Baylon that the king had been building for several years near Aranjuez[9] (figs. 133-135). This church was the first religious enterprise promoted by the crown, and it was annexed to the monastery of the Franciscan order of Alcantarines, founded by the Spanish St. Pedro d'Alcántara. Padre Eleta, the king's confessor, was also a member of the order. Built between 1765 and 1770, the church was a small and elegant building designed by the Neapolitan architect Marcel Fanton, with the financial supervision of Francesco Sabatini, who kept up relations with Padre Eleta and therefore with the court[10]. He had to wait some time for a response, which did not come until March of 1767. When it did, it arrived with the proviso that the sketches had to be approved by the King before making the assignment official. Between April and August of the same year Tiepolo prepared the sketches and sent them for approval to Sant'Ildefonso, where the King was then staying. Tiepolo would certainly have preferred to go himself to Sant'Ildefonso, near La Granja, but he was dissuaded, and the sketches had to be sufficient. In any case, the King was pleased with them and although it was not until a month later, he gave his consent that the work be executed[11].

Tiepolo set to work with the assistance of Giandomenico and Lorenzo, and by 29 August 1769 he was able to announce that the seven canvases were finished, and he was only awaiting instructions as the church was not yet finished. The cycle represents Tiepolo's last effort in religious painting and demonstrates the degree of his internalization of sacred themes reached in his final phase – even before arriving in Spain. We no longer find scenes with many characters plunged into an air thick with clouds and incense, perhaps with expressions more emphatic than devoted, supported by a sparkling sfumato style; nor do we find ostentatiously learned quotations, with classical inserts and elegant architecture bent on recalling religious themes, in a quest that reaches the limits of secular painting. Here the characters are solitary heroes who conduct silent dialogues with their own consciences: 'All were conceived, no doubt as instructed, in meditative and not dramatic terms'[12].

As in so many of his other works, the foreground is occupied by objects that either belong to everyday life, such as the carpenter's tools in the *St. Joseph and the Christ Child* and the frayed reed-matting in the *St. Francis of Assisi Receiving the Stigmata*, or the world of nature, such as the touching flowered scene on the right in *St. Pascual Baylon Adoring the Holy Sacrament* and those unforgettable distant blue and white of the mountains, seen to the left in the sketch of the same *St. Francis* now in London, and seen again in other small-scale paintings of mysteriously enigmatic landscapes from this very last phase. 'Perhaps the truest Tiepolo is to be found in the series of religious works for the church of Aranjuez, in which the landscape predominates like an echo of emotions, like a confession of insecurity and anguish'[13]. Because of this humble and deeply felt humanization, the foreground of the painting extends out into the space of the

[7] *Ibidem*, pp. 260-261.
[8] C. Whistler's work (1986) has done much to discredit the 'myth of hostility' assumed by many critics regarding Tiepolo's life at the Spanish court.
[9] G.M. Urbani de Gheltof (1981, p. 7); F.J. Sanchez Cantón (1953).
[10] C. Whistler (1985).
[11] E. Battisti (1960).
[12] M. Levey (1986, p. 272).
[13] A. Pallucchini (1966, p. 85).

138.
opposite
Flight into Egypt (by Boat). Lisbon, Museu Nacional de Arte Antigua.

spectators, involving them in 'that mood of quietism and poignant humanity which seems characteristic of his last years'[14].

Charles III would certainly have preferred something more conventional and less challenging in terms of emotional impact, as well as more rational and comprehensible on the plane of conscience. As we will see, he was to opt for the much less embarrassing Neoclassical academics. When they were first put in their positions in May 1770, the paintings were arranged in the following order: the two ovals with *St. Antony of Padua* and the *St. Peter of Alcántara* were placed in the side chapels of the entrance, respectively to the left and right, the *St. Joseph* and the *St. Charles Borromeo* must have been hung over the middle altars of the church, to the left and the right, but the latter does not even seem to have been hung, and the *St. Francis* and the *Immaculate Conception* were placed on the transept altars, to the left and the right. But this only occurred when the church of San Pascual was consecrated, as we have said, in May of 1770. Until then the paintings remained in Tiepolo's studio. Once he had finished them he waited for instructions regarding their display, and finally wrote directly to Padre Eleta, whose judgement he feared, to urge him to make some sort of comment. He did not even bother to respond. Tiepolo interpreted his silence as an implicit rejection, and decided to try another approach. He wrote directly to Múzquiz, who had always been his quickest intermediary for reaching the King[15].

In a letter of 29 August 1769 to Miguel de Múzquiz, who had become minister of finance after the death of the Marquis of Esquilache, Tiepolo confessed his fears about Padre Eleta, hoping that Múzquiz would make sure that the king approved the paintings for their final placement. These fears proved to be unfounded, since Charles III himself a few days later assured him by return of post of his most profound satisfaction regarding the work done. In addition, he gave Tiepolo 'a clear sign of approval by providing him with a further religious commission, the decoration of the dome of the collegiate church of Sant'Ildefonso at La Granja'[16]. However, the paintings definitely remained in Tiepolo's studio in Madrid and were nearly all placed on their altars only in May 1770 for the occasion of the church's consecration.

In the meantime, however, Tiepolo died suddenly on 27 March 1770. Some months later, in November 1770, the king ordered the replacement of his works with paintings of identical subjects by Mengs (for the high altar) and by his followers Francisco Bayeu and Mariano Salvador Maella: 'The picturesque realism and the stark devotional spirit of Tiepolo's late altarpieces must have jarred, to the King's eye, on the altars of his first religious foundation in Spain'[17]. Tiepolo's canvases remained in San Pascual Baylon until 1775 and only then, in a dramatically different aesthetic climate, as much changed as the King's beliefs, were they replaced by the works Charles III had ordered from Mengs and his school[18].

Other Spanish paintings: the final works

There are few works from Tiepolo's Spanish period that critics unanimously agree are separate from his work in the Royal Palace and the Alcantarine church of San Pascual Baylon. It is obvious that the two royal commissions completely absorbed Tiepolo and his sons, which was partly a result of the severely centralized policies of Charles III, which decreed that future works always depended on the success of earlier ones. The King wanted to control everything personally, from sketches to finished work, and each phase was considered concluded only when it had received the seal of his august approval. The bureaucratic process was thus lengthy and tedious, and Tiepolo constantly felt dependent on the crown, as he generally worked through a chain of intermediaries – court dignitaries and other functionaries – required by court rules. This was also the case of the third royal commission received by Tiepolo, a project to fresco the cupola of the collegiate

[14] M. Levey (1986, p. 272).
[15] In C. Whistler's 1986 article, she attributes Padre Eleta's reserve to resentment over what he saw as Tiepolo's breach of etiquette, since the confessor had chosen Francesco Sabatini as his intermediary for church-related matters, and felt that he should not have been contacted personally by Tiepolo.
[16] C. Whistler (1986, p. 202).
[17] *Ibidem.*
[18] H. Braham (1981).

139.
Rest on the Flight
into Egypt. Stuttgart,
Staatsgalerie.

church of Sant'Ildefonso at La Granja, in harsh Meseta. The frescoes were to be placed in Francesco Sabatini's stuccoes. More precisely, Sabatini, who from Madrid maintained contact between the artists active in the capital and the itinerant court, was to plan the drawings for the cornices to send or bring to the King for his customary preliminary approval, and only afterwards would Tiepolo receive the official confirmation. Giambattista himself was going through an anxious phase of uncertainty. At home he had the Aranjuez altarpieces finished and he had no idea if, how, and when they would be put into place. This was also the time when he committed his breach of etiquette by writing directly to Padre Eleta. Thus his satisfaction must have been all the greater when he heard, on 2 September 1769, that not only was the King pleased with his seven paintings for the church of San Pascual Baylon, but had also given his imprimatur for the new frescoes for Sant'Ildefonso. He immediately began to prepare the drawings for the four Evangelists to be painted on the pendentive imposts of the cupola[19]. He then set to work on the preparatory sketch for the *Triumph of Faith*, or more accurately, the *Triumph of the Immaculate*, today in the National Gallery of Dublin, which Catherine Whistler has definitively linked to the Sant'Ildefonso project[20]. The winter of 1769-70 had now arrived and the frescoes would have to wait for the return of good weather. Tiepolo, however, would not live to see the next spring, and the work was given to Bayeu two years later. We think that several works executed by Tiepolo for a patron outside the circle of Charles III can be assigned only to this brief period, in accordance with the dates proposed by Anna Pallucchini[21].

The last secular work painted by Giambattista was *Venus Entrusting Cupid to Time*, once in Lisbon. Levey believes that the painting must have been executed somewhere around February of 1768 since it was around this date that a nephew of Charles III was born, the future Emperor of Austria Francis II[22]. It seems a plausible hypothesis, since the royal insignia of Spain features an eagle between two columns with the motto 'Plus ultra', which is what we see here with only the motto omitted. However, if this was really the inspiration for the small Lisbon painting, it is still linked to the court and its ceremonies.

On the other hand, some religious paintings which date back to this period seem to reflect the votive sentiments of more reserved patrons, when they weren't actually works that Giambattista painted for himself. Here we are not referring to *Abraham and the Angels* in the Prado (figs. 136, 137), a large-scale work in which Tiepolo even seemed to be aware of the Neoclassical approach of Raphael Mengs, which must have been intended for an educated public. Instead, these works must have been the *Abraham and the Angels* and the *Annunciation*, in Pedrola (figs. 141, 142), the *Deposition in the Sepulchre* in Lisbon, and the *Deposition from the Cross* in Zurich. These are all small pieces but should be considered finished paintings, not preparatory sketches. These are works in which a beautifully proportioned sense of domestic sweetness alternates with a silent sense of interior meditation, revolving around themes relevant to Tiepolo's deepest feelings. As Terisio Pignatti writes of the Zurich *Deposition*: 'and Mary, finally a mother, raises her eyes to the heavens where the storm is already giving way to a blue sky, to ask why her son is lying dead in her lap'[23]. Even more touching, on an autobiographical level, are the four small variations on the *Flight into Egypt* (figs. 138-140). Could these have revealed an unconscious repressed desire to flee from Madrid? These are obviously bitter works, which open up – especially in the Stuttgart and New York versions – onto a miserable embittered landscape, giving us a glimpse of what may be tormenting homesickness. But on 27 March 1770 Giambattista Tiepolo died suddenly in the house in the parish of San Martin in Madrid where he had spent nearly his entire Spanish sojourn[24]. He was buried in the same church of San Martin[25]. The church and his tomb no longer exist.

The news reached Venice on 21 April 1770[26].

[19] P.E. Muller (1977).
[20] C. Whistler (1985).
[21] A. Pallucchini (1968, pp. 132-135).
[22] M. Levey (1986, p. 267).
[23] T. Pignatti (1951, p. 18).
[24] His illness and death were so sudden and unexpected that, according to the death certificate published by G.M. Urbani de Gheltof (1879, pp. 39-42): 'He was not able to receive the Holy Sacraments'.
[25] C. Whistler (1986, pp. 202-203).
[26] P. Gradenigo (1748-1774); A. Pallucchini (1968, p. 84).

140.
opposite
Detail from fig. 139.

141.
opposite
Abraham and the
Angels. Pedrola
(Portugal), Collection
of the Duchess of
Villahermosa.

142.
Annunciation.
Pedrola (Portugal),
Collection of the
Duchess of Villahermosa.

Select Bibliography

GLI AFFRESCHI NELLE VILLE VENETE dal Seicento all'Ottocento, ed. R. Pallucchini, 2 vols., Venice 1978.

AIKEMA B., "Early Tiepolo Studies. I. The Ospedaletto Problem", Mitteilungen des Kunsthistorischen Institutes in Florenz, XXVI (1982), pp. 339-381.

AIKEMA B., "Nicolò Bambini e Giambattista Tiepolo nel salone di Palazzo Sandi a Venezia", Arte Veneta (1986), pp. 167-171.

AIKEMA B., "Le decorazioni di palazzo Barbaro Curtis a Venezia fino alla metà del Settecento", Arte Veneta (1987), pp. 147-154.

AIKEMA B., 'Quattro note su Giovanni Battista Tiepolo giovane", Mitteilungen des Kunsthistorischen Institutes in Florenz, XXXI, 2/3 (1987), pp. 441-454.

AIKEMA B., "La pittura a Venezia nel Settecento", in La Pittura in Italia. Il Settecento, Milan 1989.

AIKEMA B. and D. MEIJERS, Nel regno dei poveri. Arte e storia dei grandi ospedali veneziani in età moderna. 1474-1797, Venice 1989.

ALGAROTTI F., Opere, Pisa 1764 and Venice 1791.

ARSLAN E., "Gian Battista Tiepolo e G.M. Morlaiter ai Gesuati", Rivista di Venezia, XI (1932), pp. 19-26.

ASHTON M., "Allegory, Fact and Meaning in Giambattista Tiepolo's Four Continents at Würzburg", The Art Bulletin (1978), pp. 109-125.

ASSUNTO R., "Iconismo e aniconismo", in EUA, Novara 1980-82.

ATTI del congresso internazionale di studi sul Tiepolo / Udine 1970, Milan 1972.

AVAGNINA M.E., F. RIGON and R. SCHIAVO, Tiepolo. Le ville vicentine Milan 1990.

BARBIERI F., Illuministi e neoclassici a Vicenza, Vicenza 1972.

BARCHAM W.L., "Giambattista Tiepolo's Ceiling for S. Maria di Nazareth: Legend, Traditions, and Devotions", The Art Bulletin, 61 (1979), pp. 430-447.

BARCHAM W.L., "The Cappella Sagredo in San Francesco della Vigna", Artibus et Historiae, 7 (1983), pp. 101-124.

BARCHAM W.L., "Patriarchy and Politics: Tiepolo's 'Galleria Patriarcale' in Udine Revisited", in Interpretazioni veneziane. Studi di storia dell'arte in onore di Michelangelo Muraro, ed. D. Rosand, Venice 1984, pp. 427-438.

BARCHAM W.L., The Religious Paintings of Giambattista Tiepolo. Piety and Tradition in Eighteenth-Century Venice, Oxford 1989.

BARCHAM W.L., Tiepolo, New York 1992.

BASSI E., Palazzi di Venezia. Admiranda Urbis Venetae, Venice 1976.

BATTISTI E., "Postille documentarie su artisti italiani a Madrid e sulla collezione Maratta", Arte Antica e Moderna, 9 (1960), pp. 77-89.

BOHNLEIN K., "Page und Prinzessin: zwei Studien Giovanni Battista Tiepolos zum Hochzeitsbild in der Würzburger Residenz", Welt-Kunst, 11 (1986), pp. 1574-1575.

BONORA E., "Introduction" to F. Algarotti, Dialoghi sopra l'ottica neutoniana, Turin 1977.

BORTOLAN G., "Asterischi d'archivio per il '700 veneziano", Notizie da Palazzo Albani, 3 (1973), pp. 51-53.

BRAHAM H., The Princes Gate Collection, catalogue, London 1981, pp. 75-81.

BROWN B.L., Giambattista Tiepolo Master of the oil sketch, Milan-New York 1993.

BÜTTNER F., "Die Sonne Frankens – Ikonographie des Freskos im Treppenhaus der Würzburger Residenz", Münchner Jahrbuch der bildenden Kunst (1979), pp. 159-186.

BÜTTNER F. and W.-CH. VON DER MÜLBE, Giovanni Battista Tiepolo. Die Fresken in der Residenz zu Würzburg, (1980) It. ed. Milan 1981.

CAPPELLI A., Dizionario di abbreviature latine ed italiane, Milan 1929.

CARTARI V., Imagini delli dei de gl'antichi, Venice 1556.

CHIARELLI R., I Tiepolo alla Villa Valmarana, Florence 1965.

COCHIN N., Voyage d'Italie, Paris 1758.

COLETTI L., Treviso, Bergamo 1926.

COVA M., Palazzo Valle. Gli affreschi ritrovati di G.B. Tiepolo, Vicenza 1986.

COVA M., "Vicenza: Palazzo Valle-Marchesini-Sala. Scoperta e restauro di un ciclo di affreschi (G.B. Tiepolo – G. Mengozzi Colonna)", Arte Veneta (1987), pp. 258-259.

DA CANAL V., Vita di Gregorio Lazzarini (1732), ed. G.A. Moschini, Venice 1809.

DA MOSTO A., I dogi di Venezia nella vita pubblica e privata, Milan 1966.

DANIELS J., Sebastiano Ricci, Hove 1976.

D'ARCAIS F., "Una villa affrescata da Nicolò Bambini", Arte Veneta, XX (1967).

DE VESME A., "Paralipomeni tiepoleschi", in Scritti vari di erudizione e di critica in onore di R. Renier, Turin 1912.

FOGOLARI G., *G.B. Tiepolo nel Veneto*, Milan 1913.
FOGOLARI G., "Lettere inedite a Francesco Algarotti", *Nuova Antologia*, 1621 (1942), pp. 32-37.
FREEDEN M.H. VON and C. LAMB, *Das Meisterwerk des Giovanni Battista Tiepolo. Die Fresken der Würzburger Residenz*, Munich 1956.
FREEDEN M.H. VON and C. LAMB, *Tiepolo. Die Fresken der Würzburger Residenz*, Munich 1956.

GALLI C., *Aspetti delle relazioni artistiche tra Francia e Venezia nel primo Settecento*, Dissertation, University of Venice, 1987-88.
GEALT A., *Domenico Tiepolo. I disegni di Pulcinella*, Milan 1986.
GEMIN, M., "L'Adria festosa per Federico Cristiano", in *L'invenzione del gusto*, ed. G. Morelli, Milan 1982, pp. 319-410.
GORDON D.G., *The Renaissance Imagination*, Berkeley 1975 (It. ed. 1987).
GRADENIGO P., "Notatori ed annali del N.H. Pietro Gradenigo 1748-1774, ms. della B.N.M. e della B.M.C. di Venezia", ed. L. Livan, *Regia Deputazione di Storia Patria*, V (1942).
GROPPO A., *Catalogo di tutti i drammi per musica recitati nei teatri di Venezia*, Venice 1745.
GUERRINI R., "Il Tiepolo e la stanza del Tasso a Villa Valmarana", in *Torquato Tasso tra letteratura, musica, teatro e arti figurative*, ed. A. Buzzoni, Bologna 1985, pp. 345-355.

HASKELL F., *Patrons and Painters*, London 1963. It. ed. *Mecenati e pittori. Studio sui rapporti tra arte e società italiana nell'età barocca*, II ed. (enlarged), Florence 1985.
HOWARD D., "Giambattista Tiepolo's Frescoes for the Church of the Pietà in Venice", *Oxford Art Journal*, 9 (1986), pp. 11-28.

ISHERWOOD, R.M., *Music in the Service of the King of France in the Seventeenth Century*, Ithaca and London 1973.
IVANOFF N., "Giambattista Mariotti", in *Bollettino del Museo Civico di Padova*, 1942-54.

JOHNSON JORDAN S., "The Iconography of the Sala Rossa Frescoes by Tiepolo", *Arte Veneta* (1985), pp. 170-173.

KNOX G., "Tiepolo and the Ceiling of the Scalzi", *The Burlington Magazine*, 110 (1968), pp. 394-398.
KNOX G., "Tiepolo: A Bicentenary Exhibition 1770-1970, Fogg Art Museum – Harvard University", Cambridge 1970.
KNOX G., "Giambattista Tiepolo: Variations on the Theme of Antony and Cleopatra", *Master Drawings*, 4 (1974), pp. 378-389.
KNOX G., "The Tasso Cycles of Giambattista Tiepolo and Giannantonio Guardi", *Museum Studies* (Art Institute of Chicago), 9 (1978), pp. 49-95.
KNOX G., "Giambattista Tiepolo: Queen Zenobia and Ca' Zenobio: 'una delle prime sue fatture'", *The Burlington Magazine*, CXXI (1979), pp. 409-418.
KNOX G., "Antony and Cleopatra in Russia. A Problem in the Editing of Tiepolo Drawings", *Editing Illustrated Books* (1980), pp. 35-55.

KNOX G., *Giambattista and Domenico Tiepolo. A Study and Catalogue Raisonné of the Chalk Drawings*, Oxford 1980.

LANZI L., *Storia pittorica della Italia*, Bassano 1795-96.
LAVROVA O., "Le tele di Giambattista Tiepolo nel Museo Statale di Belle Arti A.S. Pushkin (Mosca)", in *Atti del congresso internazionale di studi sul Tiepolo / Udine 1970*, Milan 1972, pp. 124-130.
LEVEY M., "Tiepolo's *Empire of Flora*", *The Burlington Magazine* (1957), pp. 89-91.
LEVEY M., *Painting in XVIII Venice*, London 1959.
LEVEY M., "Two Paintings by Tiepolo from the Algarotti Collection", *The Burlington Magazine* (1960), pp. 250-257.
LEVEY M., *Painting in XVIII Century Venice*, London 1980.
LEVEY M., *Giambattista Tiepolo. His Life and Art*, New Haven and London 1986.
LORENZETTI G. (ed.), *Tiepolo*, exhibition catalogue, Venice 1951.

MARIACHER G., "Nota sulla pala di Rampazzo di G.B. Tiepolo", *Arte Veneta* (1950), pp. 153-154.
MARINELLI S., "Giambattista Tiepolo", in *La pittura a Verona tra Sei e Settecento*, catalogue, ed. L. Magagnato, Verona 1978, pp. 217-221.
MARIUZ A., *Giandomenico Tiepolo*, Venice 1971.
MARIUZ A., *L'opera completa del Piazzetta*, Introduction by R. Pallucchini, Milan 1982.
MARIUZ A., Entries in *Gli affreschi nelle ville venete dal Seicento all'Ottocento*, ed. R.Pallucchini, 2 vols., Venice 1978.
MARIUZ A. and G. PAVANELLO, "I primi affreschi di Giambattista Tiepolo", *Arte Veneta*, XXXIX (1985), pp. 101-113.
MARIUZ A. and G. PAVANELLO, "Scoperto il primo affresco di Giambattista Tiepolo", *Il Giornale dell'Arte*, October 1985, p. 3.
MARIUZ A. and G. PAVANELLO, *La chiesa settecentesca di Biadene e il primo affresco di Giambattista Tiepolo*, Biadene 1988.
MARTINI E., *La pittura veneziana del Settecento*, Venice 1964.
MARTINI E., "I ritratti di Ca' Cornaro di Giovan Battista Tiepolo giovane", *Notizie da Palazzo Albani*, I (1974), pp. 30-35.
MARTINI E., *La pittura del Settecento veneto*, Maniago 1982.
MAZZARIOL G. and T. PIGNATTI, *Itinerario tiepolesco*, Venice 1951.
MEISSNER F.H., *Tiepolo*, Leipzig 1897.
MENEGOZZO R., *Nobili e Tiepolo a Vicenza. L'artista e i suoi committenti*, Vicenza 1990.
MIARI F., *Il nuovo patriziato veneto dopo la Serrata del Maggior Consiglio e la guerra di Candia e Morea*, Venice 1891.
MION D., *Francesco Algarotti mecenate e conoscitore d'arte*, Dissertation, University of Venice, 1980-81.
MOLMENTI P., *Les Fresques de Tiepolo dans la Villa Valmarana*, Venice 1880 (It. ed. 1928).
MOLMENTI P., *G.B. Tiepolo. La sua vita e le sue opere*, Milan n.d. (but 1909).
MORASSI A., "The Young Tiepolo", *The Burlington Magazine*, LXIV (1934), pp. 86-92.
MORASSI A., "G.B. e G.D. Tiepolo alla Villa Valmarana", *Le Arti* (1941).
MORASSI A., "Novità e precisazioni sul Tiepolo", *Le Arti* (1941-42).
MORASSI A., *Tiepolo. La villa Valmarana*, Milan 1945.
MORASSI A., "Giambattista e Domenico Tiepolo alla villa Valmarana", *Le Arti* (1951).
MORASSI A., *G.B. Tiepolo*, London 1955.
MORASSI A., "Some 'Modelli' and Other Unpublished Works by Tiepolo", *The Burlington Magazine*, XCVII (1955), pp. 4-12.
MORASSI A., *A Complete Catalogue of the Paintings of G.B. Tiepolo*, London 1962.
MORASSI A., "A Scuola del Nudo by Tiepolo", *Master Drawings*, 1 (1971), pp. 43-50.
MORETTI L., "Notizie e appunti su G.B. Piazzetta, alcuni piazzetteschi e G.B. Tiepolo", *Atti dell'Istituto Veneto di Scienze, Lettere ed Arti*, 143 (1984-85), pp. 359-395.
MORETTI L., "La data degli Apostoli della chiesa di San Stae", *Arte Veneta*, XXVII (1973), pp. 318-395.
MULLER P.E., "Francisco Bayeu, Tiepolo and the Trinitarian Dome Frescoes of the Colegiata at La Granja", *Pantheon* (1977), pp. 20-28.
MURARO M., "Ricerche su Tiepolo giovane", *Atti dell'Accademia di Scienze, Lettere e Arti di Udine*, IX (1970-72), pp. 5-64.
MURARO M., "Giovanni Battista Tiepolo tra Ricci e Piazzetta", *Atti del congresso internazionale di studi su Sebastiano Ricci e il suo tempo*, Venice 1975, pp. 59-65.

NIERO A., *La Scuola Grande dei Carmini*, Venice 1963.
NIERO A., "Giambattista Tiepolo alla Scuola dei Carmini: Precisazioni d'archivio", *Atti dell'Istituto Veneto di Scienze, Lettere ed Arti*, CXXXV (1976-77), pp. 373-391.
NIERO A., *Tre artisti per un tempio, S. Maria del Rosario – Gesuati*, Padua 1979.
NIERO A., *Guida alla chiesa di Santa Maria della Pietà a Venezia*, Venice 1988.
NIERO A., *Venezia. La Scuola Grande dei Carmini. Storia e arte*, Venice 1991.

PALLUCCHINI A., *L'opera completa di Giambattista Tiepolo*, Milan 1968.
PALLUCCHINI A., *Giambattista Tiepolo*, Milan 1971.
PALLUCCHINI R., *Gli affreschi di Giambattista e Giandomenico Tiepolo alla villa Valmarana di Vicenza*, Bergamo 1945.
PALLUCCHINI R., *La pittura nel Veneto. Il Settecento*, vol. 1, Milan 1994.
PALLUCCHINI R., *La pittura veneziana del Settecento*, Venice – Rome 1960.
PALLUCCHINI R., "Note alla Mostra di pittura veneziana a Varsavia", *Pantheon*, 1968.
PALLUCCHINI R., *La pittura veneziana del Seicento*, 2 vols., Milan 1981.
PALLUCCHINI R., "Il 'Modelletto' della pala camerte di Giambattista Tiepolo", *Notizie da Palazzo Albani*, 1-2 (1983), pp. 261-263.
PALLUCCHINI R. (ed.), *Giambattista Piazzetta. Il suo tempo, la sua scuola*, Venice 1983.
PAVANELLO G., "Un progetto di Girolamo Mengozzi Colonna per Giambattista Tiepolo: 'La Salla per il N.H. Vicenzo Pisani alla Mira'", *Bollettino dei Musei Civici Veneziani*, 1/4 (1979), pp. 52-59.
PEDROCCO F., "Giambattista Tiepolo illustratore di libri", in *Giambattista Tiepolo il segno e l'enigma*, ed. D. Succi, Ponzano Veneto 1986, pp. 64-76.
PEDROCCO F., *Giandomenico Tiepolo a Zianigo*, Treviso 1988.
PEDROCCO F., *Disegni di Giandomenico Tiepolo*, Milan 1990.
PIAI M., "Il 'Veronese revival' nella pittura veneziana del

Settecento", *Atti dell'Istituto Veneto di Scienze Lettere ed Arti*, CXXXIII (1974-75), pp. 295-312.

PIGNATTI T., *Tiepolo*, Verona 1951.

PIGNATTI T., *I disegni veneti del Settecento*, Treviso 1965.

PIGNATTI T., *Le acqueforti dei Tiepolo*, Florence 1965.

PIGNATTI T., *Tiepolo*, Brescia 1967.

PIGNATTI T., *Le acqueforti dei Tiepolo*, Florence 1979.

PIGNATTI T. and F. PEDROCCO, *Veronese. Catalogo completo dei dipinti*, Florence 1991.

PIGNATTI T., F. PEDROCCO and E. MARTINELLI PEDROCCO, *Palazzo Labia a Venezia*, Turin 1982.

PILO G.M., Entry "Gregorio Lazzarini", in *La pittura del Seicento a Venezia*, exhibition catalogue, Venice 1959.

PILO G.M., "Fresenze di Nicola Grassi all'Ospedaletto", *Il Noncello* (1982).

POMIAN K., *Collectionneurs, amateurs et curieux, Paris, Venise: XVIe-XVIIIe siècle*, Paris 1989 (It. ed. 1989).

POSSE H., "Die Briefe des Grafen Francesco Algarotti an der Sachsischen Hof und seine Bilderkaufe für die Dresdner Gemäldegalerie, 1743-1747", *Prussian Jahrbuch* (1931), pp. 1-71.

PRADELLA G., *La decorazione pittorica di ca' Dolfin*, Dissertation, University of Venice, 1979-80.

PRECERUTTI GARBERI M., *Affreschi settecenteschi delle Ville Venete*, Milan 1968.

PRECERUTTI GARBERI M., *Giambattista Tiepolo gli affreschi*, Turin 1971.

PUPPI L., "Carlo Cordellina committente d'artisti. Novità ed appunti su G. Massari, G.B. Tiepolo, F. Guardi, F. Lorenzi e O. Calderari", *Arte Veneta*, XXIII (1968), pp. 212-217.

PUPPI L., "I 'nani' di villa Valmarana a Vicenza", *Antichità Viva*, 2 (1968), pp. 34-48.

PUPPI L., "I Tiepolo a Vicenza e le statue dei 'nani' di villa Valmarana a S. Bastiano", *Atti dell'Istituto Veneto di Scienze Lettere ed Arti*, CXXVI (1968), pp. 211-250.

RIPA C., *Iconologia*, Rome 1593.

RIZZI A., *Storia dell'Arte in Friuli. Il Settecento*, Udine 1967.

RIZZI A., "Un recupero tiepolesco: i 'ritratti' del Palazzo Arcivescovile di Udine", in *Atti del congresso internazionale di studi sul Tiepolo / Udine 1970*, Milan 1972, pp. 40-43.

RIZZI A. (ed.), *Mostra della pittura veneta del Settecento in Friuli*, Udine 1966.

RIZZI A. (ed.), *Mostra del Tiepolo. Catalogo dei dipinti*, Venice 1971.

ROMANELLI G., *Venezia Ottocento*, Rome 1977.

ROMANELLI G. and F. PEDROCCO, *Ca' Rezzonico*, Milan 1986.

RUGGERI U., "San Domenico in gloria", in *Giambattista Piazzetta. Il suo tempo, la sua scuola*, Venice 1983, pp. 86-89.

SACK E., *Giambattista und Giandomenico Tiepolo. Ihr Leben und ihre Werke*, 2 vols., Hamburg 1910.

SÁNCHEZ CANTÓN F.J., *J.B. Tiepolo en España*, Madrid 1953.

SANTIFALLER M., "Carl Heinrich von Heinecken e le acqueforti di Giambattista Tiepolo a Dresda", *Arte Veneta*, XXVI (1972), pp. 145-153.

SANTIFALLER M., "Die Gruppe mit der Pyramide in Giambattista Tiepolos Treppenhausfresko der Residenz zu Würzburg", *Münchner Jahrbuch der bildenden Kunst*, XXVI (1975), pp. 193-207.

[SELVA G.A.], *Catalogo dei quadri dei disegni e dei libri che trattano dell'arte del disegno della galleria del fu Sig. Conte Algarotti in Venezia*, Venice n.d. (but 1776).

SIRÉN O., *Dessins et tableaux de la Renaissance Italienne dans les collections de Suède*, Stockholm 1902.

SOHM P.L., "Unknown Epithalamia as Sources for G.B. Tiepolo's iconography and style", *Arte Veneta* (1983), pp. 138-150.

SOHM P.L., "Giambattista Tiepolo at the Palazzo Archinto in Milan", *Arte Lombarda*, 1-2 (1984), pp. 70-78.

SPONZA S., "Della decorazione pittorica della chiesa dell'Ospedaletto ed il problema della prima attività di Giambattista Tiepolo", *Atti dell'Istituto Veneto di Scienze, Lettere ed Arti*, CXLV (1986-87), pp. 213-234.

SPONZA S., "Per il catalogo di Gregorio Lazzarini", *Arte/Documento. Rivista di Storia e Tutela dei Beni Culturali*, 3 (1989), pp. 244-261.

SUCCI D. (ed.), *Da Carlevarijs ai Tiepolo – Incisori veneti e friulani del Settecento*, Venice 1983.

SUCCI D. (ed.), *Giambattista Tiepolo, il segno e l'enigma*, Treviso 1985.

SUCCI D. (ed.), *I Tiepolo. Virtuosismo e ironia*, Turin 1988.

I TIEPOLO E IL SETTECENTO vicentino, catalogue, Milan 1990.

TIEPOLO IN WÜRZBURG. 1750-1753, exhibition, Würzburg, 1951.

TIOZZO C.B., "Giambattista Tiepolo a Ca' Pisani di Stra", *Notizie da Palazzo Albani*, 1 (1986), pp. 54-67.

URBANI DE GHELTOF G.M., *Tiepolo e la sua famiglia*, Venice 1879.

URBANI DE GHELTOF G.M., *Tiepolo in Ispagna*, Venice 1881.

WALTHER, A., "Bernardo Bellotto a Dresda" in *Bernardo Bellotto. Le vedute di Dresda. Dipinti e incisioni dai musei di Dresda*, catalogue, Vicenza 1986, pp. 31-56.

WHISTLER C., "A Modello for Tiepolo's Final Commission: the Allegory of the Immaculate Conception", *Apollo* (1985), pp. 172-173.

WHISTLER C., "G.B. Tiepolo and Charles III: the Church of San Pascual Baylon at Aranjuez", *Apollo* (1985), pp. 321-327.

WHISTLER C., "G.B. Tiepolo at the Court of Charles III", *The Burlington Magazine* (1986), pp. 199-203.

WITTKOWER R., *Art and Architecture in Italy from the Sixteenth Century to 1700*, Harmondworth 1958.

ZANETTI A.M., *Descrizione di tutte le pubbliche pitture della città di Venezia*, Venice 1733.

ZAVA BOCCAZZI F., "Gli affreschi del Celesti a villa Barbini a Caselle d'Asolo", *Arte Veneta*, XVIII (1965), pp. 119-135.

ZAVA BOCCAZZI F., *Pittoni*, Venice 1979.

ZORZI A., *Venezia scomparsa*, Milan 1984.

Index of Tiepolo's works in public and private collections

Index

Page numbers of illustrations are indicated in **boldface** type